Environmental Protection, China and International Trade

This book argues for a balanced approach to 'greening' the World Trade Organization (WTO) ban on China's export duties without opening the floodgates to protectionism.

As a result of the *China—Raw Materials* and *China—Rare Earths* decisions, China is largely prohibited from using export duties to address environmental problems, including those associated with climate change. This is despite a number of climate studies having suggested that Chinese export duties could be useful for reducing carbon leakage, an issue of international concern. This book puts the case for a more balanced approach. It shows that a harsh ban on China's export duties constrains its policy space to protect the environment, particularly in the context of climate change. The work presents feasibility tests for various legal solutions that have been discussed for adjusting the ban, and it accordingly proposes a more feasible approach that would allow China to help protect the environment without advancing protectionism. The proposed legal option provides a less protectionist alternative to export duties, namely 'export duties plus': export duties in combination with supplementary restrictions on Chinese consumption. This analysis also yields insights regarding ways to correct WTO precedents, which suggests a moderate alternative response to an important issue behind the Appellate Body crisis.

The book will be a valuable resource for academics, researchers and policymakers in the areas of International Trade Law, Environmental Law and China.

Fengan Jiang, China University of Political Science and Law.

The Rule of Law in China and Comparative Perspectives

Series Editors: Yuwen Li, Erasmus University Rotterdam, The Netherlands and Fu Hualing, University of Hong Kong, Hong Kong

There is no doctrine more effective than the rule of law in portraying the complex transformation of Chinese society from the rule of men towards the rule of law - a process inaugurated in post-Mao China which is continuing to advance legal reforms to the present day. In other parts of the world, striving for the rule of law is also evident: countries in transition face a similar mission, while the developed democratic countries are forced to tackle new challenges in retaining the high benchmark of the rule of law that has been established.

Research on the legal system in China and in comparison with other countries in the framework of the rule of law covers broad topics of public and private law, substantive law and procedural law, citizens' rights and law enforcement by courts. Based on this broad understanding of the rule of law, the series presents international scholarly work on modern Chinese law including: comparative perspectives, interdisciplinary, and empirical studies.

Other titles in this series:

Hong Kong Constitutionalism
The British Legacy and the Chinese Future
Richard Cullen

National Security Review of Foreign Investment
A Comparative Legal Analysis of China, the United States and the European Union
Cheng Bian

Law and Social Solidarity in Contemporary China
A Durkheimian Analysis
Han Peng

The Making of Chinese Criminal Law
The Preventive Shift in the Context of the Eighth Amendment
Ying Ji

Effective Environmental Regulation in China
Reflections on the Experience of European Union Legislation on Environmental Permits
Federico Pasini

Environmental Protection, China and International Trade

Greening the WTO Ban on Chinese Export Duties

Fengan Jiang

Routledge
Taylor & Francis Group
LONDON AND NEW YORK

First published 2021
by Routledge
2 Park Square, Milton Park, Abingdon, Oxon OX14 4RN

and by Routledge
605 Third Avenue, New York, NY 10158

Routledge is an imprint of the Taylor & Francis Group, an informa business

British Library Cataloguing-in-Publication Data
A catalogue record for this book is available from the British Library

Library of Congress Cataloging-in-Publication Data
Names: Jiang, Fengan, 1986- author.
Title: Environmental protection, China and international trade : greening the WTO ban on Chinese export duties / Fengan Jiang.
Description: Abingdon, Oxon ; New York, NY : Routledge, 2021. |
Series: The rule of law in China and comparative perspectives |
Based on author's thesis (doctoral - Universiteit Leiden, 2019) issued under title: 'Greening' the WTO ban on China's export duties : should WTO law allow China to use export duties to protect the environment and, if so, in what manner? | Includes bibliographical references and index.
Identifiers: LCCN 2020056821 (print) | LCCN 2020056822 (ebook) |
ISBN 9780367753832 (hardback) | ISBN 9781003162339 (ebook)
Subjects: LCSH: Foreign trade regulation--Environmental aspects. |
Export duties--Law and legislation. | Export duties--Law and legislation--China. | Raw materials--Law and legislation--China.
Classification: LCC K3943 .J534 2021 (print) | LCC K3943 (ebook) |
DDC 382/.70951--dc23
LC record available at https://lccn.loc.gov/2020056821
LC ebook record available at https://lccn.loc.gov/2020056822

ISBN: 978-0-367-75383-2 (hbk)
ISBN: 978-0-367-75395-5 (pbk)
ISBN: 978-1-003-16233-9 (ebk)

DOI: 10.4324/9781003162339

Typeset in Galliard
by Taylor & Francis Books

This book is dedicated to my parents and grandparents, especially grandfather: Zhenhua Jiang, who will celebrate his 90th birthday in 2021. 谨以此书献给父母及家中老人，特别是将于二〇二一年迎来九十大寿的祖父姜振华。

Contents

Illustrations

Figures

Tables

Acknowledgements

This book could not have been written without the help and trust of my PhD supervisor Prof. Marco Bronckers (Leiden University) and co-supervisor Prof. Armin Cuyvers (Leiden University). They have always been inspirational and encouraging by taking every opportunity to see my research 'half-full'. They have taught me how to embrace the complexity. They have helped me understand the Western way of thinking, which is essential for me to study China–EU relations in the future.

I would like to thank the members of my Doctorate Committee as well as the Opposition Committee: Prof. Freya Baetens (University of Oslo and Leiden University), Prof. Jacques Bourgeois (College of Europe), Prof. Jingdong Liu (Chinese Academy of Social Sciences), Prof. Christa Tobler (Basel University and Leiden University), Prof. Tom Ottervanger (Leiden University), Prof. Stefaan Van den Bogaert (Leiden University), Prof. Yuwen Li (Erasmus University Rotterdam), and Prof. James Crawford (International Court of Justice). Their comments are valuable.

A sincere thanks also goes to Prof. Josephine van Zeben (Wageningen University and Research) and Prof. Xianqiang Mao (Beijing Normal University) who invited me to present my research in the Annual Meeting of the Society for Environmental Law and Economics and the International Conference on Green Trade. I received helpful advice from the panellists, in particular Dr. Tao Hu (World Wide Fund for Nature) and Robert Ireland (United States International Trade Commission).

I am grateful to all my colleagues in Leiden University, especially those who spent time with me at Café L'Espérance (Kaiserstraat 1, Leiden, the Netherlands). My appreciation also goes to Christa Tobler and Jacques Beglinger. After I accepted their skiing invitation without knowing how to ski, I became a regular visitor to their mountain chalet in Braunwald (Switzerland) where I had inspiring conversation with them and their wonderful guests.

During my fellowship with the World Trade Organization (WTO), internship with the United Nations Economic and Social Commission for Asia and the Pacific (ESCAP), and academic visit to the Chinese Academy of Social Sciences (CASS), many people helped me improve my research. I hereby give my heartfelt gratitude to them.

Lastly, I would like to thank Prof. Yuwen Li who not only provided me with suggestions for publication, but also kindly invited me to dine with her family on the day before my departure for China, as a perfect ending for my research in the Netherlands. I would also like to thank two anonymous reviewers of this book and Alison Kirk and Emily Summers at Routledge for their sound advice on revisions.

Fengan Jiang 姜冯安
Shanghai, China

List of Abbreviations

AB	Appellate Body
AoA	Agreement on Agriculture
ASEAN	Association of Southeast Asian Nations
BTA	border tax adjustment
CIS	Commonwealth of Independent States
CITES	Convention on International Trade in Endangered Species of Wild Fauna and Flora
CJEU	Court of Justice of the European Union
CO2	carbon dioxide
COD	chemical oxygen demand
DSB	Dispute Settlement Body
DSU	Understanding on Rules and Procedures Governing the Settlement of Disputes
EAEU	Eurasian Economic Union
EC	European Community
ECtHR	European Court of Human Rights
EFTA	European Free Trade Association
EU	European Union
GATT	General Agreement on Tariffs and Trade 1994
GCC	Gulf Cooperation Council
HHR	high-energy-intensive, high-pollution, and resources-based
HoL	House of Lords
HS	Harmonised System
ICJ	International Court of Justice
ICTY	International Criminal Tribunal for the former Yugoslavia
ILC	International Law Commission
ILC	International Labour Conference
IMF	International Monetary Fund
IPCC	Intergovernmental Panel on Climate Change
ISDS	Investor-state dispute settlement
ITLOS	International Tribunal for the Law of the Sea
MEAs	multilateral environmental agreements
MERCOSUR	el Mercado Común del Sur (the Common Market of the South)

MEQRs	measures that had an equivalent effect on quantitative restriction
NDRC	National Development and Reform Commission
NPC	National People's Congress
NMVOCs	nonmethane volatile organic compounds
NOx	nitrogen oxides
N-NH3	ammoniacal nitrogen
OECD	Organisation for Economic Co-operation and Development
PIIE	Peterson Institute for International Economics
PM2.5	fine particulate matter
PRCEE	Policy Research Centre for Environment and Economy
RTA	regional trade agreement
SADC	Southern African Development Community
SO2	sulphur dioxide
TRIPS	Trade Related Aspects of Intellectual Property Rights
TPRs	Trade Policy Reviews
UNCITRAL	United Nations Commission on International Trade Law
UNCLOS	United Nations Convention on the Law of the Sea
UNFCCC	United Nations Framework Convention on Climate Change
UK	United Kingdom
US	United States
VAT	value-added tax
VCLT	Vienna Convention on the Law of Treaties
WIPO	World Intellectual Property Organization
WTO	World Trade Organization

1 Introduction

Global warming, according to an alarming report recently released by the Intergovernmental Panel on Climate Change (IPCC), is accelerating more rapidly than scientists had previously anticipated.[1] In order to limit its impact, countries need to take 'rapid, far-reaching and unprecedented' actions.[2] As the largest emitter and exporter of carbon dioxide emissions,[3] China is thus aiming to become carbon neutral before 2060.[4] It, however, may not legally use one potential measure to curb the export of carbon emissions, namely duties on carbon-intensive exports.[5] Owing to the *China—Raw Materials* and *China—Rare Earths* decisions,[6] China is generally prohibited from using export duties, regardless of their aims and effects.[7] China lacked convincing environmental justification in those cases, to be sure, but a general ban on China's export duties could raise environmental

1 UN, 'Statement by the Secretary-General on the IPCC Special Report Global Warming of 1.5°C', 8 October 2018, available at https://www.un.org/sg/en/content/sg/statement/2018-10-08/statement-secretary-general-ipcc-special-report-global-warming-15-%C2%BAc (visited on 14 November 2018).
2 IPCC, 'Summary for Policymakers of IPCC Special Report on Global Warming of 1.5°C approved by governments', 8 October 2018, https://www.ipcc.ch/2018/10/08/summary-for-policymakers-of-ipcc-special-report-on-global-warming-of-1-5c-approved-by-governments/ (visited on 08 November 2020).
3 China's export-related emissions constituted 7% of total global carbon emissions in 2011, which is larger than the overall emissions produced by the third or fourth largest emitters in the world, namely India (6%) and Russia (5%) in 2015. Union of Concerned Scientists, 'Each Country's Share of CO2 Emissions', 11 October 2018, https://www.ucsusa.org/global-warming/science-and-impacts/science/each-countrys-share-of-co2.html#.XAvmyCh97IV (visited on 22 November 2018).
4 Smriti Mallapaty, 'How China Could be Carbon Neutral by Mid-century', Nature, 19 October 2020, https://www.nature.com/articles/d41586-020-02927-9 (visited on 14 November 2020).
5 China described export duties as a type of instrument to 'effectively control greenhouse gas emissions'. For further information, see UNFCCC, 'Second National Communication on Climate Change of the People's Republic of China', October 2004, at 15, http://unfccc.int/resource/docs/natc/chnnc1exsum.pdf (visited on 1 January 2019).
6 For further discussion, see Chapter 3.
7 Apart from those on 84 products that fall within the maximum levels provided in Annex 6 of China's Accession Protocol. For further information, see Chapter 2.

DOI: 10.4324/9781003162339-1

concerns in the future especially in the context of climate change. A number of climate studies, including the well-known Stern Review on the economics of climate change,[8] its follow-up article,[9] and a World Bank research paper,[10] have suggested that Chinese export duties could be useful for reducing carbon leakage, an issue also worrying the West.[11] Considering the potential negative environmental impact of this jurisprudence, there is a need to consider 'greening' the World Trade Organization (WTO) ban on China's export duties.

This chapter begins with an introduction of the major research question, namely whether generally prohibiting China from using export duties limits its capacity to protect the environment, and, if so, what are the solutions to provide China with policy space without opening the floodgates to protectionism. The analysis of this question is closely related to three key issues concerning the use of export duties in this way, which are discussed in turn. It concludes with a brief discussion of the structure of the book.

1.1. Should WTO law allow China to use export duties to address trade-related environmental concerns and, if so, what form should these duties take?

Following the high-profile *China—Raw Materials* and *China—Rare Earths* cases, the United States (US) and the European Union (EU) in July 2016 brought a third case, *China—Raw Materials II.* This case again calls into question China's export duties on certain raw materials.[12] As in the earlier two cases, the products subject to export duties in *China—Raw Materials II* are key components of such high-value products as automotive parts, electronics, and chemicals. In responding to the third set of charges brought by the US and EU, China has argued that its export duties are justified as part of an environmental policy designed to tackle trade-related pollution under Article XX of the General Agreement on Tariffs and Trade 1994 (GATT).[13] The Appellate Body (AB) already ruled in the first two

8 Nicholas Stern, *The Economics of Climate Change: The Stern Review* (Cambridge, 2007), at 552.

9 Lorraine Hamid, Nicholas Stern and Chris Taylor, 'Reflections on the Stern Review (2): A Growing International Opportunity to Move Strongly on Climate Change', 8 (1) *World Economics* (2007), at 176.

10 Brian R. Copeland, 'International Trade and Green Growth', No. 6235 World Bank Policy Research Working Paper (2012).

11 For instance, as part of her European Green Deal, the President of the European Commission has proposed a 'Carbon Border Tax' aiming at avoiding carbon leakage and ensuring a level playing field for European companies. Ursula von der Leyen, 'A Union that Strives For More: My Agenda for Europe', 16 July 2019, at 5, https://ec.europa.eu/commission/sites/beta-political/files/political-guidelines-next-commission_en.pdf (visited on 1 August 2019).

12 This case is possibly on inactive status. The DSB agreed to establish a panel on 8 November 2016, but the panellists have not yet been chosen after more than two years.

13 Ministry of Commerce of People's Republic of China, 'Official from the Department of Law and Treaty Comments on EU Appealing to the WTO against China's Export

cases, however, that China cannot invoke GATT Article XX to justify violations of its export duty commitments. The pressing question here, therefore, is whether WTO law should allow China to invoke the environmental exceptions enumerated in Article XX if China's export duties truly serve environmental purposes.

To be fair, following the *China—Raw Materials* and *China—Rare Earths* decisions, China can still impose export duties on 84 products to protect the environment.[14] This policy space is, however, extremely restricted because the 84 products are identified by 8-digit Harmonised System (HS) numbers and product descriptions. These products[15] only constitute a tiny part (1.51%) of the approximately 5,300 article/product descriptions in the 6-digit code system in total.[16] In other words, China is prohibited from imposing export duties on approximately 98.49% products, regardless of their aims and effects.

After the *China—Raw Materials* and *China—Rare Earths* decisions, many scholars sympathised with China, especially given that most WTO members remain free to impose duties on exports for any purpose.[17] None of them, however, has sufficiently challenged the widely held perception that export duties are not meant to be used for environmental purposes, and China's environmental justification is a mere pretext for an industrial policy designed to limit the access of international companies to vital natural resources in China.[18] Based on this perception, even though China's right to invoke the public policy exception was denied, 'a public policy problem does not really seem to exist'.[19] In this context, the outcry over unfairness to deny China's right to invoke the WTO environmental exceptions has been criticised for being rather 'superficial'.[20]

The above negative perception is understandable because export duties have not served traditionally as an instrument in the service of environmental protection. Furthermore, in *China—Raw Materials* and *China—Rare Earths* China lacked

Management Measures on its Raw Materials', 21 July 2016, http://english.mofcom.gov.cn/article/newsrelease/policyreleasing/201607/20160701365930.shtml (visited on 1 January 2019).

14 Paragraph 11.3 of China's Protocol of Accession allows China to impose export duties on 84 products that fall within the maximum levels provided in Annex 6 of that protocol. For further information, see Chapter 2.

15 80 products at the 6-digit HS level.

16 UN International Trade Statistics Knowledgebase, 'Harmonized Commodity Description and Coding Systems (HS)', https://unstats.un.org/unsd/tradekb/Knowledgebase/50018/Harmonized-Commodity-Description-and-Coding-Systems-HS (visited on 22 November 2020).

17 For further discussion on the reception of the WTO ban on China's export duties, see Chapter 3.

18 Lothar Ehring, 'Nature and Status of WTO Accession Commitments: "WTO-Plus" Obligations and Their Relationship to Other Parts of the WTO Agreement', in Marise Cremona, Peter Hilpold, Nikos Lavranos, Stefan Staiger Schneider and Andreas R. Ziegler (eds), *Reflections on the Constitutionalisation of International Economic Law* (Brill, 2013), at 361.

19 Ibid., at 361.

20 Ibid., at 359. For further information, see Chapter 3.

convincing environmental justification. In order to minimise China's chances of circumventing WTO rules, the complaining governments thus chose to deny its right to invoke Article XX.[21]

It is, however, one thing to propose strictly scrutinising any environmental reasoning behind export duties, but quite another to ban these duties merely for the reason that they could be abused.[22] This book thus calls for a balanced approach that would provide China with policy space to protect the environment without opening the floodgates to protectionism. This policy space would not only benefit China, but also the world when it comes to addressing global environmental problems such as climate change.[23]

The environmental concerns associated with a general ban on China's export duties are not merely hypothetical.[24] For instance, in the past, China's export duties on such energy-intensive products as steel, aluminium, coal, chemical products, and fertilizers were applauded by some commentators, who see their potential to reduce carbon emissions in China.[25] Indeed, a large proportion of carbon emissions produced by China is export-related.[26] A number of climate studies thus have suggested China explore the potential of its export duties and make them a credible climate policy tool.[27] This very important issue is, however, neglected in the current discussion of the general ban on China's export duties.[28]

21 Marco Bronckers and Keith E. Maskus, '*China–Raw Materials*: A Controversial Step Towards Evenhanded Exploitation of Natural Resources', 13(2) *World Trade Review* (2014), at 402.

22 Even an author like Ehring with a critical view of the unfairness concerns may agree that such unfairness should not prevent a country from pursuing 'fundamental societal interests'. As he correctly put it, 'one needs to ask whether the values protected by Article XX truly can be threatened by the obligations at stake'. See Ehring (2013), above n 16, at 359.

23 Moreover, in the past, several major international environmental groups opposed a WTO decision prohibiting the US from adopting a measure designed to protect sea turtles outside its territorial waters. A decision that prohibits China from addressing environmental problems occurred in its own territory can be expected to elicit a similarly strong reaction from the public. ICTSD, 'Shrimp-Turtle Ruling Gets Lukewarm Reaction from All Sides', 2 (40) Bridges (1998).

24 For further discussion on the practice of WTO members to use export duties for environmental purposes, see Chapter 4.

25 For further discussion on the potential of China's export duties to tackle carbon leakage, see Chapter 6.

26 'About twenty-five percent of China's carbon emissions are caused by manufacturing products that are consumed abroad'. Export-related emissions produced by China thus constituted 7% of total global carbon emissions in 2012, see Zhu Liu, 'China's Carbon Emissions Report 2015', Energy Technology Innovation Policy Research Group (2015), at 1, https://scholar.harvard.edu/files/zhu/files/carbon-emissions-report-2015-final.pdf (visited on 1 January 2019). This number is larger than the overall emissions produced by the third or fourth largest emitters in the world, namely India (6%) and Russia (5%) in 2015. See Union of Concerned Scientists (2018), above n 5.

27 For further information, see Chapter 6.

28 It is noteworthy that, while *China—Raw Materials* and *China—Rare Earths* concerned only natural resources, the decisions in these cases also in effect prohibit China from imposing export duties on other intermediate and final goods. For further

Moreover, in order to prevent export duties from being abused for protectionist objectives, China may impose supplementary restrictions on domestic consumption as part of 'export duties plus'. Such measures are by nature much less protectionist than the ones at issue in *China—Raw Materials* and *China—Rare Earths*. While export duties, which exclusively restrict exports, should be prohibited outright, it seems reasonable to permit China to adopt 'export duties plus' for pursuing environmental purposes subject to the strict scrutiny of GATT Article XX.

Given the actual concerns over environmental protection and the possibilities to minimise the protectionist practices, the WTO ban on China's export duties seems to be rather simplistic and more based on the fear of abuse than cool-headed assessment of self-interest. What is needed, as provided in this book, is a more sophisticated response that, on the one hand, provides China with policy space to protect the environment, and, on the other hand, prevents such right from being abused. Furthermore, this book also provides solutions to expand this desirable policy space in light of the *China—Raw Materials* and *China—Rare Earths* decisions. The following discussion introduces the important issues concerning the use of export duties to address trade-related environmental concerns in China.

1.2. Trade-related environmental concerns and the controversies surrounding the use of export duties to address them

This discussion begins with an introduction of key economic hypotheses concerning the adverse effects of increasing trade on environmental quality and goes on to present empirical evidence for the existence of such concerns in China. It concludes with an assessment of the practical advantages and disadvantages associated with using export duties to address environmental concerns and of the need for more sophisticated rules to regulate them.

1.2.1. Local and global environmental problems exacerbated by trade

The relationship between increasing trade and environmental quality is complicated. On the one hand, trade promotes economic growth, which in turn tends to improve a country's environment in the long run. Thus the so-called Environmental Kuznets Curve indicates that, once a particular critical level of income has been reached, countries generally switch economic activity away from more highly polluting sectors, such as manufacturing, to less polluting sectors, such as services.[29] Moreover, within a given industry, less clean techniques tend to be replaced with cleaner ones.[30] On the other hand, though, an increase in trade can have adverse effects on environmental quality at both local and global levels.

discussion on the missing piece in the reception of *China—Raw Materials* and *China—Rare Earths* decisions, see Chapter 3.

29 Jeffrey A. Frankel, 'The Natural Resource Curse: A Survey of Diagnoses and Some Prescriptions', RWP12-014 HKS Faculty Research Working Paper Series (2012), at 6.

30 Ibid.

There is thus to begin with the problem of negative environmental externalities associated with the manufacture of products for export. These externalities could be localised in the form of ordinary water or soil pollution. Global environmental externalities, by contrast, such as increased carbon emissions generated by the manufacture of carbon-intensive products for export, can negatively affect the global climate.

The problem of negative environmental externalities in certain countries can be exacerbated by international trade. Thus, according to the so-called 'pollution haven hypothesis', polluting industries tend to relocate to jurisdictions with less stringent environmental regulations, which are thereby encouraged to specialise in relatively less clean activities and to export their products to countries with higher environmental standards.[31]

For instance, a 2019 Organisation for Economic Co-operation and Development (OECD) research suggests that non-OECD countries generally export more carbon-intensive goods to OECD countries.[32] Indeed, an empirical study based on a sample of over 12,000 Japanese manufacturing firms, for instance, showed that, although outsourcing imposes additional transport costs, large firms with high environmental regulation costs prefer either to displace entire production processes or at least the more environmentally damaging aspects of those processes to other countries, 'leav[ing] a large and profitable headquarters in the home country'.[33] China is among the popular destinations for outsourcing.[34]

1.2.2. Trade-related environmental problems in China

As the largest exporter in world merchandise trade, China's economic growth has been largely dependent on trade.[35] At the same time, however, this rapid economic growth has created environmental challenges.[36] In the period from 2001 to 2005, for instance, some 54% of the water in China's seven main rivers was deemed unsafe for human consumption.[37] In terms of air pollution, China has, since 2005, become the

31 Ibid., at 7.
32 'In OECD countries, imported carbon emissions from both OECD and countries outside the OECD area have been growing, with the latter increasing proportionally more than the former'. See Grégoire Garsous, 'Trends in Policy Indicators on Trade and Environment', No.1 OECD Trade and Environment Working Papers (2019), at 12.
33 Matthew A. Cole, Robert J.R. Elliott and Toshihiro Okubo, 'International Environmental Outsourcing', 150(4) *Review of World Economics* (2014), at 658.
34 Yanfang Lyu, 'Evaluating Carbon Dioxide Emissions in Undertaking Offshored Production Tasks: The Case of China', 116 *Journal of Cleaner Production* (2016).
35 David Barboza, 'In Recession, China Solidifies Its Lead in Global Trade', 14 October 2009, https://www.nytimes.com/2009/10/14/business/global/14chinatrade.html (visited on 1 January 2019).
36 YaleEnvironemnt360, 'China at Crossroads: Balancing The Economy and Environment', 14 November 2013, https://e360.yale.edu/features/china_at_crossroads_balancing_the_economy_and_environment (visited on 1 January 2019).
37 World Bank, 'Cost of Pollution in China: Economic Estimates of Physical Damages', 1 February 2007, http://documents.worldbank.org/curated/en/782171468027560055/

world's largest source of sulphur dioxide (SO_2) emissions.[38] Empirical research shows that an increase in exports may have contributed to these problems.

Thus, looking again at the period from 2001 to 2005, 40% of products exported from China were associated with serious consequences for air quality and 44% with serious consequences for water quality.[39] In 2007, the manufacture of products for export produced 15%, 21%, 23%, and 21% of four of the country's major air pollutants, respectively industrial primary fine particular matter ($PM_{2.5}$), SO_2, nitrogen oxides (NOx), and nonmethane volatile organic compounds (NMVOCs).[40] Research also shows that approximately 19% of the premature mortality (208,500 deaths) related to $PM_{2.5}$ in China in 2007 is attributable to the manufacture of products for export, a figure that is '150% higher than the recorded Chinese traffic fatalities in the same year'.[41] These environmental problems have also worried other countries. So it is that, while the outsourcing of high-pollution manufacturing to China has 'resulted in an overall beneficial effect for the US public health', this outcome has been achieved 'at the expense of air quality deterioration over the western US and the populous Chinese regions' owing to the combined effects of changes in emissions and atmospheric transport.[42]

Turning now to climate change, China overtook the US as the world's leading source of carbon emissions in 2008[43] and currently emits more than the US and EU combined.[44] An increase in energy-intensive exports from China has

Cost-of-pollution-in-China-economic-estimates-of-physical-damages (visited on 1 January 2019).

38 Shenshen Su, Bengang Li, Siyu Cui and Shu Tao, 'Sulfur Dioxide Emissions from Combustion in China: From 1990 to 2007', 45(19) *Environmental Science & Technology* (2011).

39 Tao Hu, 'Analysis of the Resource and Environment Deficit of China's Foreign Trade', 18(2) *China Population, Resources and Environment* (2008), at 205.

40 H. Zhao, Q. Zhang, S. Davis, D. Guan, Z. Liu, H. Huo, J. Lin, W. Liu and K. He, 'Assessment of China's Virtual Air Pollution Transport Embodied in Trade by a Consumption-based Emission Inventory', 15(12) *Atmospheric Chemistry and Physics* (2015).

41 'The European Union, North America, and East Asia, the largest three importing regions for Chinese goods (at 24, 21, and 13% of total export value, respectively), were associated with an estimated 47,000, 45,100 and 27,100 premature deaths in China from PM2.5 exposures in 2007, respectively'. See Haikun Wang, Yanxu Zhang, Hongyan Zhao, Xi Lu, Yanxia Zhang, Weimo Zhu, Chris P. Nielsen, Xin Li, Qiang Zhang, Jun Bi and Michael B. McElroy, 'Trade-driven Relocation of Air Pollution and Health Impacts in China', 738(8) *Nature Communications* (2017).

42 Jintai Lin, Da Pan, Steven J. Davis, Qiang Zhang, Kebin He, Can Wang, David G. Streets, Donald J. Wuebbles and Dabo Guanc, 'China's International Trade and Air Pollution in the United States', 111(5) *Proceedings of the National Academy of Sciences of the United States of America* (2014).

43 Elisabeth Rosenthal, 'China Increases Lead as Biggest Carbon Dioxide Emitter', 14 June 2008, https://www.nytimes.com/2008/06/14/world/asia/14china.html (visited on 1 January 2019).

44 Robert Rapier, 'China Emits More Carbon Dioxide Than The U.S. and EU Combined', 1 July 2018, https://www.forbes.com/sites/rrapier/2018/07/01/china-emits-more-carbon-dioxide-than-the-u-s-and-eu-combined/ (visited on 1 January 2019).

exacerbated the problem of carbon emissions, as indicated by, for instance, an increase in the portion of China's energy consumption embodied in exports from 14% in 1980 to 22% in 2005.[45] In 2012, China's export-related emissions even constituted 7% of total global carbon emissions, exceeding those produced by the third (6%) or fourth (5%) largest emitters.[46]

That being said, however, international trade should not be held responsible for all of China's environmental challenges. It is in this regard noteworthy that many polluting or energy-intensive products are produced and also consumed in China through, for instance, massive investments in urban infrastructure and energy systems.[47] The use of export duties, then—which by definition target exports rather than domestic consumption—to address environmental concerns in China raises a number of objections, which will now be dealt with in turn.

1.2.3. Concerns over Chinese export duties as a protectionist measure and better alternatives

Although export duties could be used to address negative environmental externalities,[48] their use in this capacity is, however, subject to the concerns over effectiveness and protectionism. Regarding the former one, export duties may in effect lower the domestic prices of targeted products relative to those paid by foreign consumers.[49] This may incentivise domestic consumption and in turn undermine the effectiveness of export duties to reduce the manufacture of targeted products. Regarding the latter one, when the targeted products are industrial inputs, export duties may in effect subsidise domestic downstream producers by providing them with preferential access to those inputs.

Following those economic rationales, it is not hard to understand why the panels and the AB in *China—Raw Materials* and *China—Rare Earths* supported the view that China should not use export duties to protect the environment. On the one hand, the duties in those cases were not an effective environmental measure because the manufacture of targeted raw materials actually increased in response to a substantial increase in Chinese domestic consumption of those products.[50] On the other hand, those duties raised concerns over protectionism as they provided Chinese companies with preferential access over their foreign competitors to the raw materials at issue. China is therefore advised to replace export

45 Liping Li, 'Research on the Construction of China's Green Trade System', 18(2) *China Population, Resources and Environment* (2008), at 201.

46 Liu (2015), above n 24.

47 UNEP, 'China Outpacing Rest of World in Natural Resource Use', 2 August 2013, https://www.unenvironment.org/news-and-stories/press-release/china-outpacing-r est-
world-natural-resource-use (visited on 1 January 2019).

48 WTO, 'World Trade Report 2010' (WTO Publications, 2010), at 128 and 136, https://www.wto.org/english/res_e/booksp_e/anrep_e/world_trade_report10_e.pdf (visited on 1 January 2019).

49 Ibid., at 131.

50 For further information, see Chapter 2.

duties with better options such as pollution taxes designed to target production rather than exportation.

However, should such ideal measures prove to be infeasible in financial or practical terms, the question remains whether China should be permitted to use export duties as an interim alternative to address trade-related concerns.[51] This question is not purely theoretical, and, in responding to it, for instance, the EU's proposal concerning the multilateral rules regulating export duties did deliberately provide countries with environmental regulatory autonomy by incorporating GATT Article XX.[52]

A number of climate studies have indeed suggested that export duties may also play a positive role in tackling carbon leakage, an issue occurs when energy-intensive industries shift production to countries that have weaker controls. This problem has largely impeded the efforts of advanced economies to keep raising their carbon prices. It thus has been argued that exporting countries such as China could either agree importing countries to adopt border tax adjustments or impose 'export taxes on energy-intensive manufacturing goods themselves'.[53] Given that the former option might risk sparking a trade war, export duties are considered an alternative to ensure a level playing field for Western manufacturers.[54] These policy recommendations are also acknowledged in a WTO working paper.[55] However, the potential of China's export duties to combat climate change has received inadequate attention in the literature on *China—Raw Materials* or *China—Rare Earths.*[56]

51 For further information, see Chapter 4.

52 Daniel Crosby, 'WTO Legal Status and Evolving Practice of Export Taxes', 12(5) *ICTSD Bridges* (2008).

53 Aaditya Mattoo and Arvind Subramanian, 'Four Changes to Trade Rules to Facilitate Climate Change Action', No.10 PIIE Policy Brief (2013), https://www.piie.com/publications/policy-briefs/four-changes-trade-rules-facilitate-climate-change-action (visited on 4 September 2019).

54 For further discussion, see Chapter 6.

55 'The GATT does not contain any discipline on export taxes or any price-based measures other than the most-favoured nation principle. It is not clear to what extent national climate change programmes will lead to action on exports. However, some authors have suggested that countries whose GHG emissions are related to products destined for export may respond to threats of border tax adjustments abroad with the adoption of their own export taxes, thus internalizing the amount of GHG tax their exports may otherwise pay in the importing country'. Patrick Low, Gabrielle Marceau and Julia Reinaud, 'The Interface between the Trade and Climate Change Regimes: Scoping the Issues', ERSD Staff Working Paper (2011), at 4.

56 To the best of the author's knowledge, in English literature about the two cases, only Baris Karapinar and Kateryna Holzer have pointed out this problem by arguing that 'as the Panel and the Appellate Body in the *China-Raw Materials* dispute clarified, China and potentially other new Members with similar commitments cannot even resort to article XX exceptions to justify the duties they impose on their exports. Therefore, the use of an export tax as a climate policy tool is not possible for these countries'. But they did not discuss the particular question concerning the potential of China's export duties to combat climate change. See Baris Karapinar and Kateryna Holzer, 'Legal Implications of the Use of Export Taxes in Addressing Carbon Leakage: Competing Border Adjustment Measures', 10(1) *New Zealand Journal of Public and International Law* (2012), at 34.

China, as the largest exporter of carbon dioxide emissions, could explore the potential of export duties to tackle carbon leakage but, admittedly, one may question the determination of China to impose export duties on a wide range of energy-intensive products at the cost of slowing down its economic growth.[57] This doubt seems to be echoed in China's recent policies to reduce export duties and to raise export tax rebate.[58] But it is noteworthy that these measures are imposed to boost trade that was hit by the US–China trade war and the coronavirus.[59] When these problems are alleviated, China may genuinely consider export duties to be a part of its environmental policy, especially given its 2020 pledge to become carbon neutral by 2060. As will be discussed in Chapter 6, boosting long-term economic growth and tackling climate change could go hand in hand. Moreover, given the fact that energy-intensive industries have created such environmental challenges as air pollution in China, the negative economic impacts caused by climate action could also be justified by an improved environment in China.

To sum up, these various disadvantages and advantages associated with the use of export duties to address trade-related concerns indicate that either complete abandonment of or unqualified support for this approach would be too simplistic. What is needed, rather, is a more sophisticated response that balances environmental and economic interests.

1.3. Structure of the analysis

This book consists of three parts. The first part sets the scene by discussing the background and reception of the WTO cases against China's export duties. The second part provides a preliminary analysis to understand whether the harsh ban on China's export duties constrain the county's capacity to protect the environment. The final part explores the options for China to use export duties legally in order to achieve environmental goals under WTO law. The brief account of each of these parts that follows here provides an overview of the study.

1.3.1. Description of Part I: setting the scene

Chapter 2 provides an overview of the *China—Raw Materials* and *China—Rare Earths* decisions and the *China—Raw Materials II* case (possibly

57 For further discussion, see Chapter 6.

58 China's Tariff Plan for 2018, see http://gss.mof.gov.cn/zhengwuxinxi/zhengcefabu/201712/P020171215531852388756.pdf (visited on 27 December 2018). China's Tariff Plan for 2019, see http://gss.mof.gov.cn/mofhome/guanshuisi/zhengwuxinxi/zhengcefabu/201812/P020181221619892272965.pdf (visited on 27 December 2018). Reuters, 'China Raises Export Tax Rebate on Almost 1,500 Products to Boost Virus-hit Trade', 17 March 2020, https://www.reuters.com/article/us-china-economy-exports-rebates-idUSKBN214223 (visited on 27 October 2020).

59 Reuters, 'China to Raise Export Tax Rebates Amid Trade War', 8 October 2018 (visited on 27 October 2020).

inactive).[60] The facts in those WTO cases and the reasoning behind the AB's interpretation disallowing the duties (in a manner consistent with Article XX) are summarised. It shows that China's export duties at issue were unlikely to be adopted for environmental purposes, largely owing to the lack of corresponding restrictions on domestic consumption of the targeted raw materials. However, the *China—Raw Materials* and *China—Rare Earths* decisions also prohibit China from justifying any future export duties, no matter on raw materials or not, even if Chinese export duties could contribute meaningfully to environmental protection. Moreover, this outcome also seems a fairly stringent finding, especially given that most WTO members remain free to impose duties on exports for any purpose. In this context, the WTO ban on Chinese export duties has raised several concerns, which are discussed in the next chapter.

Chapter 3 shows that much of the criticism of the WTO ban on China's export duties focuses on the concerns over the inequity (WTO members are generally free to impose export duties) or the rigidity of the strictly textual approach adopted by the AB regarding the applicability of Article XX to China's export duty commitments. In contrast, the potential negative environmental impact caused by this harsh ban receives much less attention, largely owing to the perception that doubts (i) the potential of using export duties to protect the environment and (ii) the genuineness of China's intent to use export duties as part of its environmental policy. This gap is unfortunate because the environmental concern is of great importance in deciding whether the WTO members or the AB should support a change of the *China—Raw Materials* and *China—Rare Earths* decisions. The next steps involve filling in the missing piece in current discussion which are presented in Part II.

1.3.2. Description of Part II: the extent to which a harsh ban on Chinese export duties would constrain China's capacity to protect the environment

The discussion in Part II, then, concerns whether China should be allowed under WTO law to use export duties to address environmental concerns. Chapter 4 surveys the practice of WTO members to restrict exports for environmental purposes (2009–2016) and the provisions limiting the use of export restrictions in WTO agreements and 50 select regional trade agreements (2012–2016). The findings show that a harsh ban on export duties is inconsistent with the practice of WTO members and economic rationale in two respects. First, the actual examples of country practices and economic research show that export duties could be useful to protect the environment because the first-best alternative is not always feasible in financial or practical terms. The environmental regulatory autonomy with respect to export duties is thus always preserved for countries at both the

60 WTO Dispute DS508, '*China — Export Duties on Certain Raw Materials*'; WTO Dispute DS509, '*China — Duties and other Measures concerning the Exportation of Certain Raw Materials*'.

multilateral and regional levels. When the EU proposed more stringent multilateral rules regulating export duties, it indeed provided countries with that environmental regulatory autonomy by incorporating Article XX. Second, the suggestion that duties could be substituted by export quotas lacks sound basis. In contrast, country practices as well as an OECD Trade Policy Paper suggested the contrary, possibly owing to the major disadvantages of quantitative restrictions compared with duties: (i) the loss of resources through rent-seeking activities, (ii) the risk of corruption, and (iii) the loss of government revenue.

Chapter 5 looks first to the legislative process that generates the export duties in China. The aim is to discover the common intention of decision-makers when designing export duties. The Five-Year Plan was subsequently identified as a trustworthy indicator to shed light on the priority of competing policy purposes. A textual analysis of the Guidelines of the Eleventh, Twelfth, and Thirteenth Five-Year Plans (which cover the period from 2006 to 2020) and relevant subsector plans reveals the policy rationales behind export duties at various points in time. Although China had prioritised the industrial purposes of export duties in the past, this role has been altered in the Guidelines of the Thirteenth Five-Year Plan (2016–2020) which makes clear that export duties together with other taxes on production or consumption could form part of a new 'eco-tax system'. An analysis of the relevant subsector five-year plans and the development of China's environmental policies (such as the resources and environmental protection taxes) shows further the increasing role of China's export duties to curtail carbon leakage. The same chapter also explains why these plans can be a trustworthy indicator by discussing a series of observations on the drafting, enactment, and implementation stages of them.

The potential of China's export duties to combat climate change has received inadequate attention in the literature on *China—Raw Materials* or *China—Rare Earths*. This neglect is unfortunate because a number of climate studies, including the Stern Review on the economics of climate change and a World Bank research paper, have suggested that export duties could be useful for curtailing carbon leakage. These policy recommendations are also acknowledged in a WTO working paper. Thus, certain Chinese export duties in the past were applauded by some commentators as a promising means to confront the country's carbon leakage problem. This practice was also recorded in China's second communication to the United Nations Framework Convention on Climate Change (UNFCCC). Chapter 6 shows that the WTO ban on Chinese export duties would undermine global efforts to fight climate change. On the one hand, export duties could be a more feasible alternative to the import carbon tariffs. On the other hand, China, as the largest emitter and exporter of carbon emissions, has incentives to genuinely adopt export duties as part of its demand-side climate policy targeting consumption.

1.3.3. Description of Part III: a basis under WTO law for China's use of export duties to address environmental concerns

The discussion in Part III relates to the potential for China to legally enact export duties as part of its environmental policy. Chapter 7 begins with an assessment of the feasibility of judicial means to ease the constraints imposed by the *China–Raw Materials* and *China–Rare Earths* decisions. It provides a comparative perspective by taking into account the practices of tribunals at various levels, including the International Court of Justice (ICJ), the International Criminal Tribunal for the former Yugoslavia (ICTY), the European Court of Human Rights (ECtHR), the Court of Justice of the European Union (CJEU), and the selected domestic courts in both common and civil law systems, all of which offer references for the AB's departure from previous decisions. A more nuanced approach has been proposed to draw a line between duties that are applied exclusively to exports on the one hand and so-called 'export duties plus', which are adopted in conjunction with corresponding restrictions on domestic consumption, on the other. Given the AB's membership crisis, it is probably not the best time to rely on a judicial approach. In terms of a political correction, the feasibility and implications of adopting an amendment, waiver, or authoritative interpretation allowing China to enact export duties under GATT Article XX are explored.

Should the environmental exceptions under Article XX become available with respect to 'export duties plus', an important follow-up question concerning China's policy space is whether Article XX requires 'export duties plus' to always treat domestic and foreign consumers in an identical manner. Chapter 8 suggests that the first condition of the chapeau generally requires China to impose equivalent charges on products destined for domestic consumption. One exception, however, might be found in the climate change regime where the parties listed in Annex I of the UNFCCC have explicitly committed to take a greater mitigation role than non-Annex I countries like China. Differential 'export duties plus' thus might be justified for the purpose of fighting climate change. That being said, however, it is equally important to address the concern that China might deliberately use differential 'export duties plus' to provide Chinese downstream producers with favourable access to industrial inputs. This chapter proposes additional limits on the use of differential 'export duties plus' as part of climate policy under the second condition of the chapeau prohibiting 'disguised restriction on international trade'. These limits would prevent China from cherry-picking the carbon-intensive products that could potentially benefit its downstream producers.

Lastly, Chapter 9 provides a review of the findings of the previous chapters in order to discuss positive implications of 'greening' the WTO ban on Chinese export duties.

Part I

Setting the scene: The background and reception of the WTO ban on Chinese export duties

2 Three WTO cases against Chinese export duties

World Trade Organization (WTO) members are generally free to impose export duties, though some of them may be restricted in doing so by special commitments.[1] China is under such a restriction, since it committed in Paragraph 11.3 of China's Protocol of Accession (Paragraph 11.3) to maintaining no export duties apart from those on 84 products that fall within the maximum levels provided in Annex 6 of that protocol (Annex 6). Although China maintained export duties on only 58 products at the time of its accession,[2] it began in 2006 to impose them on so-called high-energy-intensive, high-pollution, and resources-based products including both raw materials and other products such as aluminium, steel, coal, chemical products, and fertilizers.[3] Some of them are not included in Annex 6. Justification was offered for these practices in the name of environmental protection, but several WTO members were unconvinced and chose to litigate against the specific duties on raw materials. This chapter introduces the facts and key issues of those duties in dispute.

2.1 Annex 6 of China's Protocol of Accession

China's policy space to adopt export duties is extremely restricted under Annex 6. The listed 84 products are identified by eight-digit Harmonised System (HS) numbers and product descriptions. These products[4] only constitute a tiny part (1.51%) of the approximately 5,300 article/product descriptions in the 6-digit code system in total.[5] In other words, China is prohibited from imposing export

1 These special commitments can be found in the accession protocols of WTO–Mongolia (1997), WTO–Latvia (1999), WTO–China (2001), WTO–Saudi Arabia (2005), WTO–Vietnam (2007), WTO–Ukraine (2008), WTO–Russia (2012), WTO–Montenegro (2012), WTO–Tajikistan (2013), WTO–Kazakhstan (2015), and WTO–Afghanistan (2016). For further information, see Chapter 4.
2 WTO Panel Reports, *China — Measures Related to the Exportation of Various Raw Materials*, WT/DS394/R; WT/DS395/R; WT/DS398/R, adopted 5 July 2011, footnote 176.
3 The duties on the latter group was applauded by some commentators, who see their potential to reduce carbon emissions in China. For further discussion, see Chapter 6.
4 80 products at the 6-digit HS level.
5 UN International Trade Statistics Knowledgebase, 'Harmonized Commodity Description and Coding Systems (HS)', https://unstats.un.org/unsd/tradekb/Knowledgeba

DOI: 10.4324/9781003162339-3

duties on approximately 98.49% products, regardless of their aims and effects. Base metals and articles of base metal comprise the majority (69 products) of the 84 products on which China is permitted to impose export duties within the maximum levels. The rest of them fall within the categories of live animals and animal products (four products), mineral products (six products), products of the chemical or allied industries (four products), and raw hides and skins (other than fur skins) and leather (one product).

2.2. Facts of the export duties in *China—Raw Materials*, *China—Rare Earths*, and *China—Raw Materials II*

In late 2009, the US, EU, and Mexico brought the first case, which became known as *China—Raw Materials* because the products at issue included such raw materials as bauxite, coke, fluorspar, magnesium, manganese, silicon carbide, silicon metal, yellow phosphorus, and zinc.[6] These materials, which were subject to export duties ranging from 10% to 40%, are essential for manufacturing steel, aluminium, and various chemicals, as well as their downstream products.[7] The complainants claimed that the export duties in these cases were inconsistent with the obligations specified under Paragraph 11.3.

China did not contest this claim. It did, however, argue that those duties could be justified for environmental reasons under GATT Article XX. It thereby raised two questions. The first one regarding whether Article XX could be applied to the China's special commitments on export duties. The second one regarding whether China's export duties could meet the eligibility requirements under Article XX. A joint panel report issued in July 2011 provided negative answers to both questions, and the panel's finding was subsequently supported by the Appellate Body (AB) report of January 2012.[8] Following the recommendations of the Dispute Settlement Body (DSB), China removed the disputed export duties on 1 January 2013.[9]

In 2012, even before China had implemented the DSB's recommendations in this case, the US, EU, and Japan brought the second case, which became known as *China–Rare Earths*. This time the complainants asserted that China's export duties of from 15 to 25% on 82 products—of which 52 were rare earths products, 15 tungsten products, and 9 molybdenum products—were not covered by

se/50018/Harmonized-Commodity-Description-and-Coding-Systems-HS (visited on 22 November 2020).

6 Ibid., para 7.59.

7 Ibid., para 2.2.

8 WTO AB Reports, *China — Measures Related to the Exportation of Various Raw Materials*, WT/DS394/AB/R; WT/DS395/AB/R; WT/DS398/AB/R, adopted 30 January 2012.

9 Status report by China, *China — Measures Related to the Exportation of Various Raw Materials*, WT/DS394/19/Add.1; WT/DS395/18/Add.1; WT/DS398/17/Add.1, adopted 18 January 2013.

Annex 6.[10] For the complaining governments, this case, like the previous one, was about access to important industrial raw materials. China for its part argued that the duties in dispute had been imposed in an effort to reduce environmental risks along the production chain of the raw materials at issue and that they were therefore, once again, justified under Article XX. Largely following the reasoning in *China—Raw Materials*, the panel and the AB in *China—Rare Earths* rejected China's arguments,[11] and on 20 May 2015 China fully implemented the rulings by removing the export duties in dispute.[12]

On 13 July 2016, the US brought the third case against China's export duties.[13] The ones in dispute, ranging from 5% to 20%, had been imposed on 10 raw materials, namely antimony, cobalt, copper, graphite, lead, magnesia, talc, tantalum, tin, and chromium.[14] These export duties, in addition to one on indium, were subsequently challenged by the EU on 19 July 2016.[15] Although the duties at issue were prohibited by Paragraph 11.3, China again tried to justify its practice by referring to Article XX.[16] The two complaining governments argued that China's arguments were without merit on the grounds that Article XX had been held to be not applicable to a breach of Paragraph 11.3 in *China—Raw Materials* and *China—Rare Earths*. In November 2016, the DSB agreed to create a WTO panel to examine the third case. But the panellists have not yet been chosen after more than two years. Presumably this case is currently on inactive status.[17] On the other hand, China has already removed the export duties at issue according to its Tariff Plan for 2018 and the most recent one for 2019.[18]

10 WTO Panel Reports, *China — Measures Related to the Exportation of Rare Earths, Tungsten, and Molybdenum*, WT/DS431/R; WT/DS432/R; WT/DS433/R, adopted 26 March 2014, para 7.30. and 7.46.
11 WTO AB Reports, *China — Measures Related to the Exportation of Rare Earths, Tungsten, and Molybdenum*, WT/DS431/AB/R; WT/DS432/AB/R; WT/DS433/AB/R, adopted 7 August 2014.
12 Understanding Between China and the United States Regarding Procedures Under Articles 21 And 22 Of the DSU, WT/DS431/17, adopted 26 May 2015.
13 China—Export Duties on Certain Raw Materials—Request for consultations by the United States, WT/DS508/1; G/L/1147, adopted 14 July 2016.
14 Ibid.
15 China—Duties and other Measures concerning the Exportation of Certain Raw Materials—Request for consultations by the European Union, G/L/1148; WT/DS509/1, adopted 25 July 2016.
16 WTO Secretariat, 'China Blocks US Panel Request in Dispute over Raw Materials', https://www.wto.org/english/news_e/news16_e/dsb_26oct16_e.htm 26 October 2016 (visited on 27 December 2018).
17 The WTO website shows that 'The Dispute Settlement Body has agreed to create a panel, but the panellists have not yet been chosen', see https://www.wto.org/english/tratop_e/dispu_e/cases_e/ds508_e.htm (visited on 27 December 2018).
18 China's Tariff Plan for 2018, see http://gss.mof.gov.cn/zhengwuxinxi/zhengcefabu/201712/P020171215531852388756.pdf (visited on 27 December 2018). China's Tariff Plan for 2019, see http://gss.mof.gov.cn/mofhome/guanshuisi/zhengwuxinxi/zhengcefabu/201812/P020181221619892272965.pdf (visited on 27 December 2018).

In the above three cases, the applicability of Article XX to China's export duty commitments has been subject to continuing dispute. The next section first briefly illustrates the reasoning of the panels and the AB that disallows China to invoke the environmental exceptions under Article XX in *China—Raw Materials* and *China—Rare Earths*. Moreover, although Article XX was found not available to justify the use of export duties in these two cases, China was still given the chance to present its environmental defences for the sake of argument. These defences will be introduced subsequently in order to show the rationale of China's export duties.

2.3. The applicability of GATT Article XX to China's export duty commitments

WTO law is silent on the relationship between GATT Article XX and China's export duty commitments in its accession protocol. This kind of silence may have different meanings in different contexts,[19] so the panel and the AB are mandated to offer clarity according to 'customary rules of interpretation of public international law'.[20] Although these customary rules are not further specified in the Understanding on Rules and Procedures Governing the Settlement of Disputes (DSU), the AB has determined that Articles 31, 32, and 33 of the Vienna Convention on the Law of Treaties (VCLT) can serve as points of reference for discerning the relevant customary rules.[21] Following these methods of interpretation, the panels and the AB examined China's five major arguments in support of applying Article XX to the violations of export duty commitments. The five arguments are as follows.

2.3.1. *Incorporation theory*[22]

The silence on the applicability of Article XX to Paragraph 11.3 means that it is unclear whether WTO members intended to permit China to impose export

19 AB Reports, *Canada — Certain Measures Affecting the Automotive Industry*, WT/DS139/AB/R, WT/DS142/AB/R, adopted 31 May 2000, para 138.

20 Article 3.2 of the Understanding on Rules and Procedures Governing the Settlement of Disputes.

21 AB Report, *United States — Standards for Reformulated and Conventional* Gasoline, WT/DS2/AB/R, adopted on 29 April 1996, para 17. Article 31 of the VCLT requires a treaty interpreter to commence the process of interpretation in accordance with the ordinary meaning of the terms of the treaty, in their context, and in light of the treaty's objective and purpose. When an interpretation according to Article 31 of the VCLT 'leaves the meaning ambiguous or obscure' or 'leads to a result which is manifestly absurd or unreasonable', a treaty interpreter may have recourse to supplementary means of interpretation, such as 'the preparatory work of the treaty and the circumstances of its conclusion', as stated in Article 32 of the VCLT. Article 33 of the VCLT considers the roles languages can play in treaty interpretation.

22 Borrowed from André de Hoogh, 'The Relationship between China's Protocol of Accession and the GATT, 1994: *China—Rare Earths* and the Incorporation Theory –

duties in a manner consistent with Article XX, which thus is open to interpretation. In an effort to ascertain the common intention of WTO members, the complainants in *China—Raw Materials* referred to an 'incorporation theory' according to which the defences of Article XX were available only for two types of violations: those that involve GATT provisions and those that incorporate Article XX justifications by reference.[23]

This theory was inspired by *China—Publications and Audiovisual Products* in which China sought to apply Article XX to another commitment in Paragraph 5.1 of its accession protocol.[24] The AB in that case found that the introductory clause of Paragraph 5.1, 'without prejudice to China's right to regulate trade in a manner consistent with the WTO Agreement', provided a textual basis for incorporating Article XX.[25] In other words, if there is such language present that allows the incorporation of Article XX, then this means that WTO members intended to allow the application of Article XX to a non-GATT provision.

Following this approach, although China's export duty commitments lack the same introductory clause of Paragraph 5.1, it in *China—Raw Materials* argued that several other provisions in its Protocol of Accession and Accession Working Party Report could provide a textual basis for incorporating Article XX.[26] The panel, however, rejected this line of reasoning.[27] In its view, if the common intention of WTO members had been to make Article XX applicable to Paragraph 11.3, they would have included a reference more expressly to this effect such as the introductory clause of Paragraph 5.1.[28]

In its appeal of the decision, China argued that the mere absence of an express reference to Article XX in Paragraph 11.3 did not mean that WTO members intended to exclude its applicability.[29] In response, the AB examined the ordinary meaning and context of Paragraph 11.3 and identified three things that reflected the intention of WTO members to exclude the applicability of Article XX. First, the 'exceptional circumstances' in Annex 6 of China's Protocol of Accession that justified the use of export duty commitments did not include Article XX.[30] Second, Paragraph 11.3 confirmed that China could impose export duties in

Off with its Head! (Part 1)', available at http://www.rug.nl/news/2014/05/rare-earths (visited on 18 June 2017).

23 WTO Panel Reports, *China – Raw Materials*, para 7.111.

24 WTO DISPUTE DS363, '*China — Measures Affecting Trading Rights and Distribution Services for Certain Publications and Audiovisual Entertainment Products*'.

25 WTO AB Report, *China – Publications and Audiovisual Products*, WT/DS363/AB/R 21, adopted on 21 December 2009, paras 216–233.

26 WTO Panel Reports, *China—Raw Materials*, paras 7.125. and 7.133. From a contextual perspective, China argued that Paragraph 170 of its Accession Working Party Report, which includes a subsection titled 'Taxes and Charges Levied on Imports and Exports', can support its argument.

27 Ibid., para 7.151.

28 Ibid., para 7.154.

29 WTO AB Reports, *China—Raw Materials*, para 274.

30 Ibid., para 284.

conformity with Article VIII of the GATT 1994, and not as per Article XX.[31] Third, while both Paragraphs 11.1 and 11.2 of China's Protocol of Accession refer to the GATT 1994 in general, Paragraph 11.3 does not include such a reference that can be interpreted as incorporating Article XX.[32]

2.3.2. Inherent right

In *China—Raw Materials*, China developed a second major argument by stating that it should be allowed, based on its inherent right to regulate trade for the promotion of conservation and public health, to impose export duties in a manner consistent with GATT Article XX, unless it had explicitly abandoned this right.[33] The panel, however, found that China had, in fact, exercised this right when concluding its accession protocol.[34] In the appeal, China argued that, given the silence on the relationship between Article XX and its export duty commitments, the assumption that it had abandoned its right to invoke Article XX distorted the balance of rights and obligations established in its accession protocol, particularly in the light of the objectives of the Agreement Establishing the World Trade Organization (the 'WTO Agreement').[35] In the end, although the AB acknowledged sustainable development as one of the objectives of the WTO Agreement, it nevertheless found that none of the objectives provides 'specific guidance' on the question of applicability.[36]

2.3.3. A holistic approach

In *China—Rare Earths*, China criticised the approach of the AB in *China—Raw Materials* for being insufficiently 'holistic' in addressing its arguments relating to the purpose of the WTO Agreement.[37] For China, the result of the non-applicability ruling was inconsistent with the fundamental 'objective of sustainable development' as provided for in the preamble of the WTO Agreement.[38] Although the panel agreed with China's criticisms in this respect, going so far as to suggest that an interpretation that prevented China from enacting necessary environmental measures had the potential to become 'manifestly absurd or unreasonable',[39] it did not consider the non-applicability of Article XX to China's export duty commitments to be the proper legal context in which to address the issue. Instead, the panel pointed to environmental policy instruments other than export duties that China could legally use under WTO law.[40] Since China had

31 Ibid., para 291.
32 Ibid., para 293.
33 WTO Panel Reports, *China—Raw Materials*, para 7.155.
34 Ibid., para 7.156.
35 WTO AB Reports, *China—Raw Materials*, para 305.
36 Ibid., para 306.
37 WTO Panel Reports, *China—Rare Earths*, para 7.105.
38 Ibid., paras 7.108–7.110.
39 Ibid., para 7.111.
40 Ibid., para 7.112.

never proven that export duties were 'the only type of instrument' to address the proclaimed environmental issues, the panel believed that the *China—Raw Materials* decision would not prevent China from pursuing its environmental goals.[41] It is uncertain, however, whether the AB would also subscribe to this reasoning.[42]

*2.3.4. **Integration theory***[43]

In *China—Rare Earths*, China developed a novel argument that its export duty commitments was integrally linked to the GATT 1994 from a systemic perspective.[44] Following this approach, China argued that each provision in its accession protocol was integral to one or another of the Multilateral Trade Agreements annexed to the WTO Agreement in the light of Paragraph 1.2 of China's accession protocol and Article XII:1 of the WTO Agreement.[45] China further argued for the need to evaluate which Multilateral Trade Agreement relates intrinsically to Paragraph 11.3. For the Chinese government, since both the export duty commitments and the GATT 1944 involved regulation of trade in goods, the former one should automatically become part of the latter one. Conversely, since Article XX applied to all provisions in the GATT 1994, it should also apply to China's export duty commitments.[46]

The panel identified two underlying premises in China's argument and refuted both.[47] First, the panel adopted a narrow interpretation of the language in Paragraph 1.2 and Article XII:1, finding that these provisions only suggested that China's Protocol of Accession was an integral part of the WTO Agreement, rather than specifically making the export duty commitments an integral part of the GATT 1994.[48] Second, the panel disagreed with the premise that China's export duty commitments were intrinsically related to the GATT 1994 because the latter did not require WTO members to eliminate export duties.[49]

41 Ibid., para 7.117.
42 China did not appeal against this finding which left no chance for the AB to review this particular reasoning.
43 Borrowed from André de Hoogh, 'The Relationship between China's Protocol of Accession and the GATT 1994: China – Rare Earths and the Incorporation Theory – Off with its Head! (Part 2)', available at http://www.rug.nl/rechten/organization/vakgroepen/int/guild-blog/blogs/rare-earths-and-the-incorporation-theory-off-with-its-head-part-2 (visited on 18 June 2017).
44 WTO Panel Reports, *China—Rare Earths*, para 7.75.
45 Ibid., paras 7.76–7.90. For China, the term 'the WTO Agreement' in Paragraph 1.2 of its Protocol of Accession referred to the WTO Agreement and the Multilateral Trade Agreements annexed to it. Moreover, Article XII:1 of the WTO Agreement stipulates that the accession of WTO members shall apply to the WTO Agreement and its Multilateral Trade Agreements. In China's view, Article XII:1 suggested that the provisions in its Accession Protocol should be part of one of the Multilateral Trade Agreements.
46 Ibid., para 7.100.
47 Ibid., para 7.76.
48 Ibid., paras 7.80–7.94.
49 Ibid., para 7.95.

Notably, however, one panellist supported China's position,[50] arguing that there should be various ways for WTO members to express their common intention regarding the relationship between a provision of an accession protocol and other WTO agreements such as the GATT 1994.[51] In determining the common intention of members regarding how China's export duty commitments interacted with Article XX, the panellist found that those commitments, by their very nature, expanded China's obligations under the GATT 1994 because the export duty commitments and such GATT provisions as Article II and Article XI:1 deal with the overlapping subject matter of border tariff duties.[52] Moreover, this dissenting panellist also supported the aforementioned opinion that if WTO members had intended to exclude public policy exceptions under Article XX, they would have said so explicitly.[53] This opinion was also shared by three third-parties, namely Argentina, Brazil, and Russia.

It is noteworthy that more third-parties involved in the appeal process contesting the denial of China's right under Article XX than were involved in *China—Raw Materials.* [54] China, however, instead of appealing the whole inapplicability decision, requested the AB to only reverse part of the panel's finding, namely Paragraph 1.2 and Article XII:1 of the WTO Agreement fail to make its export duty commitments an integral part of the GATT 1994.[55] This request was rejected by the AB which emphasised that Paragraph 1.2 and Article XII:1 were only general provisions designed to connect China's Protocol of Accession with the WTO Agreement and its Multilateral Trade Agreements.[56] To further determine the relationship between Article XX and China's export duty commitments in the accession protocol, a thorough analysis of all the relevant provisions should be required. Thus, while the lack of textual reference to Article XX in China's export duty commitments under Paragraph 11.3 is not dispositive in and of itself,[57] both the text and context of Paragraph 11.3 were held to suggest that WTO members did not, after all, intend to allow for the applicability of Article XX.[58]

2.3.5. Article 30(3) of the VCLT[59]

In its appeal of *China—Rare Earths*, China developed a new argument according to which its export duty commitments constituted a subsequent agreement as

50 Ibid., para 7.3.2.1.8.
51 Ibid., para 7.131.
52 Ibid., para 7.136.
53 Ibid., para 7.137.
54 Argentina, Brazil, Colombia, and Russia.
55 WTO AB Reports, *China—Rare Earths*, para 5.13.
56 Ibid., para 5.51.
57 Ibid., para 5.61.
58 Ibid., paras 5.63–5.65.
59 In its efforts regarding *China—Raw Materials* and *China—Rare Earths*, then, it appears that China has exhausted conventional approaches for affirming the applicability of GATT Article XX to Paragraph 11.3. China's arguments based on Article 30 (3) of the VCLT thus demonstrate a desire to explore new solutions from the

described in Article 30(3) of the VCLT. For China, those commitments had modified GATT Article XI:1, for which reason Article XX should apply to the modified Article XI:1, i.e., the provision outlining China's export duty commitments.[60] China's argument here was dismissed by the AB, which found that it had failed to provide sufficient support for its reasoning in light of public international law.[61]

Although none of the above arguments was accepted, the panels in both cases continued assessing China's environmental defences under Article XX. This following section shows why these defences have been found unconvincingly.

2.4. Defences under Article XX(b) and XX(g)

GATT Article XX lays out a number of specific instances in which WTO-inconsistent measures could be justified subject to the requirements under a two-tiered test. The first tier of the test requires China's export duties to meet the requirements under any subparagraphs of Article XX. If those duties are provisionally justified, the second tier of the test further requires them to satisfy the requirements under the chapeau of Article XX.

In *China—Raw Materials*, China invoked both subparagraphs (b) and (g) of Article XX to argue that imposing export duties on the raw materials at issue would not only preserve exhaustible natural resources but also protect the local environment in China.[62] Article XX(b) permits WTO members to adopt a measure that is 'necessary to protect human, animal or plant life or health'. For the Chinese government, the duties at issue should benefit from this provision because they would reduce local pollution generated during the production of coke, magnesium, manganese, and silicon carbide.[63] In contrast, the complainants argued that these duties were actually adopted to provide Chinese companies with preferential access over their foreign competitors to the raw materials at issue.[64]

In an attempt to prove that its export duties had contributed materially to the reduction of pollution caused by the extraction of raw materials, China submitted two empirical studies showing that these duties decreased the demand for exports and therefore, in turn, decreased domestic production.[65] The accuracy of these studies was, however, questioned by the panel on the grounds that they did not account for pollution that might be generated by additional production in the domestic downstream sector.[66] In the absence of an appropriate domestic

perspective of public international law. Various options from this perspective will be examined in Chapter 7.

60 Ibid., para 5.69.
61 Ibid., para 5.70.
62 Panel Reports, *China—Raw Materials*, para 7.356 and para 7.470.
63 Ibid., para 7.519.
64 Ibid., para 7.522.
65 Ibid., para 7.519.
66 Ibid., para 7.533.

restriction, export duties were likely to increase such production and thus to undermine their material contribution to reducing pollution.[67]

Moreover, the panel also questioned the necessity of China's export duties as an environmental policy instrument. In the panel's view, China had the capacity to achieve the same environmental goal by replacing the duties at issue with various alternative measures, namely investment in more environmentally friendly technologies, further encouragement and promotion of the recycling of consumer goods, increasing environmental standards, investing in 'infrastructure necessary to facilitate recycling scrap', stimulating greater local demand for scrap material without exhausting local supply, and introducing production restrictions or pollution controls on primary production.[68] Following its analysis, the panel found that China's export duties were not justified under Article XX(b).

With respect to Article XX(g), a provision that permits WTO members to impose measures that 'relate to the conservation of an exhaustible natural resource', China argued that the export duties on fluorspar would reduce domestic production of the resource by decreasing foreign demand.[69] However, the evidence submitted to the panel showed that, after the imposition of export duties, the domestic extraction of fluorspar in fact increased in response to a substantial increase in its domestic consumption.[70] Thus these duties were found to not satisfy the purpose test under Article XX(g).[71] Moreover, the panel also found that the imposition of these duties had not been 'even-handed' because China did not impose any similar restrictions on domestic consumption. In the panel's view, although the term 'even-handed' did not require identical treatment of domestic and foreign consumers, the imposition of all limitations solely on foreign consumers was clearly not acceptable.[72]

In *China—Rare Earths*, China only invoked Article XX(b) to justify the use of export duties on the rare earth minerals, tungsten, and molybdenum.[73] Clearly having learnt some lessons from *China—Raw Materials*, when China imposed the duties on these raw materials, it made several official announcements regarding its environmental objectives in doing so.[74] These announcements, however, failed to convince the panel that the duties in dispute were truly adopted to protect the environment because no explanation had been offered regarding how controlling the exports would contribute to a decrease in the pollution associated with the production of raw materials.[75] Moreover, the panel found that China's export duties did not make a material contribution to reducing the pollution because

67 Ibid., para 7.538.
68 Ibid., para 7.566.
69 Ibid., para 7.427.
70 Ibid., para 7.429.
71 Ibid., para 7.435.
72 Ibid., para 7.465.
73 Panel Reports, *China—Rare Earths*, para 7.49.
74 Ibid., paras 7.162–7.164.
75 Ibid., para 7.166.

there was no corresponding measure restricting domestic consumption.[76] The mere imposition of export duties, rather than helping to control the production of raw materials, would encourage more intensive use of them by China's domestic downstream industries.[77] Furthermore, various alternative measures were found to be available to China.[78] In the subsequent analysis regarding the requirements of the chapeau, China's export duties were found to constitute a 'disguised restriction on international trade' because they were not actually tailored to protect the environment.[79]

The above assessment suggests that China's export duties were unlikely to be adopted for environmental purposes, largely owing to the lack of corresponding restrictions on domestic consumption of the targeted raw materials. This being the case, the *China—Raw Materials* and *China—Rare Earths* decisions that deny China's right to invoke Article XX seem to be accepted. After all, the duties in dispute would never be justified under Article XX. It is noteworthy, however, that these decisions also prohibit China from justifying any future export duties, no matter on raw materials or not, even if those duties could contribute meaningfully to environmental protection. Moreover, this outcome also seems a fairly stringent finding, especially given that most WTO members remain free to impose duties on exports for any purpose. In this context, the WTO ban on China's export duties has raised several concerns, which are discussed in the next chapter.

76 Ibid., para 7.179.
77 Ibid., para 7.176.
78 '(i) increase volume restrictions on mining and production; (ii) establish effective pollution controls on mining and production; (iii) impose a resources tax on consumption; (iv) impose a pollution tax; and (v) develop and impose an export licensing system'. Ibid., paras 7.185–7.187.
79 Ibid., paras 7.191–7.192.

3 The reception of the ban on Chinese export duties

Concerns, solutions, and the missing piece

The high-profile *China—Raw Materials* and *China—Rare Earths* cases have been the subject of considerable discussion by practitioners and scholars. A large part of this discussion has focused on two major concerns regarding the Appellate Body's (AB's) interpretation in effect denying China's right to justify the use of export duties under GATT Article XX. First, this interpretation in favour of a harsh ban on China's export duties appears to be erroneous because it neglects several important considerations. Second, such an erroneous interpretation would result in negative implications for China and for the World Trade Organization (WTO) in general. Thus various legal solutions to these concerns have been proposed, though none has been implemented to date, thereby raising the question of whether the WTO ban even merits being corrected in practice. This chapter accordingly offers a comprehensive assessment of the current literature on the necessity of providing China with the policy space to impose export duties. The following discussion first introduces the debate on the two major concerns over the ban on China's export duties and then describes the various legal solutions that have been proposed. The discussion concludes by addressing what has been missing from the current discussion, namely whether the WTO ban would in practice prevent China from protecting the environment—which is of great importance in terms of efforts to correct the *China—Raw Materials* and *China—Rare Earths* decisions.

3.1. Erroneous interpretation based on an overly rigid textual analysis

The WTO panels and Appellate Body (AB) have traditionally taken a textual approach to interpretation. This choice was initially motivated in part by a desire to avoid accusations of bias from individual members and thereby to establish the credibility of the WTO as the new institution took shape.[1] As applied in the *China—Raw Materials* and *China—Rare Earths* cases concerning China's export duty commitments, the textual analysis has incurred criticism over its rigidity in

1 Richard H. Steinberg, 'Judicial Lawmaking at the WTO: Discursive, Constitutional, and Political Constraints', 98(2) *The American Journal of International Law* (2004), at 261.

DOI: 10.4324/9781003162339-4

failing to take into account all of the necessary considerations for a correct interpretation, given the fact that China has never explicitly relinquished its right to use export duties in a manner consistent with Article XX. These neglected considerations are illustrated as follows.

First, accession protocols are essentially different from other multilateral trade agreements annexed to the WTO Agreement. The former ones are often loosely drafted because the acceding country lacks the bargaining power that could provide either the necessary checks and balances to produce carefully drafted rules or the legal competence to establish a precise meaning for a given term.[2] Thus a strict textual approach to accession protocols—as if they had been negotiated and drafted with such care that any omission, in this case the lack of reference to Article XX in China's export duty commitments, represents a 'deliberate choice' by the parties—seems in this context a dubious hermeneutic.[3]

Moreover, unlike other multilateral trade agreements, China's accession protocol does not focus on a single subject matter, such as trade in goods or services.[4] Instead, the protocol covers subjects across the entire spectrum of the WTO Agreement and therefore cannot be understood in isolation.[5] In this sense, explicit reference to GATT Article VIII in Paragraph 11.3 does not amount to the exclusion of all other provisions in the GATT, such as Article XX.[6] Otherwise, it would be necessary to make the absurd assumption that some fundamental provisions in the GATT, such as Article I, 'Most-Favoured-Nation Treatment', and Article III, 'National Treatment', are not applicable to China's export duty commitments.[7] In this context, it would be redundant for Paragraph 11.3 to state explicitly, 'consistent with the GATT 1994', a term that the AB found could establish the applicability of Article XX to Paragraph 11.3, because this is the precondition that is tacitly agreed upon in China's accession protocol.[8]

Second, the value of the interests protected by Article XX is too significant to be signed away in a silent manner. The supreme status of Article XX is based on its function as the last resort for members within the WTO framework, thus maintaining the delicate balance of the entire WTO regime.[9] It may be incorrect to assume that Article XX should apply to all WTO agreements because a few of

2 Julia Ya Qin, 'Reforming WTO Discipline on Export Duties: Sovereignty over Natural Resources, Economic Development and Environmental Protection', 46(5) *Journal of World Trade* 1147 (2012), at 1157.
3 Ibid.
4 Qin (2012), above n 2, at 1156.
5 Ibid.
6 Bin Gu, 'Applicability of GATT Article XX in *China—Raw Materials* a Clash within the WTO Agreement', 15(4) *Journal of International Economic Law* (2012), at 1024.
7 Ibid.
8 Delei Pend and Bohua Gong, 'Comments on The Findings About the Application of GATT Article XX in *China Raw–Materials*', 5 *International Business Research* (2011), at 29.
9 Ying Liu, 'The Applicability of Environmental Protection Exceptions to WTO-Plus Obligations: In View of the *China – Raw Materials* and *China – Rare Earths* Cases', 27(1) *Leiden Journal of International Law* (2014), at 127.

them do not have this exception.[10] Such an absence could, however, be carefully negotiated by all WTO members. In contrast, the absence of a reference to Article XX in China's accession protocol may well be a drafting error that should not be considered as negotiating away the right to regulate the public good, especially in the absence of 'thorough and sufficiently open debate amongst all stakeholders'.[11]

Third, the significant value under Article XX is closely related to the objective and purpose of the WTO Agreement, which should be among the considerations in treaty interpretation according to Article 31 of the VCLT. In *China—Raw Materials* and *China—Rare Earths*, China was unable to invoke Articles XX(b) and (g), the provisions referring to the values that WTO members have agreed to reaffirm in the preamble of the WTO Agreement that articulates the organization's 'mission'.[12] In this context, the silence regarding the applicability of Article XX in China's accession protocol should not amount to a waiver of China's essential rights to pursue environmental objectives.[13] In other words, the '*expressio unius* approach' adopted by the AB 'can easily be reversed by reference to a more teleological approach to interpretation'.[14] In this sense, the AB could have engaged in a 'courageous' interpretation that allowed for the availability of Article XX defences for violations of non-GATT obligations even in cases in which there is no specific language regarding their incorporation.[15]

Fourth, China's export duty commitments in Paragraph 11.3 have a special nature as a WTO-plus obligation.[16] One major reason to deny China's right under Article XX is based on a textual difference between Paragraph 11.3 and Paragraphs 11.1 and 11.2. The latter ones broadly refer to the GATT 1994 in general, which in the view of the AB textually incorporated all the GATT provisions including Article XX, whereas Paragraph 11.3 only refers to a specific GATT provision, namely Article VIII. This led the AB to conclude that there is a common intention to exclude the applicability of Article XX to Paragraph 11.3. This conclusion is, however, considered suspect. Unlike Paragraphs 11.1 and 11.2, both of which emphasize obligations already existent under the GATT 1994, Paragraph 11.3 includes two types commitments, namely the elimination of export duties as a

10 Lothar Ehring, 'Nature and Status of WTO Accession Commitments: "WTO-Plus" Obligations and Their Relationship to Other Parts of the WTO Agreement', in Marise Cremona, Peter Hilpold, Nikos Lavranos, Stefan Staiger Schneider and Andreas R. Ziegler (eds), *Reflections on the Constitutionalisation of International Economic Law* (Brill, 2013), at 359.
11 Marco Bronckers and Keith E. Maskus, '*China–Raw Materials*: A Controversial Step Towards Evenhanded Exploitation of Natural Resources', 13(2) *World Trade Review* (2014), at 401.
12 Ilaria Espa, 'The AB Approach to the Applicability of Article XX GATT In the Light of China – Raw Materials: A Missed Opportunity?', 46(6) *Journal of World Trade* (2012), at 1420–1421.
13 Gu (2012), above n 6, at 1029.
14 Eric W. Bond and Joel P. Trachtman, '*China–Rare Earths*: Export Restrictions and the Limits of Textual Interpretation', 15(2) *World Trade Review* (2016), at 208.
15 Espa (2012), above n 12, at 1421.
16 Liu (2014), above n 9, at 123.

WTO-plus obligation and the use of fees connected with importation and exportation as an existent GATT obligation.[17] In this context, while Paragraph 11.3 emphasizes the existent obligation concerning fees by referring to GATT Article VIII, it does not need to do so with regard to the WTO-plus obligation concerning export duties through reference to any GATT provision, including Article XX.[18] In this context, the absence of a reference to either the GATT 1994 in general or Article XX in specific should not be considered a common intention to prevent China from adopting export duties in a manner consistent with Article XX.

Fifth, although China's export duty commitments under Paragraph 11.3 do not have a corresponding obligation under the GATT 1994, there is a systemic relationship between them, based on which Article XX should apply to Paragraph 11.3.[19] The reason is that the use of export duties is inherently related to the GATT disciplines on customs tariffs and export restrictions.[20] In this context, contrary to the AB's finding that there should be a textual connection between Article XX and Paragraph 11.3, the latter's systemically intrinsic relationship with the GATT 1994 is sufficient to enable China to justify the violation of it under Article XX.[21] As a counter-argument, this approach may generate arbitrary results because there seems to be no clear-cut standard for determining the intrinsic relationship between a WTO-plus obligation and the subject-matter of one particular multilateral trade agreement.[22]

The above survey shows that the textual approach adopted by the AB is certainly too rigid compared with a more teleological approach, which may eventually find China's right to protect public policy. However, one can hardly argue that the preference over the textual approach in these cases is legally wrong. On the contrary, abandoning the textual approach for some good purpose may constitute a kind of activism on the part of the AB in taking up issues that should have been addressed by the 'legislative branch' of the WTO.[23] In contrast, a more compelling line of argument correctly questions the reasonableness or even legality of the premise that China could silently sign away its important right to protect public policy under Article XX.[24] Its persuasiveness, however, largely depends on whether the values protected by Article XX are truly at stake, which is discussed next.

17 Ibid.
18 Ibid.
19 Jiaxiang Hu, 'Reconsideration of Applicability of Article XX in GATT: From the Perspective of the Relationship Between GATT 1994 and Other Multilateral Trade Agreements in Goods', 6(2) *Journal of Shanghai Jiaotong University (Philosophy and Social Sciences)* (2014) at 15.
20 Qin (2012), above n 2, at 1156.
21 Hu (2014), above 19, at 34.
22 Ehring (2013), above n 10, at 357–358.
23 Danielle Spiegel-Feld and Stephanie Switzer, 'Whither Article XX? Regulatory Autonomy Under Non-GATT Agreements After *China–Raw Materials*', 38 *Yale Journal of International Law Online* (2012), at 28.
24 For further discussion, see Chapter 7.

3.2. Negative implications caused by the WTO ban on Chinese export duties

Two major concerns over environmental protection and fairness have been raised. First, the harsh ban on China's export duties may unduly limit China's policy space when it comes to protecting the environment.[25] Moreover, as the criteria set out in *China—Raw Materials* and *China—Rare Earths* may also apply to the export duty commitments of other acceded members, including Mongolia, Latvia, Saudi Arabia, Montenegro, and Tajikistan, their policy space for the use of export duties could be similarly constrained.[26] Second, the two decisions may further increase the inequality of the already existing two-tier membership structure of the WTO, thus potentially undermining the legitimacy of the organisation as a whole. In this subsection, these negative implications and counter-arguments against them are reviewed.

3.2.1. Environment-related concerns

Although China's export duties failed to meet the requirements of the environmental exceptions under Article XX in *China—Raw Materials* and *China—Rare Earths*, this, in the view of some commentators, does not necessarily mean that the duties would never be consistent with Article XX.[27] Accordingly, China's policy space for environmental protection would likely be constrained by a harsh prohibition on the imposition of export duties.[28] Moreover, these decisions might also prevent China from using export duties as a climate policy tool, an issue unaddressed in either *China—Raw Materials* or *China—Rare Earths.* [29]

Besides the potential constraints on China's policy space to protect the environment, the WTO ban may leave no room for China to develop a sound environmental policy within the WTO legal framework. It has been argued that, if Article XX is found to be applicable, China could have advanced its export duties in order to meet the requirements of the environmental exceptions, as for instance, introducing corresponding limits for domestic consumption.[30] On the

25 Bin Gu, 'Mineral Export Restraints and Sustainable Development—Are Rare Earths Testing the WTO's Loopholes?', 14(4) *Journal of International Economic Law* (2011), at 783.

26 Baris Karapinar, 'Defining the Legal Boundaries of Export Restrictions: A Case Law Analysis', 15(2) *Journal of International Economic Law* (2012), at 461.

27 For further discussion on whether China's export duties can ever be justified under Article XX, see Chapter 8.

28 Cai Fang, 'What Are the Lessons from *China – Raw Materials*?', China Environment News, available at http://cwto.mofcom.gov.cn/article/m/201202/20120207978584.shtml (visited on 18 June 2017).

29 Ibid. Also see Baris Karapinar and Kateryna Holzer, 'Legal Implications of the Use of Export Taxes in Addressing Carbon Leakage: Competing Border Adjustment Measures', 10(1) *New Zealand Journal of Public and International Law* (2012), at 34. For further discussion, see Chapter 6.

30 Bill Butcher, 'WTO Open Trade Rules and Domestic Environmental Protection Policies: A Balancing Approach', in Larry Kreiser, Soocheol Lee, Kazuhiro Ueta, Janet

contrary, however, the extreme constraint of this harsh ban appears to have pushed China to resort to such non-market means as compelling mergers of small and medium-sized producers of raw materials with a few large state-owned enterprises.[31]

The persuasiveness of the above environmental arguments is, however, diminished by two major counter-arguments. The first one calls into question of the significance of export duties as an environmental measure. It has been argued that the negative environmental impact of the WTO ban on China's export duties is very limited because the duties are at best a temporary environmental protection measure.[32] This line of thought suggests that China's export duties could well be replaced by other traditional environmental policy instruments.[33] For instance, when it comes to limit the environmental harm associated with the manufacture of certain products, one alternative would be to implement a quota or tax on the production.[34] In this way, the protectionist aspects of export duties would be eliminated while the environmental benefits would be preserved.[35] Another alternative for China is to seek advanced environmental technologies from abroad to upgrade its out-dated production technology.[36] A more controversial alternative would be to replace export duties with other types of export restrictive measures such as an export quota, which could be imposed in a manner consistent with GATT Article XX.[37] This option seems to run counter to the WTO's strong preference for tariffs over the less transparent non-tariff barriers and thus encourages China to take an undesirable path.[38]

The second counter-argument calls into question of the policy rationale behind China's export duties. It has been argued that a harsh prohibition on these duties would not practically prevent China from protecting the environment because it simply does not genuinely consider export duties to be part of its environmental

E. Milne and Hope Ashiabor (eds), *Environmental Taxation and Green Fiscal Reform* (Edward Elgar 2014), 69–81 at 77.

31 Julia Ya Qin, 'Reforming WTO Discipline on Export Duties: Sovereignty over Natural Resources, Economic Development and Environmental Protection', 46(5) *Journal of World Trade* 1147 (2012), at 1178.

32 Zhixiong Huang, 12(3) 'From "Market Access" to "Resource Acquire"—Thoughts on China Raw Materials', 1 *Studies in Law and Business* (2010), at 43.

33 Baris Karapinar, 'China's Export Restriction Policies: Complying With "WTO Plus" or Undermining Multilateralism', 10(3) *World Trade Review* (2011), at 405.

34 Mark Wu and James Salzman, 'Next Generation of Trade and Environment Conflicts: The Rise of Green Industrial Policy', 108(2) *Northwestern University Law Review* (2013), at 461. Also see Yong Li, 'Trade Disputes Caused by Export Restrictions on Rare Earths and Its Countermeasures under the WTO Framework', 13(4) *Journal of Shanghai University of Finance and Economics* (2011), at 40.

35 Ibid.

36 Brigid Gavin, 'Sustainable Development of China's Rare Earth Industry within and without the WTO', 49(3) *Journal of World Trade* (2015), at 514. For further discussion on a different proposal about a barter exchange of frontier technologies for minerals, see Gu (2011), above n 159, at 803.

37 Ehring (2013), above n 10, at 361.

38 Butcher (2014), above n 30, at 73.

policy.[39] This line of thought may have been provoked by the fact that the measures imposing the challenged export duties in the *China—Raw Materials* and *China—Rare Earths* cases did not cite any environmental purposes or explain sufficiently how they would contribute to conserving natural resources or protecting public health.[40] Moreover, the absence of restrictions on domestic consumption of the raw materials in dispute raises the suspicion that the challenged duties were adopted with the intention of creating differentials between the domestic and international prices of raw materials in order to further such industrial aims as fostering Chinese downstream sectors,[41] encouraging foreign companies to transfer production to China,[42] and maintaining control of key natural resources for domestic supply chains.[43]

Arguably, China's omission to explain the environmental rationale behind its export duties may in part be attributable to the manner in which legislation is drafted in China, which involves broad aspirational statements rather than specific and detailed provisions.[44] Regarding the lack of complementary measure to restrict the domestic consumption in China, one may argue that this country is just beginning to implement and enforce environmental legislation, so there is undoubtedly room for improvement.[45] In this context, one Chinese scholar has argued that rather than harshly prohibiting export duties, the WTO would be better advised to provide China with guidance regarding how to properly use export duties to protect the environment.[46]

In contrast, his Western counterparts appear to have a more critical view of China's actual motives. For instance, although the Chinese government removed the export duties at issue in accordance with the *China—Raw Materials* and *China—Rare Earths* decisions, the more recent *China—Raw Materials II* dispute raises the concern that Chinese industrial policy-makers are exploiting 'the WTO's "free pass" for temporary breach to their advantage without major consequence' and thus there are 'little incentives for authorities to constrain similar behavior in the future'.[47] One may challenge such perceptions by referring to China's

39 C.L. Lim and J.H. Senduk, 'You Don't Miss Your Water "Til Your River Runs Dry" Regulating Industrial Supply Shortages After *China—Raw Materials*', 18 *Stanford Journal of Law, Business & Finance* (2012), at 76.
40 Panel Reports, *China—Raw Materials*, para 7.522.
41 Karapinar (2011), above n 33, at 404.
42 Gavin (2015), above n 36, at 503.
43 Elizabeth Trujillo, 'A Dialogical Approach to Trade and Environment', 16(3) *Journal of International Economic Law* (2013), at 556.
44 Ruth Jebe, Don Mayer and Yong-Shik Lee, 'China's Export Restrictions of Raw Materials and Rare Earths: A New Balance Between Free Trade and Environmental Protection?', 44(4) *George Washington International Law Review* (2012), at 639.
45 Ibid., at 641.
46 Xiaoyong He, 'The Relationship Between Article XX of the GATT and Protocol on the Accession of the People's Republic of China—A Rational Approach to China Raw Materials', 11(6) *Law Science* (2012), at 66.
47 Mark Wu, 'China's Export Restrictions and the Limits of WTO Law', 16(4) *World Trade Review* (2017), at 674.

voluntary adjustment of its environmental policy in reaction to the *China—Rare Earths* including 'the improvement of environmental regulations on rare earths' and 'the mobilization of local governments to better implement rare earths industrial polices which cover the areas of mining, production, circulation, and industry consolidation'.[48] This line of thought, however, appears to implicitly support the first counter-argument concerning the usefulness of export duties for protecting the environment.

The above survey shows that the question relating to the usefulness of export duties to protect the environment is of the greatest importance. Its answer would determine the seriousness of the environmental problems caused by the *China—Raw Materials* and *China—Rare Earths* decisions. Moreover, without knowing the answer, no matter what China reacts to these decisions, its reaction could always be interpreted as acting in bad faith. The abolishment of export duties could be seen as supporting the claim that the declared environmental purpose of these duties was a mere pretext, whereas to keep imposing export duties is certainly exploiting the WTO dispute settlement mechanism for temporary breach. The current literature, however, provides no clear answer to this crucial question.[49]

3.2.2. Inequality-related concerns

Compared with the environment-related concerns, it is more certain that the *China—Raw Materials* and *China—Rare Earths* decisions would exacerbate the inequality-related problems in the WTO. Surely no one would disagree that the acceded WTO members generally do not enjoy *de jure* equality with the founder ones within the organization because the former ones are very often required to make so-called 'WTO-plus' commitments during their accession.[50] China's export duty commitments serve as a good example because WTO members are generally free to impose export duties. This inequality caused by the two-tier membership system, standing in sharp contrast with the original aim of the WTO,[51] raises such serious concerns as the legalist

48 Chenxi Wang, 'WTO Rare Earths Case's Influence on China's Domestic Regulatory Changes', 52(2) Journal of World Trade (2018), at 329. For the author, the change of environmental policy after the *China—Rare Earths* shows that 'China supports the WTO DSS, keeping its good compliance record with the WTO rulings, maintaining its reputation as an active player in the WTO DSS, and embracing the WTO's far-reaching impact on its domestic management regime'.

49 For further discussion on this issue, see Chapter 4.

50 Steve Charnovitz, 'Mapping the Law of WTO Accession', in Steve Charnovitz, *The Path of World Trade Law in the 21st Century* (World Scientific Publishing, 2014). Also see Matthieu Burnay and Jan Wouters, 'The EU and China in the WTO: What Contribution to the International Rule of Law? – Reflections in Light of the Raw Materials and Rare Earths Disputes', in Jianwei Wang and Weiqing Song (eds), *China, the European Union, and the International Politics of Global Governance* (Springer, 2016).

51 The original aim of the WTO was to create a single regime applying to all members, or at least to those groups of members sharing a comparable economic situation. See Bronckers and Maskus (2014), above n 19, at 400.

tendencies of the WTO.[52] In this context, a further denial of the right of China, as already a second-class member, to protect public policy under Article XX would cause a significant imbalance in the rights and obligations, and which may raise a serious constitutional issue for WTO jurisprudence[53] or even challenge the international rule of law in the long run.[54] Aside from commitments regarding export duties, the *China—Raw Materials* and *China—Rare Earths* decisions may also increase the inequality under the two-tier membership system with respect to other 'WTO-plus' commitments. Following the criteria set out in the decisions, an exception clause in a multilateral trade agreement is generally not applicable to a violation of a country-specific commitment in an accession package unless the clause is specifically incorporated into the text.[55]

Besides exacerbating the division between new and other members, the two decisions may also increase the inequality among those acceded members that have made export duties commitments. Following the criteria set out in these decisions, six of these member nations, China, Mongolia, Latvia, Saudi Arabia, Montenegro, and Tajikistan, are prohibited from imposing export duties, while the other five, Vietnam, Ukraine, Russia, Kazakhstan, and Afghanistan, retain the ability to impose export duties in a manner consistent with GATT Article XX.[56] This result is objectionable because there is no good reason why the generally accepted public policy exceptions 'cannot be invoked by *all* WTO Members in respect of the *same* type of obligation'.[57]

3.3. Proposed legal solutions and the missing piece in current discussion

Various legal solutions have been proposed to address the concerns discussed above through an alteration of the WTO ban on China's export duties. In a judicial way, there is a call for a new interpretation that allows China to justify the use of export duties under Article XX. For instance, from the perspective of public international law, Qin has proposed that China's export duty commitments be considered as either a subsequent agreement or subsequent practice of WTO members modifying GATT Article XI under Article 30 of the VCLT.[58] In the context of WTO law, a more holistic interpretation has been proposed that gives greater weight to the objective of sustainable development as recognised in the

52 Mitali Tyagi, 'Flesh on a Legal Fiction: Early Practice in the WTO on Accession Protocols', 15(2) *Journal of International Economic Law* (2012), at 297.
53 Mitsuo Matsushita, 'Export Control of Natural Resources: WTO Panel Ruling on the Chinese Export Restrictions of Natural Resources', 3(2) *Trade, Law and Development* (2011), at 286–287.
54 Burnay and Wouters (2016), above n 50, at 13.
55 Espa (2012), above 12, at 1407.
56 Qin (2012), above n 2, at 1152.
57 Bronckers and Maskus (2014), above n 11, at 400.
58 Julia Ya Qin, 'Conundrum of WTO Accession Protocols: In Search of Legality and Legitimacy', 55(2), *Virginia Journal of International Law* (2015), at 404.

preamble to the WTO Agreement in order to enable China to use export duties in a manner consistent with Article XX.[59]

In a non-judicial way, China is advised to request that the WTO's decision-making body either approve an amendment to current WTO disciplines on export restrictions in order to incorporate Article XX into China's commitment on export duties[60] or adopt an authoritative interpretation that corrects the *China—Raw Materials* and *China—Rare Earths* decisions.[61] In the case of an amendment, Russia's export duty commitments offer guidance.[62] Having learned the lessons of China's omission in the drafting of its export duty commitments, Russia created a new section in the 'Schedules of Concession and Commitments' annexed to the GATT 1994 in which to record its export duty commitments.[63] In order to make use of such an approach, China could request that the WTO's Ministerial Conference approve an amendment to its export duty commitments that either transfers them to its own 'Schedules of Concession and Commitments' or directly incorporates Article XX.[64] Alternatively, China may also request that the Ministerial Conference or General Council adopt an authoritative interpretation that corrects *China—Raw Materials* and *China—Rare Earths* decisions.[65]

China, however, seems to lack confidence in convincing the WTO members or the AB to support the proposed legal solutions. On the one hand, it has not sought help from the WTO's decision-making body to date. On the other hand, China is also reluctant to develop a new interpretation in the more recent *China—Raw Materials II* case, otherwise it could have responded more actively in the settlement process. This raises the question of whether the harsh ban on China's export duties even merits being corrected in practice.

This book argues that neither the WTO members nor the AB would be interested in altering the WTO ban merely because the textual approach adopted by the AB in *China—Raw Materials* and *China—Rare Earths* was criticised for being too rigid. As shown in Section 3.1, the adherence to the text-first approach in these cases may not be a clear-cut error in a strictly legal sense though the silence on the relationship between Article XX and China's export duty commitments does provide the AB with interpretive space to adopt a more ideal approach, for avoiding all the negative implications caused by a rigid textual analysis as discussed in Section 3.2.

Similarly, the general concerns for unfairness alone would also be insufficient to convince the WTO members or the AB to support the proposed legal solutions. Indeed, although the preamble of the WTO Agreement calls for 'the elimination

59 Liu (2014), above n 9, at 132.
60 Minyou Yu and Chuanhai Hu, 'Be Careful About the Negative Implications from *China–Raw Materials* Rulings' 11(14) *Journal of International Trade* (2012), at 64.
61 Jingdong Liu, 'Accession Protocols: Legal Status in the WTO Legal System', 48 *Journal of World Trade* (2014), at 751.
62 Qin (2012), above n 2, at 1160.
63 Ibid.
64 Yu and Hu (2012), above n 60.
65 Liu (2014), above n 61.

of discriminatory treatment in international trade relations', discriminatory treatment against certain acceded members is in practice permitted.[66] In this context, the WTO decisions that exacerbate the inequality among WTO members concerning the use of export duties seems to be just adding one more example to the existing discriminatory treatment in the WTO. As argued by Ehring, nothing in WTO law or 'superior international law' prohibits WTO members from taking advantage of an acceding member during negotiations.[67]

In contrast, the environmental concern is of great importance in deciding whether WTO members or the AB should support a correction of the *China—Raw Materials* and *China—Rare Earths* decisions. Even an author like Ehring with a critical view of the unfairness concerns may agree that the discrimination applied to the negotiation of accession protocols should not prevent a country from pursuing 'fundamental societal interests'.[68] As he correctly put it, 'one needs to ask whether the values protected by Article XX truly can be threatened by the obligations at stake'.[69] Thus, to justify his argument in favour of a harsh ban on China's export duties, he claimed that the environmental concerns are merely 'the fog created by political statements and litigation advocacy' and 'a public policy problem does not really seem to exist'.[70] Interestingly, this similar view was also repeatedly emphasised by the complainants and the panels as an attempt to justify the denial of China's right under Article XX.[71] In this sense, all of them seem to agree that, if disallowing China to impose export duties would indeed prevent it from protecting the environmental under certain circumstances, the decisions placing a harsh ban on China's export duties should be reconsidered. Otherwise, the discussion of those environmental concerns is of more academic interest than practical importance.[72]

The current literature, however, provides no clear answer to the crucial question of whether the WTO ban on China's export duties would in practice constrain its policy space to protect the environment. In particular, there is a lack of research examining the validity of the two counter-arguments relating to the usefulness of

66 As a result, 'the argument that non-discrimination is constitutional principle of the WTO is facetious at best'. See Charnovitz (2014), above n 50.

67 'There is, however, no legal basis for this claim of discrimination because the WTO prohibitions on discrimination apply to Members' treatment of trade, but not to the negotiation of WTO agreements, nor does superior international law contain a norm prohibiting the unequal treatment of equal situations (despite the principle of sovereign equality) when it comes to negotiating international agreements'. See Ehring (2013), above n 10, at 344.

68 Ibid., at 361.

69 Ibid., at 359.

70 Ibid., at 361.

71 The panel in *China—Rare Earth* went so far as to suggest that an interpretation that prevented China from enacting necessary environmental or public health measures had the potential to become 'manifestly absurd or unreasonable'. See Panel Reports, *China—Rare Earth*, para 7.111.

72 For instance, no environmental group has condemned the WTO ban on China's export duties to date. See Wu and Salzman (2013), above n 34, at 450.

export duties to protect the environment and to the real purpose of China's export duties. The next steps involve filling in the missing piece in current discussion through an examination of practices of WTO members that support the use of export duties to protect the environment (Chapter 4), the policy rationale behind China's export duties (Chapter 5), and the potential role of the duties in tackling carbon leakage, which remained unaddressed in *China—Raw Materials* and *China—Rare Earths* (Chapter 6).

Part II

Preliminary analysis: Would a harsh prohibition on Chinese export duties constrain China's capacity to protect the environment?

4 A harsh ban on export duties would prevent a country from protecting the environment under certain circumstances

The previous chapter presents a popular view, which appears to suggest that a harsh ban on export duties would not prevent a country from protecting the environment. According to this view, on the one hand, targeting exports tends to be less effective than directly regulating the production that causes local or global pollution, for which reason the duties should be generally replaced with such traditional environmental measures as pollution taxes. On the other hand, even if it may sometimes be meaningful to target exports, counties could use quantitative export restrictions, such as quotas. Thus the World Trade Organization (WTO) ban on China's export duties would not prevent China from protecting the environment because it could still impose quantitative export restrictions in a manner consistent with WTO law.

The above perception is, however, rather arbitrary because it ignores the practice of WTO members in two respects. First, although export resections can hardly be the best option to protect the environment, they are certainly not rarely used for that purpose. Section 4.1 provides a survey of this kind of practice in the period from 2009 to 2016 based on the WTO's environmental database.[1] Furthermore, the same survey reveals the preference of countries for export duties over quantitative restrictions, owing to some major drawbacks of the latter option compared with export duties. The actual examples of country practices to use export duties to reduce local or global pollution are also discussed.

The second type of ignorance is in the field of the practice to regulate export restrictions. Section 4.2 shows that environmental regulatory autonomy of countries is always protected in the regulation of such export restrictions as duties or quotas at both the multilateral and regional levels by incorporating general or specific exceptions. This observation is based on a survey of the provisions or

1 It contains all environment-related notifications submitted by WTO members as well as environmental measures and policies mentioned in the Trade Policy Reviews of WTO members.

DOI: 10.4324/9781003162339-6

proposals limiting the use of export restrictions in WTO agreements and 50 select regional trade agreements (RTAs) that have entered into force in the period from 2012 to 2016. The same survey also illustrates the regulatory preference of WTO members for export duties over quantitative restrictions.

4.1. Practice of WTO members to restrict exports for environmental purposes in the period from 2009 to 2016

Based on a survey of the practice of WTO members to impose export restrictions as a means to achieve environmental goals in the period from 2009 to 2016, this section offers two observations. First, it is fair to claim that export restrictions are widely used to fulfil the requirements under multilateral environmental agreements (MEAs). Second, compared with the practice to achieve MEA-related goals, the use of export restrictions to address non-MEA-related issues is less frequent but certainly not unusual. Third, when it comes to using export restrictions to tackle non-MEA-related problems, WTO members prefer duties over quantitative export restrictions. This section discusses these observations and offers actual examples of country practices to use export duties to reduce local or global pollution.

4.1.1. General observations and actual examples of country practices to use export duties to reduce local or global pollution

Regarding the first observation of the practice to use export restrictions to implement MEAs, the WTO Trade Policy Reviews (TPRs) data show that such restrictive measures as export bans are widely used to achieve the goals under two major MEAs, namely the Montreal Protocol on Substances that Deplete the Ozone Layer (the Montreal Protocol) and the Convention on International Trade in Endangered Species of Wild Fauna and Flora (CITES). The former one is designed to protect the ozone layer by phasing out the consumption and production of numerous substances that are responsible for ozone depletion, whereas the latter one is an agreement calling for international cooperation to safeguard certain species from over-exploitation, in order to preserve limited natural resources.

The wide use of export restrictions especially export bans to achieve the objectives of the Montreal Protocol and the CITES can be explained by the fact that these treaties explicitly authorise the participant countries to impose export restrictions on certain targeted products. The Montreal Protocol, for instance, requires contracting parties to not only ban the import of controlled substances from non-parties but also restrict the exports of controlled substances to non-parties.[2] The CITES also includes such import and export restrictions with

2 Article 4 of the Montreal Protocol.

non-parties in order to prevent them from functioning as transit countries for illegal trade in certain species.[3]

One major reason for requiring countries to restrict exports under these treaties is to prevent trade from exacerbating the existing problems. For instance, at the 2013 meeting of the Conference of the Parties to CITES, the large exports of whale products from Iceland to Japan and Norway under their respective reservations to the convention raised the concern that the increased trade in whale products would risk undermining the global efforts to protect endangered whales.[4] Thus Iceland was recommended to remove its reservation and then to restrict the exports of whale products.[5] Moreover, export restrictions may also induce behaviour change. For instance, part of the rationale behind the obligations to restrict exports under the Montreal Protocol is to 'maximizing participation in the protocol'.[6] The reasoning is that, compared with the situation of losing access to the controlled substances entirely, non-party countries would prefer joining the Protocol which only limits their consumption of the controlled substances.[7]

This above observation shows that export restrictions could contribute to treaty-based environmental objectives though, as mentioned above, those restrictions are mostly adopted in the form of ban. In contrast, when it comes to protecting non-treaty-based environmental values, WTO members prefer such comparatively mild restrictions as duties over embargos. One possible reason could be that, unlike the substances that are responsible for ozone depletion, most of the targeted products for non-treaty-based environmental purposes are not required to be completely eliminated. According to the survey of the use of export restrictive measures to achieve non-MEA-related goals, WTO members (nearly 18% of all members)[8] had restricted the exports of various products ranging from raw materials to finished product in the period from 2009 to 2016 (Table 4.1). The following part offers actual examples of country practices to use export duties to reduce local or global pollution.

For instance, Sri Lanka, a country with an abundance of quartz deposits, once adopted export duties on quartz minerals in order to reduce the pollution

3 OECD, 'Trade Measures in Multilateral Environmental Agreements', 9 February 2000, https://www.oecd-ilibrary.org/trade/trade-measures-in-multilateral-environmental-agreements_9789264180611-en;jsessionid=SnsDsvs6SiUMXGCjZWliMkLV.ip-10-240-5-115 (visited on 1 January 2019), at 174.
4 AWI, 'AWI Comments on Iceland's Commercial Whaling and Trade in Whale Products', https://awionline.org/sites/default/files/uploads/documents/AWICommentsonIcelandRev9-15-14.pdf (visited on 28 May 2018).
5 Ibid.
6 UNEP Ozone Secretariat, 'Briefing Note on Non-Party Trade Provisions', April 2016, http://conf.montreal-protocol.org/meeting/oewg/oewg-37/presession/Background_documents/Briefing_note_on_non-party_trade.pdf (visited on 1 January 2019).
7 OECD (2000), above n 3, at 176.
8 The WTO currently has 164 members.

Table 4.1 Practice of WTO Members: export restrictive measures to protect the environment (non-international obligations)

No	*Members*	*Export Restrictions*	*Products*	*Environmental Purposes*
			2009	
1	Brazil	'prior authorization'	'a relatively large number of products'	'environmental reasons'[9]
2	Fiji	export bans	'round logs'	'environmental reasons'[10]
3	Guatemala	export bans	'logs of more than 11 cm in diameter'	'environmental reasons'[11]
4	Maldives	export bans	'certain marine species'	'environmental reasons'[12]
5	Solomon Islands	export duties	timber, fish and other raw materials	'help protect the environment'[13]
			2010	
6	Benin	export bans	'unprocessed teak wood and charcoal'	'protect natural resources'[14]
7	China	export duties	'highly polluting and high-energy-consuming products'	'promoting environmental protection; improving sustainable economic development; and conserving natural resources'[15]

9 WT/TPR/S/237/Rev.1, para 110.

10 WT/TPR/S/213, at 67. 'Exports of round logs are banned for environmental reasons and to promote downstream processing, which provides an implicit subsidy to processors at the expense of forest owners, by lowering the domestic price'.

11 WT/TPR/S/210, at 53–54. 'Export prohibitions are mainly imposed for reasons of national security, protection of Guatemala's heritage or for environmental reasons'.

12 WT/TPR/S/221, at 28. 'Exports of certain marine species are prohibited for environmental reasons'.

13 WT/TPR/S/215, at 35. 'The authorities indicate that export taxes are a practical and cost-efficient means of raising revenue and that they encourage downstream domestic processing and help protect the environment'.

14 WT/TPR/S/236/BEN, at 111. 'Following a shortage on the domestic market and in order to protect natural resources, since 1997 exports of unprocessed teak wood and charcoal have been banned'.

15 WT/TPR/S/230, at 44. 'From time to time, China has been revising its export tax rates or adjusting the list of commodities subject to export taxes, or levying special export taxes, with a view to curtailing exports of certain products, including restricting exports of highly polluting and high-energy-consuming products; promoting environmental protection; improving sustainable economic development; and conserving natural resources'.

No	*Members*	*Export Restrictions*	*Products*	*Environmental Purposes*
8	Malaysia	export duties	'timber, live animals, ash and residues, precious metals, copper, and ferrous waste and scrap'	'conserve the environment'[16]
9	Sri Lanka	export duties	quartz	'protect the environment'[17]
10	United States	'export control'	crude oil	energy conservation[18]
			2011	
11	Australia	'export control'	'wood and wood chips'	'protecting environmental and heritage values'[19]
12	Cambodia	export duties	'certain unprocessed raw materials and products'	'protect human health'[20]
		export quotas	'certain wood products'	'preserve exhaustible natural resources'[21]
13	Congo	export duties	'certain types of timber'	'forest species to be promoted'[22]

16 WT/TPR/S/225, at 35. 'According to the authorities, the main objective of these taxes is to promote the use of locally produced commodities in domestic downstream industries as well as to conserve the environment. The authorities are of the view that export taxes on timber allow them to better manage sustainable development of Malaysian forest'.

17 WT/TPR/S/237/Rev.1, para 110. 'Sri Lanka's legislation allows the use of export duties and cesses to ensure the availability of raw materials for higher-value-added industries and to promote further processing of local materials; finance export promotion activities; and protect national security, archaeological items, and the environment'.

18 WT/TPR/S/235, at 50. 'the Bureau of Industry and Security is responsible for the administration of export controls under the Energy Policy and Conservation Act, the Mineral Leasing Act, the Naval Petroleum Reserves Production Act, and the Outer Continental Shelf Lands Act'.

19 WT/TPR/S/244, at 60. 'Export controls on wood and woodchips are for the purpose of protecting environmental and heritage values'.

20 WT/TPR/S/253, at 44, 'Cambodia levies export taxes on certain unprocessed raw materials and products to encourage local processing, encourage exports of finished products, and protect human health'.

21 Ibid. 'According to the authorities, these procedures conform to GATT Article XX(g), which allows trade measures to be taken to preserve exhaustible natural resources, when such measures complement domestic conservation policies'.

22 WT/TPR/S/240, at 42. 'The export of certain types of timber (forest species to be promoted) are subject to a charge of 2 per cent of the Ex-Works (EWK) value per cubic metre of raw timber exported, which goes to the Ministry of the Environment'.

No	*Members*	*Export Restrictions*	*Products*	*Environmental Purposes*
14	India	export duties	'various raw materials'	'preserve natural resources'[23]
15	Nepal	export bans	various products	'protection of wild-life, human health, and to conserve the biodiversity and environment'[24]
		'export permission'	'some timber products and forest resources'	'biodiversity and environment conservation'[25]
		export duties	'mainly vegetables, maize, rice, wheat, oil cake, sand and stones, and some wood'	'protect environment (discourage environment degradation)'[26]
16	Papua New Guinea	export bans	'certain trees (balsa, blackbean, cordial, ebony, rose wood, teak and all conifers)'	'environmental reasons'[27]
		export duties	skins	'conservation reasons'[28]
17	Paraguay	export bans	'unprocessed or semi processed wood (roundwood or logs) of any species'	'environmental reasons'[29]

23 WT/TPR/S/249, at 76. 'Export taxes are used as a policy instrument to, *inter alia*, ensure domestic supply of raw materials for higher-value-added industries, promote further processing of natural resources, ensure an "adequate" domestic price, and preserve natural resources'.

24 WT/TPR/S/257, at 39. 'Nepal bans the export of certain products for various reasons (Table III.7)'.

25 Ibid. at 40.

26 Ibid. 'According to the authorities, they are levied to protect environment (discourage environment degradation), ensure food security, and discourage trade diversion to neighbouring countries (such as India)'. 'The authorities state that export tax on wood is needed to protect the environment'.

27 WT/TPR/S/239, at 48. 'Exports of certain trees (balsa, blackbean, cordial, ebony, rosewood, teak and all conifers) are prohibited for environmental reasons'.

28 Ibid. 'Exports of skins are taxed for conservation reasons'.

29 WT/TPR/S/245, at 68. 'Some other restrictions are for both environmental purposes and the development of a domestic industry, with the resulting increase in the value added of production. For example, under Law No. 515/94 of 9 December 1994, as amended by Law No. 2.848/05, the export of all unprocessed or semi processed wood (roundwood or logs) of any species is banned'.

No	*Members*	*Export Restrictions*	*Products*	*Environmental Purposes*
18	Thailand	export licensing	a few items of animal products and raw materials	'animal preservation, public health, forest conservation, and conserve exhaustible natural resources'
19	Zimbabwe	export duties	'live wildlife specimens and fertile eggs'	conservation reasons[30]
		'export permit'	'indigenous plants and wildlife'	conservation reasons[31]
			2012	
20	Turkey	export bans	various agricultural goods	'environmental, health or cultural reasons'[32]
21	Philippines	export duties	'plantation (non-native) logs'	'sustainable supply of domestic timber'[33]
22	China	export bans	various products	'domestic considerations regarding environmental and human health protection, and preservation of natural resources'[34]
		export quotas	raw materials including coal and rare earths	'help conserve natural resources or protect the environment'[35]

30 WT/TPR/S/252, at 44. 'Exports of live wildlife specimens and fertile eggs are reportedly subject to an ad valorem levy of 20%, collected by the National Parks and Wild Life Management Authority'.

31 Ibid. 'The Authority administers the permit system governing the movement of all wildlife within Zimbabwe and across its borders (sections (2)(vi) and (3)(iii))'.

32 WT/TPR/S/259, at 53. 'Turkey prohibits exports of 12 items (by broad category, mostly agricultural goods) for environmental, health or cultural reasons (Table III.14)'.

33 WT/TPR/S/261, at 50. 'Only plantation (non-native) logs are subject to an export tax (20% of f.o.b.)'.

34 WT/TPR/S/264, at 59–60. 'mainly because of China's international obligations and domestic considerations regarding environmental and human health protection, and preservation of natural resources'.

35 Ibid. 'The authorities believe that these export restrictions could help conserve natural resources or protect the environment'.

No	*Members*	*Export Restrictions*	*Products*	*Environmental Purposes*
23	Côte d'Ivoire	export duties	'wood in log form'	'forest conservation and development'[36]
		export 'prior authorization' or bans	certain goods such as ivory and some species of logs	'protect the fauna and flora'[37]
24	Korea	export bans	'uncut pieces of natural granite stones'	'preserve natural resources'[38]
25	Bangladesh	export duties	bricks	'brick production is not environmentally friendly'[39]
			2013	
26	Costa Rica	export 'authorization'	'coffee, bulk sugar, fish, molluscs and crustaceans'	'public health, environmental protection'[40]
27	Indonesia	export bans	'sand, soil and top soil'	'protection of the environment and ecology'[41]
		export 'authorization'	'oil and gas'	'sustainable and efficient management of oil and gas as non-renewable natural resources; prevention of excessive exploitation and environmental damage'[42]
		export duties	'leather and wood; crude palm oil; raw cocoa; and mineral ore products'	'safeguard the environment'[43]

36 WT/TPR/S/266/CIV, at 127. 'Exports of wood in log form are subject to a reforestation tax of 2 per cent of the reference value used as the basis for the DUS; the Customs Administration collects this tax on behalf of the Treasury. In addition, Ivorian logs exported or sold on the domestic market are subject to a felling tax and a special forest conservation and development tax'.

37 Ibid., at 129. 'The exportation of certain goods requires prior authorization; there are also prohibitions in place, chiefly to protect the fauna and flora (Table III.9)'.

38 WT/TPR/S/268, at 81. 'The negative list of banned exports … … and preserve natural resources (uncut pieces of natural granite stones)'.

39 WT/TPR/S/270, at 49. 'ceramic building bricks (25%) in order to discourage production of these products'.

40 WT/TPR/S/286, at 9. 'Certain exports (such as coffee, bulk sugar, fish, molluscs and crustaceans) are subject to authorization for reasons of public health, environmental protection or quality assurance. The exportation of various species of wood logs is prohibited'.

41 WT/TPR/S/278, at 55.

42 Ibid., at 56.

43 Ibid., at 58.

No	*Members*	*Export Restrictions*	*Products*	*Environmental Purposes*
			2014	
28	Malaysia	export duties	'timber, live animals, ash and residues, crude petroleum, precious metals, nickel, copper, and ferrous waste and scrap'	'conserve the environment'; 'better manage sustainable development of the Malaysian forest'[44]
29	Myanmar	export duties	'gems, gas, crude oil, teak and conversions, and timber and conversions'	'preserve natural resources'[45]
30	Tonga	'export restriction'	'out-of-season exports of sea cucumber'	'conservation purposes'[46]
			2015	
31	Madagascar	export duties	forestry products	'These levies are paid into the National Forestry Fund, whose aim is sustainable exploitation of this subsector'.[47]
32	Thailand	export duties	'certain sawn wood and hides'	'conserving the environment'[48]
			2016	
33	Fiji	export bans	'round logs'	'environmental reasons'[49]

44 WT/TPR/S/292, at 59. 'According to the authorities, the main objective of these taxes is to promote the use of locally produced commodities in domestic downstream industries as well as to conserve the environment; export taxes on timber allow them to better manage sustainable development of the Malaysian forest'.

45 WT/TPR/S/293, at 42. 'according to the authorities, this is to preserve natural resources'.

46 WT/TPR/S/291, at 34.

47 WT/TPR/S/318, at 88.

48 WT/TPR/S/326, at 64. 'the authorities had indicated that export taxes are primarily for the purpose of conserving the environment, are applied in a non-discriminatory manner and are not intended to be protection for domestic industries nor trade barriers'.

49 WT/TPR/S/330, at 42. 'Exports of round logs are banned for environmental reasons and to promote downstream processing, which provides an implicit subsidy to processors at the expense of forest owners, by lowering the domestic price'.

No	*Members*	*Export Restrictions*	*Products*	*Environmental Purposes*
34	Sri Lanka	export duties	'cashew nuts (fresh and in shells), raw vein quartz and semi-finished products of iron or non-alloy steel'	'protecting the environment'[50]
35	Solomon Islands	export duties	various goods including logs, fish, and timber	'a practical and cost-efficient means of … … protect the environment'[51]

associated with the mining activities.[52] These activities are known to cause such local environmental problems as surface water pollution, soil erosion, or groundwater pollution.[53] Thus when the Supreme Court of Sri Lanka in 2007 stopped the mining activities of a quartz production company on environmental grounds, this decision was praised for achieving a major victory for environmental justice.[54]

A critical view of the above example may suggest that the proclaimed environmental concerns could be used as a pretext for providing quartz processing companies in Sri Lanka with a favourable access to the industrial inputs. This line of thought, however, could hardly apply to the case of Bangladesh in which its government once imposed export duties on bricks to protect the environment.[55] It is difficult to discern any industrial purpose in these duties which, on the contrary, have very strong environmental grounds. According to a Pulitzer Center report, entitled 'Bangladesh's Air Pollution Problem Grows, Brick by Brick', the brick-making businesses in Bangladesh should be blamed for the serious air pollution in that country.[56] Its capital city Dhaka was ranked by the World Health

50 WT/TPR/S/347, at 57. 'With a view to ensuring the availability of raw materials, promoting further processing of local materials, financing export promotion activities, protecting national security, and protecting the environment, Sri Lanka applies both export duties and a cess on certain goods'.
51 WT/TPR/S/349, at 34. 'The authorities consider export taxes a practical and cost-efficient means of raising revenue that could also encourage downstream domestic processing and help protect the environment'.
52 WT/TPR/S/237/Rev.1, para 110.
53 Environmental Justice Atlas, 'Dambulla Quartz Mining Case, Sri Lanka', https://www.ejatlas.org/print/dambulla-quartz-mining-case (visited on 15 June 2019).
54 Ibid. 'Specifically, the court appealed to Article 12(1) of the constitution claiming the right to a clean environment and the principle of inter-generational equity with respect to the protection and preservation of the environment that in this case was under threat for quarry mining'.
55 WT/TPR/S/270, at 49. 'ceramic building bricks (25%) in order to discourage production of these products'.
56 'The kiln operations alone — while representing just 1 percent of the country's GDP — generate nearly 60 percent of the particulate pollution in Dhaka'. See Sohara Mehroze

Organization (WHO) as the top 50 cities with the highest annual $PM_{2.5}$ pollution.[57] Moreover, brick manufacturing would also cause soil degradation and thus threaten the sustainable agriculture in Bangladesh.[58] These environmental problems, however, was once exacerbated by an increase in exports of bricks to India. These increasing exports are believed to be caused by an environmental campaign in India to reduce carbon emissions, which includes a restriction on domestic brickmaking industry and a duty-free treatment on brick imports from Bangladesh.[59] This may explain why the Bangladesh government believed that the use of export duties on bricks would 'discourage production of these products'.[60]

An interesting aspect of the Bangladesh example is that the export duties at issue could contribute to reduce both the local pollution such as $PM_{2.5}$ and the global carbon emissions. Similarly, China also once claimed to have adopted export duties on such so-called 'highly polluting and high-energy-consuming products' as aluminium, coal, chemical products, and fertilizers in order to address both local and global environmental problems.[61] Although some of the duties were clearly WTO-inconsistent, no dispute was raised, possibly for the reason that these duties could not potentially provide Chinese industry with advantages compared with those disputed in *China—Raw Materials* and *China—Rare Earths.* Moreover, these duties were applauded by some commentators, who see their potential to reduce carbon emissions in China as the largest emitter and exporter of carbon dioxide emissions,[62] though a critical view suggests that China should target more energy-intensive products including such higher value-added ones as electronics, machinery, metal products, and textiles in order to make these duties a credible climate policy tool.[63] A detailed discussion is presented in Chapter 6.

Shachi and Larry C. Price, 'Bangladesh's Air Pollution Problem Grows, Brick by Brick', Pulitzer Center, 5 September 2018, https://pulitzercenter.org/reporting/bangladeshs-air-pollution-problem-grows-brick-brick (visited on 15 June 2019).

57 Ibid.

58 Debashish Biswas, 'The Drivers and Impacts of Selling Soil for Brick Making in Bangladesh', 62(4) *Environmental Management* (2018).

59 Kongkon Karmaker, 'Brick Exports: Brisk Business, but Eco-worries Mount', *The Daily Star*, 12 April 2011, https://www.thedailystar.net/news-detail-181387 (visited on 15 June 2019).

60 WT/TPR/S/270/Rev.1, para 74.

61 WT/TPR/S/230, at 44. 'From time to time, China has been revising its export tax rates or adjusting the list of commodities subject to export taxes, or levying special export taxes, with a view to curtailing exports of certain products, including restricting exports of highly polluting and high-energy-consuming products; promoting environmental protection; improving sustainable economic development; and conserving natural resources'.

62 For instance, China's export duties may be reinterpreted as an indirect carbon-pricing system, which is similar to the EU-ETS at the time. See Tancrede Voituriez, Xin Wang, 'Can Unilateral Trade Measures Significantly Reduce Leakage and Competitiveness Pressures on EU-ETS-Constrained Industries? The Case of China Export Taxes and VAT Rebates', Climate Strategies Working Paper (2009).

63 Susanne Dröge, 'Tackling Leakage in a World of Unequal Carbon Prices', Climate Strategies Working Paper (2009), at 67.

The above actual examples of country practices show that export duties would contribute to reducing local or global pollution under certain circumstances, possibly because the theoretically best environmental policies are not always feasible in financial or practical terms. Instructive in this context is a 2003 research study suggesting that if the implementation of pollution taxes is too 'costly' to get public support in the MERCOSUR countries, they could apply export duties as an alternative to improve environmental quality.[64] Similarly, a 2005 International Monetary Fund (IMF) study recommended that Liberia impose an export duty as part of environmental policy until the country has sufficient tax 'administration capacity' to regulate production.[65] Thus, as will be discussed in Section 4.2, the environmental regulatory autonomy with respect to export duties is always preserved for WTO members at both the multilateral and regional levels, except for the WTO ban on China's export duties.

4.1.2. Preference for export duties over quantitative export restrictions in practice

One may argue that the environmental regulatory autonomy with respect to China's export duties is still there because China could simply adopt such quantitative restrictions as quotas which 'fall simply under Article XI:1 of the GATT 1994 and benefit from exceptions under Article XX'.[66] Indeed, export quotas could in theory replace duties in order to achieve the same purpose of limiting exports. In practice, however, WTO members express a strong preference for duties over quotas. Thus the former-mentioned survey shows that 17 WTO members (59%) in the period from 2009 to 2016 chose to use export duties compared with the fact that only 2 members (7%) preferred export quotas to pursue non-treaty-based environmental purposes. Such preference could be explained in the following three respects.

First, compared with export duties, export quotas have to be allocated to various exporting firms, which thus have a great incentive to obtain the privilege to trade, for such quotas often make a product's world market price higher than the domestic price. As a result, exporting firms may waste additional resources in rent-seeking activities.[67] In other words, export quotas are not as economically efficient as export duties.

64 Carlos M. Gómez G. and Carlos E. Gómez C, 'Could the Desire for a Better Environment Lead to Political Options Against Free Trade? Insights from MERCOSUR' (2003), at 3, available at http://www3.uah.es/econ/Papers/TradeEnvGomezG03.pdf (visited on 18 June 2017).

65 Arnim Schwidrowski and Saji Thomas, 'Forestry taxation in Africa: the case of Liberia', *International Monetary Fund Publications* (2005), at 3.

66 Lothar Ehring, 'Nature and Status of WTO Accession Commitments: "WTO-Plus" Obligations and Their Relationship to Other Parts of the WTO Agreement', in Marise Cremona, Peter Hilpold, Nikos Lavranos, Stefan Staiger Schneider and Andreas R. Ziegler (eds), *Reflections on the Constitutionalisation of International Economic Law* (Brill, 2013), at 361.

67 Shantayanan Devarajan, Delfin Go, Maurice Schiff and Sethaput Suthiwart-Narueput, 'The Whys and Why Nots of Export Taxation', No.1684 World Bank Policy Research Working Paper Series (1996), at 10.

Second, rent-seeking activities may also increase the risk of corruption and the attendant welfare losses. Ukraine's export quotas on grain in 2006, for example, raised such concerns, with a Working Paper from the World Bank suggesting that the export quotas should be replaced with export duties.[68] Indeed, when it comes to ensure food security, the EU chose to impose export duties rather than export quotas on cereals as 'a precautionary measure to avoid an overheating of the EU cereals market'.[69] As another example, in 2004, as part of its efforts to protect the environment, the Chinese government imposed export quotas on coke that resulted in the doubling of the world market price for this commodity; as a consequence, many Chinese firms bribed officials in order to obtain the export quotas and thus reap the benefits of the higher international price.[70] In the aftermath, many experts suggested that the Chinese government should replace export quotas with export duties.[71]

Third, export quotas may also result in a greater loss of government revenue.[72] When a government imposes export duties, it enjoys the benefits of the tax; but it cannot always acquire the quota rent from export quotas, even when they are auctioned.[73] Therefore, if a country replaces export duties with export quotas, it stands to lose a large amount of tax revenue, money that could have been used to protect the environment. Thus, for example, China once imposed export duties on textile products and used the revenue to reduce the environmental damage caused by the textile industry.[74]

Aside from the three major drawbacks just detailed—the loss of resources through rent-seeking activities, the risk of corruption, and the loss of government revenue—the replacement of export duties with export quotas would entail losses for import countries. Export quotas, almost by definition, do not allow for a supply response to an increase in demand, and as a result they create larger welfare losses than export duties when the targeted products are inelastic staple goods, such as industrial raw materials.[75] It is for this reason that there was no strong objection to China's export duties on rare earths, while global markets responded strongly when the export quotas were subsequently introduced on these goods.[76]

68 Stephan v. Cramon and Martin Raiser, 'The quotas on grain exports in Ukraine: ineffective, inefficient, and non-transparent', No. 38596 World Bank Working Paper (2006), at 10.
69 European Commission, 'Export Tax on Cereals', IP/97/408, 14 May 1997, available at http://europa.eu/rapid/press-release_IP-97-408_en.pdf (visited on 8 July 2018).
70 EEO, 'Corruption Scandals Concerning Export Quotas on Coke in Shanxi', 2007.
71 Xinhuanet, 'The Adjustment of China's Export Quotas on Rare Earths Products', 7 November 2013.
72 K.C. Fung and Jane Korinek, 'Economics of Export Restrictions as Applied to Industrial Raw Materials', No. 155 OECD Trade Policy Papers (2013), at 18.
73 Ibid., at 18.
74 CCICED, '2006 Annual Report', http://www.china.com.cn/tech/zhuanti/wyh/2008-02/13/content_9734281_5.htm (visited on 8 July 2018).
75 Siddhartha Mitra, Tim Josling, 'Agricultural Export Restrictions: Welfare Implications and Trade Disciplines', IPC Position Paper (2009), at 9.
76 Fung and Korinek (2013), above n 72, at 32.

Therefore, if a country replaces export duties with export quotas, its trading partners may find it more difficult to obtain industrial inputs that are necessary for manufacturing supply chains.

Thus, any argument for the replacement of export duties with quantitative restrictions would be inconsistent with the general economic rationales and common practice of WTO members. Indeed, considering all the disadvantages of quantitative restrictions, an OECD Trade Policy Paper even suggested that RTAs 'could be used as a regulatory tool in order to favour the use of export taxes in situations where export restraint is desirable, rather than quantitative export restrictions'.[77] The regulatory preference for export duties over quantitative restrictions on exports is discussed in the next section.

4.2. Environmental regulatory autonomy and regulatory preference at both the multilateral and regional levels

Based on the WTO's environmental database, the above survey provides two important observations of country practices to use export duties. First, export duties could be useful to reduce local or global pollution under certain circumstances. Second, WTO members generally prefer export duties over quantitative restrictions, owing to some major drawbacks of the latter option compared with duties. These findings are also echoed in a survey of the WTO members' practice to regulate export restrictions at both the multilateral and regional levels. A detailed discussion follows.

4.2.1. Environmental regulatory autonomy with respect to export restrictions

The environmental regulatory autonomy with respect to both export quantitative restrictions and export duties is generally preserved for WTO members at the multilateral level. With respect to quantitative restrictions, although they are generally prohibited under GATT Article XI, Article XX(b) and (g) permit WTO members to impose quantitative restrictions on exports for various environmental purposes. The former one could be used to address such local pollution problems as those threatening 'human, animal or plant life or health', whereas the latter one is more suitable for tackling such global environmental problems as climate change.[78]

Similarly, the founding members of the WTO also have the environmental regulatory autonomy with respect export duties since duties are generally available to them, except for Australia, which committed to refraining from export duties on certain mineral products in the Goods Schedules annexed to the GATT 1994. But these duties could be justified for environmental purposes under Articles XX(b) or XX(g).

In the context of acceded members, 17 of them have committed to restrict the use of export duties in their accession protocols which, unlike other standard WTO agreements, do not have any exception clause (Table 4.2). According to the

77 Ibid.
78 For further discussion, see Chapter 8.

Table 4.2 WTO limits on export duties

No.	*(1994–2011)*	*Export Duties*		
		Scope	*Specific Exception*	*General Exception*
1	GATT 1994	Not covered	Not covered	Not covered
2	GATT Australia Goods Schedules	Positive list	No	Article XX
3	WTO–Mongolia (1996)	Positive list	No	No
4	WTO–Latvia (1998)	Positive list	No	No
5	WTO–China (2001)	Negative list	Yes	No
6	WTO–Saudi Arabia (2005)	Positive list	No	No
7	WTO–Vietnam (2006)	Positive list	No	Article XX
8	WTO–Ukraine (2008)	Positive list	No	Article XX
9	WTO–Russia (2011)	Positive list	No	Article XX
10	WTO–Montenegro (2011)	Ban	No	No
11	WTO–Tajikistan (2012)	Negative list	No	No
12	WTO–Kazakhstan (2015)	Negative list	No	Article XX
13	WTO–Afghanistan (2015)	Negative list	Yes	Article XX

criteria set out in *China—Raw Materials* and *China—Rare Earths* decisions, 11 of those members can justify the use of export duties under Article XX(b) or (g), whereas the other 6 seem to have implicitly negotiated away their environmental regulatory autonomy with respect to export duties.[79]

One might wonder whether those countries would ever have agreed to give up such autonomy if this issue was explicitly raised during the accession negotiations. Or perhaps, reputational-wise, no one would ever ask a sovereign state to give away its right to protect the environment, especially in such imbalanced negotiations as those for access to the WTO, for not being perceived to be unjust or immoral. Indeed, one could hardly do so even in a more balanced multilateral negotiation as, for instance, the EU's proposal generally prohibiting the use of export duties did recognise the environmental regulatory autonomy of WTO members by incorporating Article XX.[80] Interestingly, this proposal was rejected by several countries including China.[81] About three years later, the EU launched the *China—Raw Materials* case and claimed that China had silently signed away its right to protect the environment under Article XX, as part of the 'entry fee' to the WTO.[82] If China would have been informed of this hidden cost earlier, it might have acted differently towards the EU's proposal.

79 China, Mongolia, Latvia, Saudi Arabia, Montenegro, and Tajikistan.
80 Daniel Crosby, 'WTO Legal Status and Evolving Practice of Export Taxes', 12(5) ICTSD Bridges (2008).
81 Ibid.
82 Panel Report, *China—Raw Materials*, para 7.112.

These observations of the environmental regulatory autonomy are also echoed at the regional level. Based on WTO databases, this book examines the provisions limiting the use of export restrictions in 50 select RTAs that have entered into force in the period from 2012 to 2016.[83] Thirty-nine out of the them directly incorporate GATT Article XX as the general exception clause. Although Article XX is not fully incorporated in 11 of the RTAs (22%), these latter agreements include general exceptions that are similar to Article XX(a) to XX(h). In other words, all 50 RTAs in this survey either fully incorporate Article XX(b) and (g) or include environmental exceptions that are similar to the former provision (Tables 4.3 and 4.4). Thus the environmental regulatory autonomy with respect to both export duties and quantitative restrictions are preserved for all contracting parties at the regional level.

Table 4.3 RTAs limits on quantitative export restrictions

No.	*RTAs*	*Quantitative Export Restrictions*		
		Scope	*Specific Exception*	*General Exceptions*
		2012		
1	Canada–Jordan[84]	General ban	Article XI:2(a)	Article XX
2	Chile–Malaysia[85]	General ban	Article XI:2(a)	Article XX
3	EFTA–Hong Kong[86]	General ban	Article XI:2(a)	Article XX
4	EFTA–Montenegro[87]	General ban	Article XI:2(a)	Article XX
5	EFTA–Ukraine[88]	General ban	Article XI:2(a)	Article XX
6	EU–ESA[89]	Negative list	No	Yes
7	Japan–Peru[90]	Negative list	Article XI:2(a)	Article XX

83 There are 61 RTAs that have entered into force in the period from 2012 to 2016, of which 50 RTAs provide texts in English according to WTO databases.
84 Canada–Jordan (2012): Free trade agreement between Canada and Jordan, 1 October 2012, WT/REG335.
85 Chile–Malaysia (2012): Free trade agreement between Chile and Malaysia, 25 February 2012, W/REG330.
86 EFTA–Hong Kong (2012): Free trade agreement between Hong Kong, China and the EFTA States, 1 October 2012, WT/REG322.
87 EFTA–Montenegro (2012): Free trade agreement Montenegro and the EFTA states, 1 September 2012, WT/REG323.
88 EFTA–Ukraine (2012): Free trade agreement between Ukraine and the EFTA States, 1 June 2012, WT/REG315.
89 EU–ESA (2012): Interim economic partnership agreement between the European Union and the ESA states (Madagascar, Mauritius, Seychelles and Zimbabwe), 14 May 2012, WT/REG307.
90 Japan–Peru (2012): Free trade agreement between Japan and Peru, 1 May 2012, WT/REG309.

No.	*RTAs*	*Quantitative Export Restrictions*		
		Scope	*Specific Exception*	*General Exceptions*
8	Korea–United States[91]	General ban	Article XI:2(a)	Article XX
9	CIS[92]	General ban	Article XI:2(a)	Article XX
10	United State–Colombia[93]	General ban	Article XI:2(a)	Article XX
11	United States–Panama[94]	General ban	Article XI:2(a)	Article XX
		2013		
12	Canada–Panama[95]	Negative list	Article XI:2(a)	Article XX
13	Costa Rica–Singapore[96]	General ban	Article XI:2(a)	Article XX
14	EU–Central America[97]	General ban	Article XI:2(a)	Article XX
15	EU–Colombia and Peru[98]	General ban	Article XI:2(a)	Yes
16	EU–Serbia[99]	General ban	No	Yes
17	GCC–Singapore[100]	General ban	Restricted	Yes
18	Korea–Turkey[101]	General ban	Article XI:2(a)	Yes

91 Korea–United States (2012): Free trade agreement between the United States and the Republic of Korea, 15 March 2012, WT/REG311.
92 CIS (2012): Treaty on a Free Trade Area between members of the Commonwealth of Independent States (CIS), 20 September 2012, WT/REG343.
93 United State–Colombia (2012): Free trade agreement between the United States and Colombia, 15 May 2012, WT/REG314.
94 United States–Panama (2012): Free trade agreement between the United States and Panama, 31 October 2012, WT/REG324.
95 Canada–Panama (2013): Free trade agreement between Canada and Panama, 1 April 2012, WT/REG334.
96 Costa Rica–Singapore (2013): Free trade agreement between Costa Rica and Peru, 1 June 2013, WT/REG342.
97 EU–Central America (2013): Agreement establishing an Association between the European Union and its Member States, on the one hand, and Central America on the other, 1 August 2013, WT/REG332.
98 EU–Colombia and Peru (2013): Trade Agreement between the European Union and its Member States, of the one part, and Colombia and Peru, of the other part, 1 March 2013, WT/REG333.
99 EU–Serbia (2013): Stabilisation and Association Agreement between the European Communities and their Member States of the one part, and the Republic of Serbia, of the other part, 1 September 2013, WT/REG285.
100 GCC–Singapore (2013): Agreement between the Gulf Cooperation Council (GCC) and the Republic of Singapore, 1 September 2013, WT/COMTD/N/45/Rev.1.
101 Korea–Turkey (2013): Free trade agreement between the Republic of Korea and Turkey, 1 May 2013, WT/REG339.

No.	*RTAs*	*Quantitative Export Restrictions*		
		Scope	*Specific Exception*	*General Exceptions*
19	Malaysia–Australia[102]	General ban	Article XI:2(a)	Yes
20	New Zealand–Chinese Taipei[103]	General ban	Article XI:2(a)	Article XX
21	Turkey–Mauritius[104]	General ban	Article XI:2(a)	Yes
22	Ukraine–Montenegro[105]	Negative list	Article XI:2(a)	Yes
		2014		
23	Canada–Honduras[106]	Negative list	Article XI:2(a)	Article XX
24	Chile–Viet Nam[107]	Negative list	Article XI:2(a)	Article XX
25	EFTA–Central America[108]	General ban	No	Article XX
26	EU–Cameroon[109]	General ban	No	Yes
27	EU–Georgia[110]	General ban	Article XI:2(a)	Article XX
28	EU–Moldova[111]	General ban	Article XI:2(a)	Yes
29	EU–Ukraine[112]	General ban	Article XI:2(a)	Article XX

102 Malaysia–Australia (2013): Free trade agreement between Australia and Malaysia, 1 January 2013, WT/REG340.

103 New Zealand–Chinese Taipei (2013): Agreement between New Zealand and The Separate Customs Territory of Taiwan, Penghu, Kinmen and Matsu on economic cooperation, 1 December 2013, WT/REG348.

104 Turkey–Mauritius (2013): Free trade agreement between Turkey and Mauritius, 1 June 2013, WT/REG341.

105 Ukraine–Montenegro (2013): Free trade agreement between Ukraine and Montenegro, 1 January 2013, WT/REG338.

106 Canada–Honduras (2014): Free trade agreement between Canada and Honduras, 1 October 2014, WT/REG364.

107 Chile–Viet Nam (2014): Free trade agreement between Viet Nam and Chile, 1 January 2014, WT/REG365.

108 EFTA–Central America (2014): Free trade agreement between the EFTA states and Central America – Costa Rica and Panama, 19 August 2014, WT/REG357.

109 EU–Cameroon (2014): Interim Agreement with a view to an Economic Partnership Agreement between the European Community and its Member States, of the one part, and the Central Africa Party, of the other part – Protocol, 4 August 2014, WT/REG274.

110 EU–Georgia (2014): Deep and comprehensive free trade area concluded as a part of the association agreement between the European Union and Georgia, 1 September 2014, WT/REG354.

111 EU–Moldova (2014): Deep and comprehensive free trade area concluded as a part of the association agreement between the European Union and the Republic of Moldova, 1 September 2014, WT/REG352.

112 EU–Ukraine (2014): Deep and comprehensive free trade area concluded as a part of the association agreement between the European Union and Ukraine, 23 April 2014, WT/REG353.

No.	*RTAs*	*Quantitative Export Restrictions*		
		Scope	*Specific Exception*	*General Exceptions*
30	Hong Kong–Chile[113]	General ban	Article XI:2(a)	Article XX
31	Iceland–China[114]	General ban	Article XI:2(a)	Article XX
32	Korea–Australia[115]	General ban	Restricted	Article XX
33	Singapore–Chinese Taipei[116]	General ban	Article XI:2(a)	Article XX
34	Switzerland–China[117]	General ban	Article XI:2(a)	Article XX
		2015		
35	ASEAN–India[118]	General ban	Article XI:2(a)	Article XX
36	Australia–China[119]	General ban	Article XI:2(a)	Yes
37	Canada–Korea[120]	Negative list	Article XI:2(a)	Article XX
38	China–Korea[121]	General ban	Article XI:2(a)	Article XX
39	EFTA–Bosnia and Herzegovina[122]	Positive list	Article XI:2(a)	Article XX
40	EU–Bosnia and Herzegovina[123]	General ban	No	Yes

113 Hong Kong–Chile (2014): Free trade agreement between Hong Kong, China and Chile, 9 October 2014, WT/REG356.

114 Iceland–China (2014): Free trade agreement between Iceland and China, 1 July 2014, WT/REG355.

115 Korea–Australia (2014): Free trade agreement between the Republic of Korea and Australia, 12 December 2014, WT/REG359.

116 Singapore–Chinese Taipei (2014): Agreement between Singapore and the Separate Customs Territory of Taiwan, Penghu, Kinmen and Matsu on economic partnership, 19 April 2014, WT/REG350.

117 Switzerland–China (2014): Free trade agreement between Switzerland and China, 1 July 2014, WT/REG351.

118 ASEAN–India (2015): Framework Agreement on Comprehensive Economic Cooperation Between the Republic of India and the Association of Southeast Asian Nations, 1 July 2015, WT/REG372.

119 Australia–China (2015): Free trade agreement between Australia and China, 20 December 2015, WT/REG369.

120 Canada–Korea (2015): Free trade agreement between Canada and the Republic of Korea, 1 January 2015, WT/REG362.

121 China–Korea (2015): Free trade agreement between China and the Republic of Korea, 20 December 2015, WT/REG370.

122 EFTA–Bosnia and Herzegovina (2015): Free trade agreement between the EFTA States and Bosnia and Herzegovina, 1 January 2015, WT/REG360.

123 EU–Bosnia and Herzegovina (2015): The Stabilisation and Association Agreement between the European Union and Bosnia and Herzegovina, 1 July 2015, WT/REG242.

No.	*RTAs*	*Quantitative Export Restrictions*		
		Scope	*Specific Exception*	*General Exceptions*
41	EAEU[124]	General ban	No	Yes
42	Japan–Australia[125]	General ban	Restricted	Article XX
43	Korea–New Zealand[126]	General ban	Restricted	Article XX
44	Korea–Viet Nam[127]	General ban	Article XI:2(a)	Article XX
45	SADC–Accession of Seychelles[128]	General ban	No	Yes
46	Turkey–Malaysia[129]	General ban	Article XI:2(a)	Article XX
		2016		
47	EU–Côte d'Ivoire[130]	General ban	No	Yes
48	Japan–Mongolia[131]	General ban	Article XI:2(a)	Article XX
49	Korea–Colombia[132]	Negative list	Article XI:2(a)	Article XX
50	Turkey–Moldova[133]	General ban	Article XI:2(a)	Article XX

Furthermore, two EU RTAs, namely EU–Cameroon (2014) and EU–Côte d'Ivoire (2016), specifically permit the other parties to use export duties on a temporary basis to protect the environment under certain circumstances. On the

124 EAEU (2015): Treaty on the Eurasian Economic Union, 1 January 2015, WT/REG358.

125 Japan–Australia (2015): Economic partnership agreement between Japan and Australia, 15 January 2015, WT/REG361.

126 Korea–New Zealand (2015): Free trade agreement between the Republic of Korea and New Zealand, 20 December 2015, WT/REG367.

127 Korea–Viet Nam (2015): Free trade agreement between The Republic of Korea and Viet Nam, 20 December 2015, WT/REG371.

128 SADC–Accession of Seychelles (2015): Accession of Seychelles to the Southern African Development Community Trade Protocol, 25 May 2015, REG368.

129 Turkey–Malaysia (2015): Free trade agreement between Turkey and Malaysia, 1 August 2015, WT/REG379.

130 EU–Côte d'Ivoire (2016): Economic partnership agreement between Côte d'Ivoire and the European Union, 3 September 2016, WT/REG258.

131 Japan–Mongolia (2016) has additional exception clauses that allow either party to consult with the other regarding the imposition of export restrictions for the purpose of stabilizing the prices of primary commodities or promoting a particular industry 'with a view to raising the general standard of living of its people'.

132 Korea–Colombia (2016): Free trade agreement between Colombia and the Republic of Korea, 15 July 2016, WT/REG375.

133 Turkey–Moldova (2016) has additional exception clauses that allow either party to impose export restrictions in accordance with procedures set out in the dispute settlement clause in circumstances in which compliance with the limits on export restrictions leads to a serious shortage of one of the exporting country's essential products.

Table 4.4 RTAs limits on export duties

No.	*RTAs*	*Export Duties*		
		Scope	*Specific Exception*	*General Exception*
		2012		
1	Canada–Jordan	Not covered	Not covered	Not covered
2	Chile–Malaysia	No covered	Not covered	Not covered
3	EFTA–Hong Kong	Positive list	No	Article XX
4	EFTA–Montenegro	Positive list	No	Article XX
5	EFTA–Ukraine	Positive list	No	Article XX
6	EU–ESA	Negative list	Yes	Yes
7	Japan–Peru	General ban	Yes	Article XX
8	Korea–United States	General ban	Yes	Article XX
9	CIS	Negative list	No	Article XX
10	United State–Colombia	General ban	Yes	Article XX
11	United States–Panama	General ban	Yes	Article XX
		2013		
12	Canada–Panama	General ban	Yes	Article XX
13	Costa Rica–Singapore	Positive list	No	Article XX
14	EU–Central America	General ban	No	Article XX
15	EU–Colombia and Peru	General ban	No	Yes
16	EU–Serbia	General ban	No	Yes
17	GCC–Singapore	Not covered	Not covered	Not covered
18	Korea–Turkey	General ban	Yes	Yes
19	Malaysia–Australia	Not covered	Not covered	Not covered
20	New Zealand–Chinese Taipei	Not covered	Not covered	Not covered
21	Turkey–Mauritius	General ban	No	Yes
22	Ukraine–Montenegro	Negative list	No	Yes
		2014		
23	Canada–Honduras	General ban	Yes	Article XX
24	Chile–Viet Nam	Not covered	Not covered	Not covered
25	EFTA–Central America	Negative list	No	Article XX

No.	*RTAs*	*Export Duties*		
		Scope	*Specific Exception*	*General Exception*
26	EU–Cameroon	Negative list	Yes	Yes
27	EU–Georgia	General ban	No	Article XX
28	EU–Moldova	General ban	No	Yes
29	EU–Ukraine	Negative list	Yes	Article XX
30	Hong Kong–Chile	Not covered	Not covered	Not covered
31	Iceland–China	Not covered	Not covered	Not covered
32	Korea–Australia	General ban	Yes	Article XX
33	Singapore–Chinese Taipei	General ban	No	Article XX
34	Switzerland–China	Not covered	Not covered	Not covered
		2015		
35	ASEAN–India	Not covered	Not covered	Not covered
36	Australia–China	Not covered	Not covered	Not covered
37	Canada–Korea	General ban	Yes	Article XX
38	China–Korea	Not covered	Not covered	Not covered
39	EFTA–Bosnia and Herzegovina	Positive list	No	Article XX
40	EU–Bosnia and Herzegovina	General ban	No	Yes
41	EAEU	General ban	No	Yes
42	Japan–Australia	General ban	Yes	Article XX
43	Korea–New Zealand	General ban	Yes	Article XX
44	Korea–Viet Nam	Not covered	Not covered	Not covered
45	SADC–Accession of Seychelles	General ban	No	Yes
46	Turkey–Malaysia	Not covered	Not covered	Not covered
		2016		
47	EU–Côte d'Ivoire	Negative list	Yes	Yes
48	Japan–Mongolia	Not covered	Not covered	Not covered
49	Korea–Colombia	Negative list	Yes	Article XX
50	Turkey–Moldova	General ban	No	Article XX

one hand, the EU appears to have recognised the usefulness of export duties as an environmental measure. On the other hand, there seems to be a regulatory preference for export duties over other export restrictive measures. A detailed discussion of such regulatory preference is presented in the following subsection.

4.2.2. Regulatory preference for export duties over quantitative restrictions

There is a clear regulatory preference for export duties over quantitative restrictions at the multilateral level. As introduced above, the latter ones are generally prohibited under the GATT 1994, whereas only 18 members have committed to restrict the use of export duties. In the period before 2011, WTO-plus provisions on export duties were incorporated into the accession protocols of six acceded members, including WTO–Mongolia (1996),[134] WTO–Latvia (1998),[135] WTO–China (2001),[136] WTO–Saudi Arabia (2005),[137] WTO–Vietnam (2006),[138] and WTO–Ukraine (2008).[139] Like the commitments made by Australia, most of these WTO-plus provisions provide a list of products that are not to be subject to export duties ('positive list').[140] Unusually, China's Protocol of Accession provides a negative list that allows the imposition of export duties on only 84 specific products with a maximum level ('negative list').[141]

By contrast, the 11 that concluded after 2011 reflect a tough approach to export duties, in that 5 of them, namely WTO–Russia (2011),[142] WTO–Montenegro

134 WTO–Mongolia (1996): Protocol for the Accession of Mongolia to the Marrakesh Agreement Establishing the World Trade Organization, 25 July 1996, WT/ACC/MNG/11; Report of the Working Party on the Accession of Mongolia, 27 June 1996, WT/ACC/MNG/9, para 24.

135 WTO–Latvia (1998): Protocol of Accession of Latvia to the Marrakesh Agreement Establishing the World Trade Organization, 23 October 1998, WT/ACC/LVA/35; Report of the Working Party on the Accession of Latvia to the World Trade Organization, 30 September 1998, WT/ACC/LVA/32, paras 67–69.

136 WTO–China (2001): Protocol on the Accession of the People's Republic of China, 23 November 2001, WT/L/432, para 11.3; Report of the Working Party on the Accession of the People's Republic of China, 1 October 2001, WT/ACC/CHN/49, paras 155–156.

137 WTO–Saudi Arabia (2005): Protocol on the Accession of the Kingdom of Saudi Arabia, November 2005, WT/L/627 11; Report of the Working Party on the Accession of the Kingdom of Saudi Arabia to the World Trade Organization, 1 November 2005, WT/ACC/SAU/61, para 184.

138 WTO–Vietnam (2006): Protocol on the Accession of the Socialist Republic of Viet Nam, 15 November 2006, WT/L/662; Report of the Working Party on the Accession of Viet Nam, 27 October 2006, WT/ACC/VNM/48, paras 256–260.

139 WTO–Ukraine (2008): Protocol on the Accession of Ukraine, 13 February 2008, WT/L/718; Report of the Working Party on the Accession of Ukraine to the World Trade Organization, 25 January 2008, WT/ACC/UKR/152, paras 228–240.

140 This term was borrowed from the use of 'positive' and 'negative' lists in the context of trade in services and investment. See European Commission, 'Services and investment in EU trade deals Using 'positive' and 'negative' lists', April 2016.

141 Ibid.

142 WTO–Russia (2011): Protocol on the Accession of the Russian Federation, 17 December 2011, WT/MIN(11)/24; WT/L/839; Report of the Working Party on

(2011),[143] WTO–Tajikistan (2012),[144] WTO–Kazakhstan (2015),[145] and WTO–Afghanistan (2015),[146] include provisions regulating export duties (Table 4.2). In these provisions, the earlier practice of providing a positive list that prohibits countries from imposing export duties on certain products has been gradually replaced by a negative list that specifies the products on which countries are permitted to impose export duties. However, compared with the general prohibition on quantitative export restrictions under GATT Article XI, the limits on export duties in accession protocols are still much less stringent, which appears to reflect the regulatory preference for duties over quantitative restrictions.[147]

Similarly, at the regional level, this regulatory preference is found in the select 50 RTAs that have entered into force in the period from 2012 to 2016 in two respects.[148] First, regarding the limits on the scope of products subject to export restrictions, most RTAs (82%) generally prohibit contracting parties from using quantitative export restrictions by directly incorporating GATT Article XI. In contrast, less than half RTAs (44%) have a general prohibition on export duties.[149] Moreover, another 15 RTAs lack any provision for restricting the use of export duties.[150]

the Accession of the Russian Federation to the World Trade Organization, 17 November 2011, WT/ACC/RUS/70; WT/MIN(11)/2, paras 621–638.

143 WTO–Montenegro (2011): Protocol on the Accession of Montenegro, 17 December 2011, WT/MIN(11)/28; WT/L/841; Report of the Working Party on the Accession of Montenegro to the World Trade Organization, 5 December 2011, WT/ACC/CGR/38; WT/MIN(11)/7, paras 130–132.

144 WTO–Tajikistan (2012): Protocol on the Accession of the Republic of Tajikistan, 11 December 2012, WT/L/872; Report of the Working Party on the Accession of Tajikistan to the World Trade Organization, 6 November 2012, WT/ACC/TJK/30, paras 166–169.

145 WTO–Kazakhstan (2015): Protocol on the Accession of the Republic of Kazakhstan, 30 July 2015, WT/L/957; Report of the Working Party on the Accession of the Republic of Kazakhstan to the World Trade Organization, 23 June 2015, WT/ACC/KAZ/93, paras 528–540.

146 WTO–Afghanistan (2015): Protocol on the Accession of the Islamic Republic of Afghanistan, 21 December 2015, WT/MIN(15)/39; WT/L/974; Report of the Working Party on the Accession of the Islamic Republic of Afghanistan to the World Trade Organization, 13 November 2015, WT/ACC/AFG/36; WT/MIN(15)/6, paras 140–145.

147 Exceptionally, according to Paragraph 132 of its Working Party Report, Montenegro committed not to apply or reintroduce any export duty as from the date of accession. See Report of the Working Party on the Accession of Montenegro to the World Trade Organization, WT/ACC/CGR/38, 5 December 2011.

148 There are 61 RTAs that have entered into force in the period from 2012 to 2016, of which 50 RTAs provide texts in English according to WTO database.

149 2012: Japan–Peru, Korea–United States, United State–Colombia, United States–Panama; 2013: Canada–Panama, EU–Central America, EU–Colombia and Peru, EU–Serbia, Korea–Turkey, Turkey–Mauritius; 2014: Canada–Honduras, EU–Georgia, EU–Moldova, Korea–Australia, Singapore–Chinese Taipei; 2015: Canada–Korea, EU–Bosnia and Herzegovina, EAEU, Japan–Australia, Korea–New Zealand, SADC–Accession of Seychelles; 2016: Turkey–Moldova.

150 Most of the RTAs that do not limit export duties involve at least one party from Asia, including Chile–Malaysia (2012), GCC–Singapore (2013), Malaysia–Australia (2013),

It is noteworthy that, all the RTAs involving China does not limit the use of export duties,[151] whereas those involving the EU requires the contracting parties to either stop imposing export duties on any products[152] or provide a negative list.[153] This striking contrast between their attitudes towards the regulation of export duties may have developed into a series of confrontations between the EU and China in front of the WTO. However, even a party like the EU with enthusiasm for banning export duties, it provides contracting parties with the policy space to use duties for environmental purposes in all the RTAs. Furthermore, when export restraint is desirable for its trading partners to achieve certain objectives such as environmental protection, the EU prefers the use of duties over quantitative restrictions by incorporating specific exception clauses in some RTAs.

These specific exceptions that are tailor-made for the use of export duties represent the second type of regulatory preference at the regional level. Indeed, compared with WTO law, 24% of RTAs choose to restrict or exclude the use of the WTO specific exception to quantitative export restrictions, namely GATT Article XI:2(a), whereas 32% of RTAs actively create new specific exception to export duties which include three RTAs involving the EU. Thus, under EU–Cameroon (2014), Cameroon could impose export duties in the event of 'serious public finance problem' or 'the need for greater environmental protection'. Likewise, EU–Côte d'Ivoire (2016) permits Côte d'Ivoire to impose export duties on a temporary basis for 'income, protection for infant industry or environmental protection'. Moreover, EU–Ukraine (2014) in a more general sense allows Ukraine to apply a safeguard measure in the form of a surcharge to the export duty on certain products when the cumulative volume of the exports of these products exceeds a trigger level.[154]

In fact, these regulatory preferences as observed above have existed for a long time. For instance, an OECD Trade Policy Paper in 2012 examined 93 RTAs, which have been concluded before 2010, and found some of the agreements clearly show contracting parties' preference for export duties over quantitative restrictions by allowing the former one to be imposed on a wider range of products than the latter one.[155] The same paper thus suggests that this type of practice 'could be used as a regulatory tool in order to favour the use of export taxes in situations where export restraint is desirable, rather than quantitative export

New Zealand–Chinese Taipei (2013), Chile–Viet Nam (2014), Hong Kong–Chile (2014), Iceland–China (2014), Switzerland–China (2014), Association of Southeast Asian Nations (ASEAN)–India (2015), Australia–China (2015), Korea–Viet Nam (2015), Turkey–Malaysia (2015), and Japan–Mongolia (2016).

151 Iceland–China (2014), Switzerland–China (2014), Australia–China (2015), and China–Korea (2015).

152 It is noteworthy that 6 of 10 RTAs involving the EU, namely EU–Central America (2013), EU–Colombia and Peru (2013), EU–Serbia (2013), EU–Georgia (2014), EU–Moldova (2014), and EU–Bosnia and Herzegovina (2015), generally prohibit export duties.

153 EU–ESA (2012), EU–Cameroon (2014), EU–Ukraine (2014), and EU–Côte d'Ivoire (2016).

154 Annex I – D of EU–Ukraine (2014).

restrictions'.[156] The rationale behind this policy recommendation is to avoid the disadvantages of quantitative restrictions compared with export duties as discussed in the previous section.

4.3. Conclusions

This chapter shows that a harsh ban on export duties is inconsistent with the practice of WTO members and economic rationale in two respects. First, the actual examples of country practices and economic research show that export duties could be useful to reduce local or global pollution under certain circumstances, because the theoretically best environmental policies are not always feasible in financial or practical terms. Thus the environmental regulatory autonomy with respect to export duties is always preserved for WTO members at both the multilateral and regional levels,[157] except for the WTO ban on China's export duties. In this sense, it is one thing to propose strictly scrutinising any environmental reasoning behind export duties, but quite another to ban these duties without any reasoning. The arbitrary nature of the latter one is apparent.

Second, the suggestion that export duties could be substituted by export quotas lacks sound basis. In sharp contrast, an OECD Trade Policy Paper suggested the contrary,[158] possibly owing to the major disadvantages of quantitative restrictions compared with duties: (i) the loss of resources through rent-seeking activities, (ii) the risk of corruption, and (iii) the loss of government revenue. Moreover, quantitative restrictions also create additional challenges for importing countries that need access to such inelastic staple goods as raw materials. The OECD opinion is echoed by the practice of WTO members, which shows a clear preference for export duties over quantitative restrictions.

To conclude this chapter, both the practice and rationales suggest that export duties would remain meaningful for countries to reduce local or global pollution under certain circumstances. Thus, at least in theory, the WTO ban on China's export duties could prevent this country from enacting important environmental protections. Relevant to these considerations is the issue of China's actual rationale for seeking to impose export duties, which is taken up in the following chapter.

156 Ibid.

157 This observation is based on the surveys of WTO members' practice in the period from 2009 to 2016 and the provisions limiting the use of export restrictions in 50 select RTAs that have entered into force in the period from 2012 to 2016. For further information, see Sections 4.1.1 and 4.2.1.

158 Korinek and Bartos (2012), above n 155.

5 Policy rationales behind Chinese export duties

As introduced in Chapter 3, one perception that flourished despite the harsh ban on China's export duties is that the declared environmental purposes of these duties are a mere pretext for a policy designed to further an economic goal. This perception may have been provoked by the fact that the measures imposing the challenged export duties in the *China—Raw Materials* and *China—Rare Earths* cases did not cite any environmental purposes or explain sufficiently how they would protect the environment. Moreover, the absence of restrictions on domestic consumption of the raw materials in dispute in effect created differentials between the domestic and international prices of raw materials, which raises the suspicion that the challenged duties were actually adopted to indirectly subsidise Chinese downstream sectors.

There are at least two good reasons for doubts. First, measures could fall short of their original purposes when they are put into effect. Thus some scholars have argued that the WTO would be better advised to provide China with guidance regarding how to properly use export duties to protect the environment.[1] Second, most importantly, even if the duties in dispute were actually adopted for an industrial purpose, the question is how greatly could this result be generalised. As introduced in the previous chapter, China's export duties on such so-called 'highly polluting and high-energy-consuming products' as aluminium, coal, chemical products, and fertilizers were applauded by some commentators, who see their potential to reduce carbon emissions in China as the largest emitter and exporter of carbon dioxide emissions. It is insensible to ban them outright without any assessment.

Admittedly, the tendency for Chinese legislation to take the form of broad aspirational statements rather than detailed provisions complicates efforts to determine the specific rationales for a given measure.[2] This chapter, accordingly, rather than focusing on textual analysis of relevant legal documents, looks first to the legislative process that generated the export duties in order to identify the

1 For further information, see Chapter 3.

2 Ruth Jebe, Don Mayer and Yong-Shik Lee, 'China's Export Restrictions of Raw Materials and Rare Earths: A New Balance Between Free Trade and Environmental Protection?', 44(4) *George Washington International Law Review* (2012), at 639.

DOI: 10.4324/9781003162339-7

common intention, if there was one, of decision-makers when designing China's export duties. The fundamental premise of this analysis is that the rationales behind a measure or policy are likely to be determined by the missions of the government organs that participate in its formation process. The key actors are accordingly discussed in Section 5.1 along with an analysis of the mandate of each.

While this approach has the capacity to determine the possible rationales behind a measure, it also has limits. When a measure has been formulated by various government organs, each with its own mandate, the mandate that takes priority is not always clear. A key indicator is thus necessary. Section 5.2 proposes that China's five-year plans could serve in terms of discerning the policy rationales behind export duties. The same section also explains why these plans are a trustworthy indicator by discussing a series of observations on the drafting, enactment, and implementation stages of them. Section 5.3 subsequently provides a textual analysis of the Guidelines of the Eleventh, Twelfth, and Thirteenth Five-Year Plans (which cover the period from 2006 to 2020) and relevant subsector Five-Year Plans in order to reveal the policy rationales behind China's export duties at various points in time. Section 5.4 suggests that China might in earnest make use of export duties in the future as part of its environmental policy.

5.1. The possible rationales behind Chinese export duties

This section first introduces the formation process of export duties in China by reviewing relevant legislation. Subsequently, the key actors in this process and their different missions are discussed in order to expose policy rationales behind China's export duties.

5.1.1. The formation process of export duties in China

According to the *Regulations of the People's Republic of China on Import and Export Duties*, which is the major legislation regarding export duties, the State Council, as the highest organ of State administration which is chaired by the premier and consists of the heads of each cabinet-level executive departments,[3] is responsible for formulating the 'the tariff items, tariff nomenclature heading numbers and tariff rates as prescribed in the Customs Import and Export Tariffs of the People's Republic of China (hereinafter referred to as the Tariffs)'.[4] Thus the State Council has the power to decide which products are subject to export duties.

3 State Council Organization Chart, http://english.gov.cn/state_council/2014/09/03/content_281474985533579.htm (visited on 22 June 2018). 'The State Council of the People's Republic of China, namely the Central People's Government, is the highest executive organ of State power, as well as the highest organ of State administration. The State Council is composed of a premier, vice-premiers, State councilors, ministers in charge of ministries and commissions, the auditor-general and the secretary-general'.

4 Article 3 of the *Regulations of the People's Republic of China on Import and Export Duties*, No.392, 1 January 2004, http://english.mofcom.gov.cn/article/lawsdata/

Article 4 of the same regulation stipulates that the 'tariff items, tariff nomenclature heading numbers and tariff rates in the Tariff' could be readjusted by the Customs Tariff Commission which 'shall be established by the State Council'.[5] Moreover, the Customs Tariff Commission can also decide 'the goods subject to temporary tariff rates, the tariff rates and time limit'.[6] The Customs Tariff Commission can not only modify the existing regular export duties (upon the approval of the State Council) but also create new interim duties on exports (without the approval of the State Council).

The interim export duties are of significance with regard to the implementation of China's export duty commitments. Unlike the regular export duties which are decided strictly in accordance with Paragraph 11.3 of China's Accession Protocol that only permit China to impose duties on 84 products within maximum rate, interim export duties are those duties that violate Paragraph 11.3 in two ways: either to be imposed on impermissible products which are outside the scope of 84 products, or to be imposed on one of 84 products, but above the maximum rate. Thus, the export duties at issue in *China—Raw Materials*, *China—Rare Earths*, and *China—Raw Materials II* are all interim export duties that were solely decided by the Customs Tariff Commission. In this context, the Customs Tariff Commission seems to be the key to investigate the policy rationales behind those WTO-inconsistent export duties.

The Customs Tariff Commission was created in 1987 and initially consisted of 16 members from various cabinet-level executive departments under the State Council.[7] From an institutional perspective, this Commission functions as a consultative platform in the context of which officials can collaborate in designing various duties including regular or interim duties on imports and exports, tariff quota, antidumping duties, countervailing duties, duty under safeguard measures,

chineselaw/200411/20041100311020.shtml (visited on 21 June 2018). 'The tariff items, tariff nomenclature heading numbers and tariff rates as prescribed in the Customs Import and Export Tariffs of the People's Republic of China (hereinafter referred to as the Tariffs) and the Import Tariff Rates of the People's Republic of China for Entry Articles (hereinafter referred to as the Import Tariff Rates for Entry Articles), which are formulated by the State Council shall form an integral part of the present Regulations'.

5 Ibid., Article 4.

6 Ibid. 'The Customs Tariff Commission shall be established by the State Council. The Customs Tariff Commission shall be responsible for readjusting and interpreting tariff items, tariff nomenclature heading numbers and tariff rates in the Tariffs and the Import Tariff Rates for Entry Articles, which shall take effect upon the approval of the State Council; it makes decisions on the goods subject to temporary tariff rates, the tariff rates and time limit; it makes decisions on the rate of tariff quota, the imposition of antidumping duties, countervailing duties, duty under safeguard measures, retaliatory duties; makes decisions on the implementation of other measures in relation to customs duties and the application of tariff rates under special circumstances, and exercises the other functions as provided for by the State Council'.

7 Notice of the General Office of the State Council on Adjusting the Composition of the Customs Tariff Commission of the State Council, the State Council, Guo Ban Fa [1987] No. 12.

retaliatory duties, and other duties under special circumstances.[8] According to the Rules of Procedure of the Customs Tariff Commission, the Commission normally meets every three months; its daily business is carried on through an office in the Ministry of Finance (the 'Office').[9] A major task of this Office is to provide preliminary opinion on the proposal submitted by members of the Customs Tariff Commission.[10]

Once a preliminary consensus among the heads of the Office and representatives of the relevant members of the Customs Tariff Commission on a proposal, for instance imposing interim export duties on rare earth products, is reached, the imposition of these duties is to be further discussed in the Customs Tariff Commission meeting, which requires all members to attend.[11] In order to approve theses export duties, a consensus among the Commission members is necessary.[12] Therefore, it seems fair to claim that the imposition of China's export duties is motivated by a common intention of the Commission members. In this context, the mandates of these members are of importance to expose the rationales behind China's export duties.

5.1.2. Different missions of the relevant actors in deciding export duties

Following several changes in its membership, the Customs Tariff Commission has always consisted of 12 members since 2003 though the departments from which these members come are different. The members who decided the disputed export duties in *China—Raw Materials* and *China—Rare Earths* were from the Customs Tariff Commission in the period from 2008 to 2012. The official list of the composition of these members is as follows (Table 5.1). This composition of Customs Tariff Commission members has not much changed to date (Table 5.1).[13]

It is noteworthy that, none of the Customs Tariff Commission members is from the Ministry of Environmental Protection, which is responsible for 'establishing a sound basic system for environmental protection' and 'attaining national pollution reduction targets' relevant to 'pollution to water, air, soil and by noise, light, odor, solid wastes, chemicals, and vehicles'.[14] In this context, compared with the Commission members, people from the Ministry of Environmental Protection are likely

8 Article 4 of the *Regulations of the People's Republic of China on Import and Export Duties.*
9 Rules of Procedure of the Customs Tariff Commission of the State Council, the Customs Tariff Commission, Shui Wei Hui [1999], No. 3, http://sczjd.jl.gov.cn/fgdh/gjjbwfg/lvyj/200606/t20060629_147408.html (visited on 21 June 2018).
10 Ibid., Article 5.
11 Ibid., Article 4.
12 Ibid., Article 9.
13 Notice of the General Office of the State Council on Adjusting the Composition of the Customs Tariff Commission of the State Council, the State Council, Guo Ban Fa [2017] No. 66, http://www.gov.cn/zhengce/content/2017-07/20/content_5211986.htm# (visited on 21 June 2018).
14 Ministry of Environmental Protection, 'Mandates', http://english.sepa.gov.cn/About_MEE/Mandates/ (visited on 22 June 2018).

Table 5.1 Customs Tariff Commission members in the period from 2008 to 2012

Members	*2008 to 2012*
Director	Minister of Finance
Deputy Director	Deputy Secretary General of the State Council
Other members	Deputy Director of National Development and Reform Commission
	Deputy Minister of Commerce
	Deputy Minister of Industry and Information Technology
	Deputy Minister of Land and Resources
	Deputy Minister of Agriculture
	Deputy Director of General Administration of Customs
	Chief Economist of the State Administration of Taxation
	Deputy Director General of General Administration of Quality Supervision, Inspection and Quarantine
	Deputy Director of Legal Affairs Office
	Assistant Minister of Finance

Table 5.2 Comparing the Customs Tariff Commission members in the period from 2008 to 2012 and from 2017 to now

Members	*2008 to 2012*	*2017 to Now*
Director	Minister of Finance	Minister of Finance
Deputy Director	Deputy Secretary General of the State Council	Deputy Secretary General of the State Council
Other members	Deputy Director of National Development and Reform Commission (NDRC)	Deputy Director of National Development and Reform Commission (NDRC)
	Deputy Minister of Commerce	Deputy Minister of Commerce
	Deputy Minister of Industry and Information Technology	Deputy Minister of Industry and Information Technology
	Deputy Minister of Land and Resources	Deputy Minister of Land and Resources
	Deputy Minister of Agriculture	Deputy Minister of Agriculture
	Deputy Director of General Administration of Customs	Deputy Director of General Administration of Customs
	Chief Economist of the State Administration of Taxation	**Changed to:** Deputy Director of the State Administration of Taxation
	Deputy Director General of AQSIQ	Deputy Director General of AQSIQ
	Deputy Director of Legal Affairs Office	Deputy Director of Legal Affairs Office
	Assistant Minister of Finance	**Changed to:** Deputy Minister of Finance

to have less influence in deciding export duties during the Customs Tariff Commission meeting.[15] This may explain why China failed to provide strong environmental justification for its export duties under GATT Article XX(b) in *China—Raw Materials* and *China—Rare Earths.*

By contrast, one of the Tariff Commission members is from the Ministry of Land and Resources, which has the mission 'to be responsible for the planning, administration, protection and rational utilization of such natural resources as land, mineral and marine resources in the People's Republic of China'.[16] Thus, when it comes to a proposal to impose export duties on natural resources in a Customs Tariff Commission meeting, the member from the Ministry of Land and Resources is likely to consider whether these proposed duties would help the Ministry to achieve the aforementioned conservation purposes. In other words, the policy rationales for China's export duties might include conservation of natural resources. This assumption is, however, inconsistent with China's failure to justify its export duties under GATT Article XX(g) in *China—Raw Materials.* The evidence in this case showed that, after the imposition of export duties, the extraction of targeted products in China in fact increased in response to a substantial increase in its domestic consumption.[17]

This inconsistency could be possibly explained by the fact that the formation process of export duties also involves an important Tariff Commission member from the Ministry of Industry and Information Technology, as part of which the Industrial Raw Materials Division is responsible for regulating the raw materials industry concerning non-ferrous materials, gold, rare earth minerals, and so on.[18] One of the responsibilities of this Ministry is to promote industrial development, which could compete with conservation of natural resources.[19] These two goals cannot go hand in hand to the extent that export duties are adopted to provide domestic industry with a favourable access to raw materials, which often incentivises the domestic consumption. In this case, export duties would in effect

15 Though the Ministry of Environmental Protection could attend the Customs Tariff Commission office meeting to give an opinion on a preliminary proposal of export duties. In practice, the Ministry of Environmental Protection has also made several policy recommendations for restricting the production of high-energy-intensive, high-pollution, and resources-based products, such as cancelling export tax rebates, prohibiting the processing trade, and imposing export duties. See Ministry of Environmental Protection, '2007 Category of High-Pollution and High-Environmental-Risk Products'; Ministry of Environmental Protection, '2011 Category of High-Pollution and High-Environmental-Risk Products'.

16 Ministry of Land and Resources, 'Responsibilities of the Ministry of Land and Resources', http://www.mlr.gov.cn/mlrenglish/about/mission/200710/t20071015_656461.htm (visited on 22 June 2018).

17 Panel Reports, *China—Raw Materials*, para 7.429.

18 State Council, 'Ministry of Industry and Information Technology', http://english.gov.cn/state_council/2014/08/23/content_281474983035940.htm (visited on 18 June 2018).

19 The Ministry of Industry and Information Technology, 'Function' http://www.scio.gov.cn/ztk/xwfb/jjfyr/35081/jgjs35086/Document/1490727/1490727.htm (visited on 18 June 2017).

accelerate the extraction of targeted natural resources; this goes against the goal of conserving natural resources.

For a similar reason, the above industrial goal could also compete with the purpose of reducing carbon emissions, a proclaimed environmental goal of China's export duties according to the survey provided in the previous chapter,[20] to the extent that these duties aim to provide domestic industry with a favourable access to energy-intensive industrial inputs and thus to incentivise the domestic consumption and manufacture of these products. This result is inconsistent with the mission of another important Tariff Commission member, namely the National Development and Reform Commission (NDRC) which operates as the national climate change agency. For the Chinese government, fighting climate change, in contrast with addressing domestic environmental concerns, needs a strong cooperation of different government agencies which calls for 'a powerful facilitative focal point at the macro level'.[21] In this context, the NDRC, which is often referred to as 'the little State Council' due to its broad range of responsibilities, is a suitable agency to lead China's climate change actions that include 'organizing the formulation of key strategies, plans and policies in addressing climate change', 'taking the lead with related ministries in attending international negotiations of climate change', 'undertaking relevant work in regard to the fulfilment of the United Nations Framework Convention on Climate Change at national level', and 'undertaking comprehensive coordination of energy saving and emission reduction'.[22]

The above analysis of the relevant actors in deciding export duties in the period from 2008 to now offers two useful observations to assess the policy rationales behind these duties. First, export duties are less likely to be designed for addressing such concerns as air or water pollutions because the Ministry of Environmental Protection is absent from the formation process of export duties.[23] Second, the presence of relevant agencies in deciding export duties suggest that the policy rationales might cover conserving natural resources, fighting climate change, or promoting industrial development. However, as discussed above, the industrial purpose cannot go hand in hand with the former two environmental purposes. The next section proposes that China's Five-Year Plans could serve as a key indicator to shed light on the priority of competing policy purposes.

20 For further information, see Table 1: Practice of WTO Members: export restrictive measures to protect the environment (non-international obligations).

21 NDRC, 'Institutional Arrangements on Climate Change in China', 23 April 2014, https://unfccc.int/sites/default/files/china-institutional_arrangement_in_china.pdf (visited on 1 January 2019).

22 NDRC, 'Main Functions of the NDRC', available at http://en.ndrc.gov.cn/mfndrc/ (visited on 22 June 2018).

23 But the Ministry of Environmental Protection has made several policy recommendations for restricting the production of high-energy-intensive, high-pollution, and resources-based products, such as cancelling export tax rebates, prohibiting the processing trade, and imposing export duties. For further discussion, see Section 5.3.

5.2. China's Five-Year Plan as a trustworthy policy indicator

Having learnt some lessons from *China—Raw Materials*, when China imposed the export duties on rare earth minerals, it made several official announcements regarding its environmental objectives in doing so.[24] As introduced in Chapter 2, these announcements failed to convince either the complainants or the panel in *China—Rare Earths*. Thus one may ask why should China's Five-Year Plan be a trustworthy policy indicator rather than a pretence.

It is, however, far too costly and time consuming to use these plans as a pretext since their formulation process is long and complex.[25] For instance, the formulation of the Guidelines of China's Thirteenth Five-Year Plan (2016–2020) took three years and included four major stages.[26] Phrase I (March to December 2013) aimed to provide a mid-term evaluation of implementation of China's Twelfth Five-Year Plan (2011–2015). This evaluation, which was drafted by the NDRC, needs to be approved by the State Council and the National People's Congress Standing Committee, a permanent organ of the national legislature.[27] Based on the mid-term evaluation report, Phrase II (December 2013 to March 2015) aimed to produce so-called Basic Ideas of China's Thirteenth Five-Year Plan. At this stage, the NDRC entrusts think tanks with policy research concerning 25 important topics through public procurement. Based on the research outcomes, the NDRC drafted the Basic Ideas and submitted it to the Central Committee of the Communist Party of China (CPC) and the State Council. Subsequently, at Phrase III (March to October 2015), the Politburo Standing Committee of the CPC, a committee consisting of the top leadership of the CPC, organised a team including scholars and local officials in order to publish the CPC Central Committee's Proposal on Formulating the Thirteenth Five-year Plan. Based on this proposal, at Phrase IV (October 2015 to March 2016), the NDRC started to draft the Guidelines of China's Thirteenth Five-Year Plan, which involves public consultation[28] and expert review.[29] The final draft was subject to the approval of the State Council.

Moreover, China's Five-Year Plan is one of the few leading matters that need to be endorsed by the National People's Congress, the most authoritative organ of state power in China. For instance, aside from 'examine and approve' the Five-year Plan, the Congress also exercises other functions and powers such as 'to

24 Panel Reports, *China—Rare Earths*, paras 7.162–7.164.
25 At the stage of drafting the Five-Year Plan, the State Council, as the highest organ of State administration, is constitutionally tasked with drafting each Five-Year Plan, officially the 'Guidelines of the Five-Year Plan for National Economic and Social Development' (or 'Guidelines of the Five-Year Plan').
26 Cyberspace Administration of China, 'How to draft a Five-Year Plan', http://www.cac.gov.cn/2016-03/23/c_1118414992.htm (visited on 21 June 2018).
27 Ibid.
28 The public can make suggestions through various forms such as email, SMS, and letter.
29 Fifty-five involved experts are specialising in different fields such as economics, science and technology, public administration, law, and environmental protection.

amend the Constitution', 'to supervise the enforcement of the Constitution' and 'to enact and amend basic laws governing criminal offences, civil affairs, the State organs and other matters'.[30] This shows the important role of Five-Year Plan in China's governance system.

To ensure the implementation of these plans, the Guidelines of the Eleventh Five-Year Plan (2006–2010) began to introduce two corresponding concepts, which are referred to as expected targets and restricted targets, in order to ensure its implementation. The former one includes soft targets to be achieved primarily through market forces with indirect support from the government.[31] The Eleventh Five-Year Plan included 14 expected targets, including 2 economic growth targets, namely gross domestic product (the goal being a 7.5% annual increase) and GDP per capita (the goal being a 6.6% annual increase). Restricted targets, on the other hand, are hard targets that the government should actively fulfil. For instance, officials need to reach the restricted targets in order to ascend the career ladder.[32] In order to implement the Guidelines of China's Five-Year Plan, various cabinet-level executive departments under the State Council would develop relevant subsector Five-Year Plans based on their missions.

The implementation appears successful according to the popular perception in the West of 'China, Inc.'.[33] It suggests that one major factor making the organization of China unique among countries is the 'state control over planning and inputs', whereby 'the Chinese state translates shareholder control into coordinated action to fulfil its policy objectives'.[34] In this process, China's Five-Year Plan plays an important role in setting the policy tone, 'unlike other countries, such as India, where the Five-Year Plan serves merely as an aspirational guide'.[35]

This is why the content of China's Five-Year Plan is often used as evidence to show the intention of China. For instance, the Made in China 2025 initiative, which has worried the EU and US, is explicitly stated in the Guidelines of the Thirteenth Five-Year Plan (2016–2020). Moreover, the complaining governments in *China—Rare Earths* also referred to several subsector Five-Year Plans in order to prove the industrial purpose of China's export duties.[36] These practices provide additional reasons for using the Five-Year Plans to discern the policy rationales behind China's export duties. The next section thus assesses the function of export duties in the context of the Guidelines of the Eleventh to Thirteenth Five-Year

30 Article 62 of the *Constitution of the People's Republic of China*.

31 Central Government, 'The Change of Targets in the New Five-Year Plan', http://www.gov.cn/ztzl/2006-03/07/content_220639.htm (visited on 21 June 2018).

32 Tiechuan Hao, 'The Legal Binding Effect of China's Five-Year Plan', http://theory.people.com.cn/GB/41038/5354249.html (visited on 18 June 2017).

33 Mark Wu, 'The "China, Inc." Challenge to Global Trade Governance', 57(2) *Harvard International Law Journal* (2016), at 264.

34 Ibid., at 275.

35 Ibid., at 276.

36 For instance, the Twelfth Five-Year Development Plan for New Materials Industry, see AB Report, *China—Rare Earths*, para 7.401.

Plan (2006–2020) and relevant subsector Five-Year Plans in order to discover the policy rationales behind China's export duties at various points in time.

5.3. The different roles of export duties in the context of Eleventh to Thirteenth Five-Year Plans (2006–2020)

This section examines the different roles of export duties in Eleventh to Thirteenth Five-Year Plans in order to offer observations of whether these duties are considered as environmental measures or industrial policies during the period of 2006 to 2020. The outcome of this analysis is summarised in the tables at the end of this chapter (Tables 5.3 to 5.5).

5.3.1. Period of 2006–2015: economic development as a dominant purpose

To begin with, according to the Guidelines of the Eleventh Five-Year Plan (2006–2010), China was to impose export restrictive measures on so-called high-energy-intensive, high-pollution, and resources-based products, known as 'HHR products', in order to 'optimize the trade mix'.[37] These export restrictive measures, according to the interpretation of the NDRC, included export duties.[38]

The specific role of export duties is difficult to glean from the vague phrase 'optimize the trade mix', but the position of the phrase within the Five-Year Plan may shed some light on the issue. From a contextual perspective, this phrase is the title of a section in Chapter 35. This chapter is titled 'Accelerating the Transformation of Approaches to Developing Foreign Trade', and it is concerned with increasing the exports of high-value-added products. For instance, the introduction part of this chapter states that

> in accordance with the requirements of exerting comparative advantages, making up for insufficient resources, expanding development space, and increasing added value, the country will actively develop foreign trade and promote the transformation of foreign trade from quantity increase to quality improvement.

By contrast, the two chapters that stipulate the goals of reducing pollution and conserving natural resources make no reference to any export restrictive measures, including export duties.[39] In this context, the major role of export duties during

37 Guidelines of the Eleventh Five-Year Plan for National Economic and Social Development, 14 March 2006, http://www.gov.cn/ztzl/2006-03/16/content_228841_10.htm (visited on 18 June 2017).

38 National Development and Reform Commission, 'Improving Export Structure', http://www.gov.cn/node_11140/2006-03/18/content_230121.htm (visited on 18 June 2017).

39 Chapter 24 'Enhancing Environmental Protection' and Chapter 25 'Improving Resources Management'.

Table 5.3 Comparing the Guidelines of the Eleventh to Thirteenth Five-Year Plan (2006–2020)

Period	*2006–2010*	*2011–2015*	*2016–2020*
Chapter	**Chapter 35 'Accelerating the Transformation of Approaches to Developing Foreign Trade'** In accordance with the requirements of exerting comparative advantages, making up for insufficient resources, expanding development space, and increasing added value, the country will actively develop foreign trade and promote the transformation of foreign trade from quantity increase to quality improvement. By 2010, the total import and export of goods and services trade aims to reach 2.3 trillion US dollars and 400 billion US dollars respectively.	**Chapter 51 'Optimize the Trade Mix'** Continue to stabilize and expand external demand, accelerate the transformation of foreign trade development mode, and promote the transformation of foreign trade development from scale expansion to quality efficiency improvement, and from cost advantage to comprehensive competitive advantage.	**Chapter 47 'Improve Mechanisms for Ensuring Ecological Security'** We will build up institutions for ecological progress, establish sound systems for ecological risk prevention and control, and improve capabilities to respond to ecological and environmental emergencies in order to keep China ecologically secure.
Section	Section 1 'Optimize the trade mix'	Section 1 'Gaining new export strengths'	Section 1 'Ecological and Environmental Protection Systems'
Content	Focusing on self-owned brands, independent intellectual property rights and independent marketing, the government will guide enterprises to enhance their comprehensive competitiveness. Support the export of autonomous high-tech products, electromechanical products and high value-added labour-intensive products. Strictly implement labour, safety, and environmental protection standards, and regulate the composition of export costs, **restrict the exports of 'HHR products'**.	Maintain the existing export competitive advantage and accelerate the cultivation of new advantages in technology, brand, quality and service as the core competitiveness. Enhance the quality and grade of labour-intensive export products and expand the export of mechanical and electrical products and high-tech products, **restrict the exports of 'HHR products'**.	We will accelerate the establishment of diverse compensation mechanisms for ecological restoration and conservation efforts, and improve the mechanism linking fund allocation to ecological protection performance. **We will establish an eco-tax system that covers certain areas including mining, resource consumption, pollutant discharge, and the import and export of resource products**.

Table 5.4 Comparing the subsector Five-Year Plans relevant to environmental protection (2006–2020)

Period	*2006–2010*	*2011–2015*	*2016–2020*
Chapter	Chapter 5 'Implementation'	Chapter 8 'Improve policy measures'	Export duties are not mentioned.
Section	Section 4 'New mechanism'	Section 12 'International cooperation'	
Subsection	Subsection 2 'Improve environmental economic policies' In the resource tax, consumption tax, **import and export tax reform**, full consideration of environmental protection requirements, explore the establishment of an environmental tax.	Paragraph 2 Actively participate in environmental and trade-related negotiations and the formulation of relevant rules, strengthen the coordination of environment and trade, and safeguard China's environmental rights and interests. Study and adjust **the import and export tax policy** for products with 'high pollution and high environmental risks' to curb the export of high-energy and high-emission products.	

the period from 2006 to 2010 would appear to have been that of supporting domestic industry.

This prioritisation of industrial goals likewise characterized the Guidelines of the Twelfth Five-Year Plan (2011–2015).[40] In Chapter 51 titled 'Optimize the Trade Mix', the introduction part of which states that to 'continue to stabilize and expand external demand, accelerate the transformation of foreign trade development mode, and promote the transformation of foreign trade development from scale expansion to quality efficiency improvement, and from cost advantage to comprehensive competitive advantage', export restrictive measures on HHR products are described as a means of 'gaining new export strengths', an aim that again includes the increase of high-tech exports. By contrast, the three chapters that stipulate the aims of conserving natural resources, reducing pollution, and reducing carbon emissions make no reference to any export restrictive measures, including export duties.[41] As in the period from 2006 to 2010, then, so also in the period from 2011 to 2015 any export duties would appear to have been largely considered industrial policies.

Indeed, the term 'optimize the trade mix' are also found in the subsector Twelfth Five-Year Plan for Developing the Non-ferrous Metal Industry. As an

40 Guidelines of the Twelfth Five-Year Plan for National Economic and Social Development, 16 March 2011, http://news.sina.com.cn/c/2011-03-17/055622129864.shtml (visited on 18 June 2017).

41 Chapter 21 'Combating Climate Change', Chapter 22 'Improving Resources Management', and Chapter 24 'Enhancing Environmental Protection'.

Table 5.5 Comparing the subsector Five-Year Plans relevant to climate change (2006–2020)

Period	*2006–2010*	*2011–2015*	*2016–2020*
Section	Section 2 'Control production, adjust and optimize the structure'	Section 8 'Improve energy conservation and emission reduction economic policies'	Section 3 'Create a low carbon industry system'
Subsection	Subsection 3 'Control the excessive growth of industries with high energy consumption and high pollution'	Subsection 34 'Improve tax support policies'	Subsection 1 'Accelerate the adjustment of industrial structure'
Content	Strictly control new high-energy, high-pollution projects… Implement policies that limit the export of high-energy-consumption and high-pollution products. Continue to use measures **such as adjusting export tax rebates, increasing export tariffs**, reducing export quotas, and including some products in the prohibited categories of processing trade, and **controlling the export of high-energy-consumption and high-pollution products**.	Implement the national preferential policies for supporting energy conservation and emission reduction income tax and value-added tax… Improve and implement tax incentives for comprehensive utilisation of resources and renewable energy development. **Adjust import and export tax policies to curb the export of high-energy and high-emission products**.	The low-carbon development will be regarded as an important driving force for economic upgrading and efficiency improvement under the new normal and promote the transformation and upgrading of industrial structure… **We will change the export model, strictly control the export of HHR products, and focus on optimizing the export structure**.

industrial plan issued by the Ministry of Industry and Information Technology (a Tariff Commission member mandated to promote industrial development), in Chapter 6 'Implementation', Section 5, titled 'Promote international exchanges and cooperation', it states that 'We encourage the import of non-ferrous metal resources and products, and strictly limit the export of HHR products and primary deep-processing products in accordance with WTO rules'. The same section shows that the aim of such export restriction is to 'optimize the trade mix'.

It is noteworthy that the vague phrase 'optimize the trade mix' and undefined scope of HHR products could have confused some other government agencies to the extent that they considered export duties as an environmental measure in their subsector Five-Year Plans. For instance, the Ministry of Land and Resources, as another Tariff Commission member mandated to conserve natural resources, once issued a subsector Eleventh Five-Year Plan relevant to export duties.[42] In Chapter 10, titled 'Technological progress and innovation', Section 35, titled 'Deepen reform and promote the construction of market system', considered export policy a means to control mineral production by stating that 'we will adjust the total supply of land and minerals through measures concerning planning and investment, taxes, environmental protection, and import and export' in order to 'improve the macro-control mechanism of land and resources'.

The same as the Ministry of Environmental Protection, although this agency mandated to address domestic pollution is absent in the formation process of export duties, these duties are explicitly referred to in the subsector Eleventh Five-Year and Twelfth Plans for Environmental Protection.[43] In the former Plan, Chapter 5 titled 'Implementation', Section 2 titled 'New mechanism', it suggests that export duties, together with resource taxes and consumption taxes, could be used to 'improve environmental economic policies'. In the latter one, Chapter 8 titled 'Improve policy measures', Section 12 titled 'International cooperation', export duties are considered an instrument to 'safeguard China's environmental rights and interests' by curbing the 'export of high-energy and high-emission products' (Table 5.4).

The rationale behind the imposition of export duties has been explained in research by the Policy Research Centre for Environment and Economy (PRCEE), a think-tank affiliated with the Ministry of Environmental Protection. After calculating the pollution caused by exports from 2003 to 2007, the PRCEE concluded that 20% of sulphur dioxide (SO_2), 20% of chemical oxygen demand (COD), and 30% of carbon dioxide (CO_2) in China could be attributed to exports of HHR products.[44] This being the case, export duties could be adopted as a means to fulfil the restricted environmental targets in the Guidelines of the Eleventh and Twelfth Five-Year Plans.[45] Indeed, the restricted environmental targets in the former Guidelines are to reduce the SO_2 and COD, as useful measures of air and water pollution, by 10% annually; In the Guidelines of the Twelfth Five-Year Plan, the restricted environmental targets call for annual reductions of SO_2 and COD by 8%.[46] Thus, the Ministry of Environmental Protection has made several policy recommendations for restricting the production of HHR products, such as cancelling export tax rebates, prohibiting the processing trade, and imposing export duties.[47]

42 The Eleventh Five-Year Plan for the Ministry of Land and Resources (2006–2010), http://www.yic.cas.cn/xxfw/ggxx/200701/t20070117828754.html (visited on 18 June 2017).
43 The National Eleventh Five-Year Plan for Environmental Protection (2006–2010), Guo Fa [2007] No. 37, promulgated by the State Council on 22 November 2007.
44 Tao Hu, 'Analysis on The Environment Deficit of China's Export', 18(2) *China Population Resources and Environment* (2008), at 13.
45 Jun Pang, 'Green Trade in China's Twelfth Five-Year Plan' 3 *Environment and Sustainable Development* (2011), at 27.
46 Chapter III of the Guidelines of the Twelfth Five-Year Plan (2011–2015).
47 The Ministry of Environmental Protection, '2007 Category of High-Pollution and High-Environmental-Risk Products'. The Ministry of Environmental Protection, '2011 Category of High-Pollution and High-Environmental-Risk Products'.

Owing to the prioritisation of the industrial purposes of export duties in the Guidelines of the Eleventh and Twelfth Five-Year Plans, the above considerations of the Ministry of Land and Resources and the efforts made by the Ministry of Environmental Protection did not produce the desired effect. Their unrealized environmental initiatives, however, may have incentivised China to try its luck under the environmental exceptions of Article XX in *China—Raw Materials* and *China—Rare Earths*. Without convincing environmental justification, this move then provoked the complaining governments to take an extremist stance and reject China's right to invoke the provision.

Beyond the proclaimed environmental purposes in these cases, export duties could also have been considered a measure to combat climate change in the period from 2006 to 2015 in order to meet the restricted targets in the Guidelines of the Eleventh and Twelfth Five-Year Plans. The target in the former Guidelines is to reduce 20% GDP per unit of energy use ('energy intensity') annually. In the Guidelines of the Twelfth Five-Year Plan, the restricted environmental targets call for annual reductions of energy intensity by 16%, and greenhouse gases by 17% per capita and per unit of GDP ('carbon intensity'). Thus, the State Council once issued the Plan for Energy Conservation and Emission Reduction for the Eleventh Five-Year Plan Period.[48] In Section 2, titled 'Control production, adjust and optimize the structure', this sub-sector Five-Year Plan suggests that 'adjusting export tax rebates, increasing export tariffs' could be used to restrict 'the export of high-energy-consumption and high-pollution products' in order to eventually 'control the excessive growth of industries with high energy consumption and high pollution' (Table 5.5). In a same manner, the Plan for Energy Conservation and Emission Reduction for the Twelfth Five-Year Plan in Chapter VIII, titled 'Developing Energy Conservation and Emission Reduction Economic Policy', Section 8, titled 'Improve energy conservation and emission reduction economic policies', mandated the imposition of export duties to restrict the exports of energy-intensive and high-pollution products.

This consideration may explain why, despite the export duties at issue in the *China—Raw Materials* and *China—Rare Earths* cases, the Chinese government during the above period also imposed duties on the exports of certain energy-intensive products including steel, aluminium, coal, chemical products, and fertilizers, which was applauded by some commentators as discussed in the previous chapter. The limited scope of targeted products, however, raised the concern over the real contribution of these duties in targeting carbon emissions. In other words, to make export duties as a credible climate policy tool, China could have targeted more energy-intensive products, especially those higher value-added ones which significantly contribute to its economic growth.[49] This shortcoming again could be attributed to the prioritisation of the economic purposes of export duties in the above Guidelines of Five Year Plans.

48 Plan for Energy Conservation and Emission Reduction for the Eleventh Five-Year Plan Period, the State Council, Guo Fa [2007] No. 15.

49 Susanne Dröge, 'Tackling Leakage in a World of Unequal Carbon Prices', Climate Strategies Working Paper (2009), at 67.

5.3.2. Period of 2016–2020: a clear shift to environmental protection

In contrast with the Guidelines of the Eleventh and Twelfth Five-Year Plans, the Guidelines of the Thirteenth Five-Year Plan (2016–2020), however, has shifted the focus to environmental protection in two respects.[50] First, the industrial role of export duties is completely abandoned in the new Guidelines. Compared with the Guidelines of the Twelfth Five-Year Plan, in the section titled 'Optimize the Trade Mix', the reference to export restrictive measures targeting HHR products has been deleted. Second, export duties are explicitly referred as part of China's environmental policy. In Chapter 47, titled 'Improve Mechanisms for Ensuring Ecological Security', the use of export duties as an environmental measure is raised in the statement that 'We will establish *an eco-tax system* that covers certain areas, including mining, resource consumption, pollutant discharge, and *the import and export of resource products*' (emphasis added).[51]

This shift is also reflected in the relevant subsector Five-Year Plans concerning the industrial development as none of them refers to either export duties or export restrictions in general. However, the specific environmental considerations behind China's export duties are difficult to glean from the vague phrase 'an eco-tax system'. The phrase 'resource products' seems to suggest the purpose of conserving natural resources. This assumption, however, seems to be inconsistent with the fact that export duties are not mentioned in the relevant subsector Five-Year Plans concerning the conservation of natural resources.

The new development of China's resource taxes suggests that these taxes are more suitable than export duties to protect natural resources. China has been making use of resource taxes on the manufacture of various mineral products since 1984.[52] The rate and scope of such taxes, however, have been too limited to solve the problem of overexploitation of resources, as shown in the *China—Raw Materials* and *China—Rare Earths* cases.[53] To reinforce current resource taxes, the subsector Thirteenth Five-Year Plan concerning protecting natural resources mandates changing the method by which they are calculated from 'a fixed amount of tax per unit of a product' to 'a percentage tax of the value of a product'.[54] This latter calculation method, in effect a value-based resource tax, is believed to be more effective in addressing the concern of overexploitation of resources.[55] According to a recent notice from the

50 Guidelines of the Thirteenth Five-Year Plan for National Economic and Social Development (2016–2020), March 2016, available at http://www.sdpc.gov.cn/zcfb/zcfbghwb/201603/P020160318573830195512.pdf (visited on 18 June 2017).

51 Translated by Compilation and Translation Bureau, Central Committee of the Communist Party of China, http://en.ndrc.gov.cn/newsrelease/201612/P020161207645765233498.pdf (visited on 18 June 2017).

52 Xinhuanet, 'Reform on Resource Taxes', May 2016, http://news.xinhuanet.com/fortune/2016-05/10/c_128974414.htm (visited on 18 June 2017).

53 Panel Reports, *China—Rare Earths*, paras 7.182.–7.185.

54 People, 'The Countdown to the Reform on Resource Taxes', 4 June 2016, http://finance.people.com.cn/n1/2016/0604/c1004-28411574.html (visited on 18 June 2017).

55 Xinhuanet (2016), above n 52. Also see NDB, 'Environmental Highlights in Thirteenth Five-Year Plan', 4 March 2016, http://www.nbd.com.cn/articles/2016-03-04/988819.html (visited on 18 June 2017).

Ministry of Finance, the scope of products subject to value-based resource taxes has been broadened from 6 types, including rare earths, to 24 types beginning 1 July 2016.[56] Given the progress achieved by reinforcing resource taxes, China is not likely to choose export duties for conserving natural resources.

China is also not likely to choose export duties for reducing local pollution. Unlike the previous subsector Five-Year Plans for Environmental Protection, the subsector Thirteenth Five-Year Plan for Environmental Protection lists various policy instruments for use in fulfilling their environmental aims without referring to export duties.[57] This change could be explained by the new development of China's environmental protection tax.[58] The introduction of these taxes aims to replace pollution fees, which was the instrument that China traditionally used to target such environmental problems as air or water pollutions.[59] As instituted in 1982, the system of pollution fees, however, has long been criticised for its dependence on administrative intervention by local governments.[60] Such dependence in practice leads to weak enforcement of pollution fees because local governments tend to promote polluting companies in the pursuit of economic development. Unlike pollution fees, environmental protection taxes are collected by local tax authorities who are independent of local governments.[61] This latter manner of collection would thus solve the problem of weak enforcement, an issue that China once claimed could be addressed by export restrictions.[62] In this sense, the new environmental protection taxes could alleviate the need for export duties to address local environmental concerns.

The Thirteenth Five-Year Plan for Reducing Carbon Emissions, by contrast, considers export restrictions on HHR products as a climate policy tool to 'accelerate the adjustment of industrial structure' in Section 3 titled 'Create a low carbon industry system'.[63] In this context, a potential policy rationale for export

56 Ministry of Finance, 'The Notice to Reform Resource Taxes', May 2016, http://szs.mof.gov.cn/zhengwuxinxi/zhengcefabu/201605/t201605101984605.html (visited on 18 June 2017).
57 The subsector Thirteenth Five-Year Plan for Environmental Protection, available at http://www.gov.cn/zhengce/content/2016-12/05/content_5143290.htm (visited on 18 June 2017).
58 Xinhuanet, 'To Impose Environmental Protection Taxes in 2018', December 2016, http://news.xinhuanet.com/fortune/2016-12/26/c_1120184613.htm (visited on 18 June 2017).
59 People, 'The Environmental Protection Tax Law of the People's Republic of China', 10 June 2015, http://politics.people.com.cn/n/2015/0610/c1001-27134414.html (visited on 18 June 2017).
60 Chinadialogue, 'China Issues Draft on Environmental Protection Taxes to Combat Pollution', 11 June 2015, https://www.chinadialogue.net/article/show/single/en/7975-China-issues-draft-on-environmental-taxes-to-combat-pollution (visited on 18 June 2017).
61 Xinhuanet, 'Environmental Taxes In 2016', 21 March 2016, http://news.xinhuanet.com/fortune/2016-03/21/c_1118396224.htm (visited on 18 June 2017).
62 WTO Panel Reports, *China—Rare Earths*, para 7.416.
63 Thirteenth Five-Year Plan for Reducing Carbon Emissions, Guofa [2016] No. 61, http://www.gov.cn/zhengce/content/2016-11/04/content_5128619.htm (visited on 18 June 2017).

duties could be to reduce carbon emissions by targeting energy-intensive products. A major consideration for this policy choice is that, compared with those environmental concerns that have been addressed by the newly introduced resources taxes and environmental protection taxes in China,[64] the issue of climate change is too complex to be addressed by carbon taxes owing to economic and administrative considerations.[65] The next chapter provides a comprehensive analysis of the potential of China's export duties to combat climate change.

5.4. Conclusions

This chapter investigated the policy rationales behind China's export duties in two respects. First, from a policy formation perspective, an analysis of the composition of China's Customs Tariff Commission—which has played a vital role in designing its export duties—shows that the Ministry of Environmental Protection has long been absent from the formation process for China's export duties. By contrast, the mandates of the other three long-standing members of the commission—to promote industrial development, conserve natural resources, and combat climate change—seem to have had more influence over the formation of China's export duties.

In the second part of this chapter, the Five-Year Plan was identified as a trustworthy indicator to shed light on the priority of competing policy purposes.[66] The Guidelines of the Eleventh and Twelfth Five-Year Plans (for 2006–2010 and 2011–2015, respectively) imposed export duties on so-called HHR product—those defined as high-energy-intensive, high-pollution, and resources-based—as part of efforts to 'optimize the trade mix' or 'gain new export strengths', vague phrases from which it is difficult to deduce a specific purpose. A textual analysis of these plans in context showed clearly, however, that China had prioritised the industrial purposes of the duties. This finding goes a long way towards explaining why China lacked convincing environmental justification in *China—Raw Materials* and *China—Rare Earths.*

The vague language, especially the term 'high-energy-intensive, high-pollution, and resources-based', in the plans may also have confused the Ministry of Environmental Protection. In the subsector Eleventh and Twelfth Five-Year Plans for Environmental Protection, this ministry referred explicitly to export duties as a part of 'environmental economic policies' intended to 'safeguard China's

64 The environmental protection taxes, however, only target air, water, and noise pollution, leaving unaddressed the target of reducing carbon emissions. Annex I of the *Environmental Protection Tax Law of the People's Republic of China.*

65 For further discussion, see Chapter 6.

66 For instance, it is far too costly and time consuming to use these plans as a pretext since their formulation process is long and complex. Moreover, these plans are often used as evidence to show the intention of China in practice. The complaining governments in *China—Rare Earths* thus referred to several Five-Year Plans in order to prove the actual purpose of China's export duties. For further information, see Section 5.2.

environmental rights and interests'.[67] In pursuit of this objective, it developed a list of high-pollution and high-environmental-risk products and recommended imposing export duties on some of them together with proper measures to also restrict domestic consumption. These initiatives from the ministry, however, possibly owing to its insignificant role in the formation process of the export duties and their prioritised industrial purpose under the Guidelines of the Eleventh and Twelfth Five-Year Plans, were not reflected in the policy that eventually took shape.

It is ironic that although the efforts of the Ministry of Environmental Protection have not produced the desired effect, its environmental initiatives, as a form of evidence, may have incentivised China to try its luck under Article XX. For China, while the export duties in dispute were adopted for an industrial purpose, they might have indeed reduced the pollution associated with the manufacture of certain targeted products.[68] Based on those potential good side-effects, China was trying to justify the bad aim of its duties.[69] This move provoked the complaining governments to take an extremist stance and reject China's right to invoke the environmental exceptions at all.

Possibly owing to lessons learned from the *China—Raw Materials* and *China—Rare Earths* cases, China has done away with all of the disputed export duties and stopped their industrial role in its Guidelines of the Thirteenth Five-Year Plan (2016–2020). Moreover, departing from the previous vagueness, the new guidelines also make clear that export duties in combination with other taxes on production and consumption could form part of a new 'eco-tax system' designed to 'ensure ecological security'.[70] An analysis of the relevant subsector five-year plans and the development of China's environmental policies shows further the decreasing role of export duties in conserving natural resources or reducing local pollution associated with manufacturing as first-best options, such as resources and environmental protection taxes, have been adopted to address these concerns.

As a consequence of these shifts in policy, the most likely environmental role for China's export duties in the future is to combat climate change. According to the language regarding climate change in the new subsector five-year plans, exports of HHR products are to be strictly controlled in order to 'create a low-carbon

67 For further information, see Section 5.3.1. Moreover, the vague language might have also confused the Ministry of Land and Resources which, as a Tariff Commission member mandated to conserve natural resources, once issued a subsector Eleventh Five-Year Plan relevant to export duties.

68 For instance, China adduces two empirical studies in *China—Raw Materials* which show that 'elimination of the export duty of 20% on manganese metal would imply an increase in production by 4.28%'; 'eliminating the 40% export duty on coke would increase domestic production of coke by 2.2%'. See Panel Reports, *China—Raw Materials*, paras 7.519–7.520.

69 This line of thoughts is clearly inconsistent with Article XX. It is unclear, however, whether a good aim would always be defeated by some bad side-effects under Article XX. For further discussion, see Chapter 8.

70 For further information, see Section 5.3.2.

industrial system'. In this context, considering their advantages over quantitative export restrictions as discussed in the previous chapter, export duties could be a suitable border measure to combat climate change. The following chapter provides a detailed assessment of the potential role of export duties in this regard, an issue that has not yet been addressed adequately in the literature about the negative impacts of the *China—Raw Materials* and *China—Rare Earths* decisions.

6 A neglected issue

Negative impacts on China's capacity to fight climate change

Thus far, this book has shown that a harsh ban on export duties could hamper China's progress for fighting climate change, especially on addressing the issue of carbon leakage. Such problems occur when energy-intensive industries shift production to countries that have weaker or no such controls in order to evade the effects of a state's carbon pricing policies.[1] This important issue, however, has received inadequate attention in the literature on the *China—Raw Materials* and *China—Rare Earths* decisions.[2]

A possible reason for this neglect is that export duties have only rarely been used to reduce carbon emissions. The survey in Chapter 4 shows that only two countries had imposed export duties for addressing issues associated with climate change. One is Bangladesh which once imposed export duties on bricks in order to counter a climate action of India that in effect outsourced the polluting brick-making industry to Bangladesh.[3] In a much more extensive manner, China, as the other one, had imposed duties on the exports of a range of energy-intensive products in the period from 2009 to 2016.[4] This practice has been recorded in China's second communication to the United Nations Framework Convention on

1 R.K. Pachauri and A. Reisinger (eds), *Contribution of Working Groups I, II and III to the Fourth Assessment Report of the Intergovernmental Panel on Climate Change* (IPCC, 2007), at 665.

2 To the best of the author's knowledge, in English literature about the two cases, only Baris Karapinar and Kateryna Holzer have pointed out this problem by arguing that 'as the Panel and the Appellate Body in the *China-Raw Materials* dispute clarified, China and potentially other new Members with similar commitments cannot even resort to Article XX exceptions to justify the duties they impose on their exports. Therefore, the use of an export tax as a climate policy tool is not possible for these countries'. But they did not discuss the particular question concerning the potential of China's export duties to combat climate change. See Baris Karapinar and Kateryna Holzer, 'Legal Implications of the Use of Export Taxes in Addressing Carbon Leakage: Competing Border Adjustment Measures', 10(1) *New Zealand Journal of Public and International Law* (2012), at 34.

3 Sohara Mehroze Shachi and Larry C. Price, 'Bangladesh's Air Pollution Problem Grows, Brick by Brick', Pulitzer Center, 5 September 2018, https://pulitzercenter.org/reporting/bangladeshs-air-pollution-problem-grows-brick-brick (visited on 15 June 2019).

4 For further information, see Chapter 4.

DOI: 10.4324/9781003162339-8

Climate Change (UNFCCC) as a type of instrument to 'effectively control greenhouse gas emissions'.[5]

This neglect is unfortunate because a number of climate studies have suggested that export duties could be useful for curtailing carbon leakage,[6] especially in the context of China as 'the world's most unbalanced virtual emissions' trader, for its emissions associated with its exports being eight times higher than those associated with its imports.[7] In the global context, China in 2012 was responsible for 28% of global carbon emissions, about one-quarter of which were created by the manufacture of export products,[8] meaning that 7% of total global carbon emissions in that year were attributable to Chinese exports.

To explore this neglected issue of China's constrained policy space to fight climate change, this chapter provides a comprehensive assessment of the advantages and disadvantages of considering export duties as part of climate change policy. This chapter also examines arguments that cast doubt on the significance of export duties for China's overall climate policy and refutes them based on the country's recent actions to combat climate change.[9]

6.1. Measures to tackle carbon leakage

Climate change is an environmental externality caused by market failure, and one key policy measure to correct this failure is to place a price on carbon emissions.[10] Current climate policies are, however, applied asymmetrically, a circumstance that creates incentives for emission-intensive economic activity to migrate away from regions where the price of carbon emissions is higher.[11] This is the situation often

5 China described export duties as a type of instrument to 'effectively control greenhouse gas emissions'. For further information, see UNFCCC, 'Second National Communication on Climate Change of the People's Republic of China', October 2004, at 15, http://unfccc.int/resource/docs/natc/chnnc1exsum.pdf (visited on 1 January 2019).

6 For instance, the well-known Stern Review on the economics of climate change, its follow-up article, and a World Bank research paper, etc. For further discussion, see Section 6.2.

7 Zhu Liu, 'China's Carbon Emissions Report 2015', Energy Technology Innovation Policy Research Group (2015), at 1, https://scholar.harvard.edu/files/zhu/files/carbon-emissions-report-2015-final.pdf (visited on 1 January 2019).

8 Ibid.

9 First, given the fact that China's export duties, mostly on primary products, have so far only targeted a 'small fraction of the emissions from its exports', China may not be willing to extend export duties to major wealth-creating export sectors given its overarching goal of economic development. Second, China could replace export duties with alternative measures targeting the production of high-energy-intensive products in order to achieve the same climate goal. See Glen P. Petersb, Dabo Guanc and Klaus Hubacekd, 'The Contribution of Chinese Exports to Climate Change', 36(9) *Energy Policy* 3572 (2008), at 3576.

10 UNEP and WTO, 'Trade and Climate Change: A Report by the United Nations Environment Programme and the World Trade Organization' (2009), at 90.

11 IPCC, *Climate Change 2014: Mitigation of Climate Change* (Cambridge University Press, 2015), at 63.

referred to as carbon leakage, and it seriously undermines collective efforts to combat climate change. Three basic ways have been proposed to address this problem.[12]

The first option is to pursue a global international agreement that imposes a similar carbon cost on all emitters.[13] The recent achievement in this area is the Paris Agreement, which went into force on 4 November 2016. Unlike the earlier Kyoto Protocol, which exempts developing countries from restrictions on emissions, the Paris Agreement requires that all nations take measures to combat climate change, though it bases this requirement on the principle of 'common but differentiated responsibility', which recognises historical differences between the contributions of developed and developing countries to climate change. As a result, whereas the Paris Agreement requires that developed countries 'continue taking the lead by undertaking economy-wide absolute emission reduction targets', developing countries are 'encouraged' to move, over time, towards the reduction targets set by developed countries.[14] It would therefore be overly optimistic to expect all countries to have similar carbon prices in the near future.

As an alternative, the second option for confronting carbon leakage is to reduce the net carbon costs of domestic production in emission outsourcing countries.[15] Thus, for instance, when the EU launched the emissions trading system (EU ETS) in 2005, which requires emitters to purchase carbon emission permits, it included the free allocation of allowances, a mechanism to exempt certain companies from limits on carbon emissions. Under this mechanism, the manufacturing industry received 80% of its allowances for free at the beginning of the EU ETS.[16] While the free allocation of allowances shields internationally competing industries in the EU from carbon leakage, it also raises concerns about the potential of this mechanism to undermine the overall effectiveness of the EU ETS.[17] To address this problem, 57% of the total amount of allowances was to be auctioned, instead of being freely allocated, in the current trading period (2013–2020).[18] However, assuming that the decrease in free allocation will make the EU ETS more effective, the problem of carbon leakage may recur owing to increased carbon prices in the EU. This may explain why the new President of the European Commission has recently proposed a 'Carbon Border Tax' aiming at avoiding carbon leakage and ensuring a level playing field for European companies as part of her European Green Deal.[19]

12 Michael Grubb, Thomas Counsell, 'Tackling Carbon Leakage: Sector-Specific Solutions for a World of Unequal Carbon Prices', *Carbon Trust Report* (2010), at 30.
13 Ibid.
14 Article 4(4) of the Paris Agreement, done at Paris, 12 December 2015, UN / FCCC.
15 Grubb and Counsell (2010), above n 12, at 32.
16 European Commission, 'Free Allocation', https://ec.europa.eu/clima/policies/ets/allowances_en (visited on 1 January 2019).
17 Energypost, 'To Make European Climate Policy Work, We Need to Put a Carbon Price on Imports', reporter Emil Dimantchev, 5 March 2015.
18 European Commission, above n 16.
19 Ursula von der Leyen, 'A Union that Strives for More: My Agenda for Europe', 16 July 2019, at 5, https://ec.europa.eu/commission/sites/beta-political/files/political-guidelines-next-commission_en.pdf (visited on 1 August 2019).

This 'Carbon Border Tax' is a third option that has been proposed to address the difference in carbon prices across international borders, also known as carbon-based border tax adjustment (BTA).[20] It requires carbon-outsourcing countries to impose duties on the energy-intensive imports from carbon-outsourced countries. In addition to the newly proposed 'Carbon Border Tax' in 2019, the French government once proposed a EU-wide carbon tax on imports in 2010,[21] though this proposal has been heavily opposed by such EU members as Germany. Another example can be found in the American Clean Energy and Security Act, also known as the Waxman-Markey Bill after the US legislators who cosponsored it, which requires that importers purchase emissions credits from an 'international reserve allowance program'.[22] This bill was passed by the US House of Representatives in 2009, but was eventually rejected by the Senate.[23]

To date, no import BTA has been implemented. Concerns have been raised over the legality of these measures, an issue that has long been discussed within the legal profession. As concluded by many lawyers, although requirements for a carbon-based tax on imports may potentially violate GATT Article II and Article III, such a violation could be justified by the environmental exceptions under Article XX.[24] It thus has been so fully argued that 'governments cannot hide behind the pretext that WTO law prevents them from using their markets, through trade-related measures, for environmental progress: WTO law is no excuse for environmental inaction'.[25]

Perhaps the more important reason for the inaction on import BTAs is on the political side. For instance, while the French President Emmanuel Macron has recently introduced his idea of imposing import BTAs, a major concern is whether such proposal would ever receive political support from major European business groups, given the risk that these carbon tariffs could spark a trade war.[26] They have good reasons to worry because import BTAs would almost certainly face strong political opposition from developing countries. Especially in the context of

20 Grubb and Counsell (2010), above n 12, at 36. See more discussion in Stéphanie Monjon and Philippe Quirion, 'Border Adjustments – Implications of Design Options', in Arttu Makipaa (ed), 'Competitive Distortions and Leakage in a World of Different Carbon Prices' (European Parliament, 2008), 35–43.

21 Nature, 'France Unveils Carbon Tax', reporter Declan Butler, 15 September 2009.

22 Harro van Asselta and Thomas Brewerb, 'Addressing Competitiveness and Leakage Concerns in Climate Policy: An Analysis of Border Adjustment Measures in the US and the EU' 38(1) *Energy Policy* 42 (2010), at 45.

23 TIME, 'Why the Climate Bill Died', reporter Bryan Walsh, 26 July 2010.

24 For instance, Joost Pauwelyn, 'Chapter 15: Carbon Leakage Measures and Border Tax Adjustments Under WTO Law', in Geert Van Calster and Denise Prévost (eds), *Research Handbook on Environment, Health and the WTO* (Edward Elgar Publication, 2013).

25 Barbara Cooreman, *Global Environmental Protection through Trade: A Systematic Approach to Extraterritoriality* (Edward Elgar, 2016), at 281.

26 Frédéric Simon, 'BusinessEurope warms to Macron's EU carbon tariff idea', EURACTIV, 29 April 2019, https://www.euractiv.com/section/emissions-trading-scheme/news/businesseurope-warms-to-macrons-eu-carbon-tariff-idea/ (visited on 16 June 2019).

the above-mentioned principle of 'common but differentiated responsibility', it would be considered 'inherently unfair' to penalise developing countries through the imposition of BTAs,[27] and this unfairness may further undermine efforts to engage emerging economies to binding commitments to reduce emissions.[28]

Against this background, export duties, another type of border-levelling mechanism, have been proposed as an alternative to import BTAs which will be discussed next (Figure 6.1).

6.2. Export duties as an alternative to import BTAs

The idea of export BTAs was perhaps inspired by a success story with voluntary export restraints in a dispute involving the US and Canada in 1996.[29] In this case, Canada was accused by the US of unfairly subsidising its lumber industry. In order to avoid potential import duties on its lumber products, Canada agreed to impose

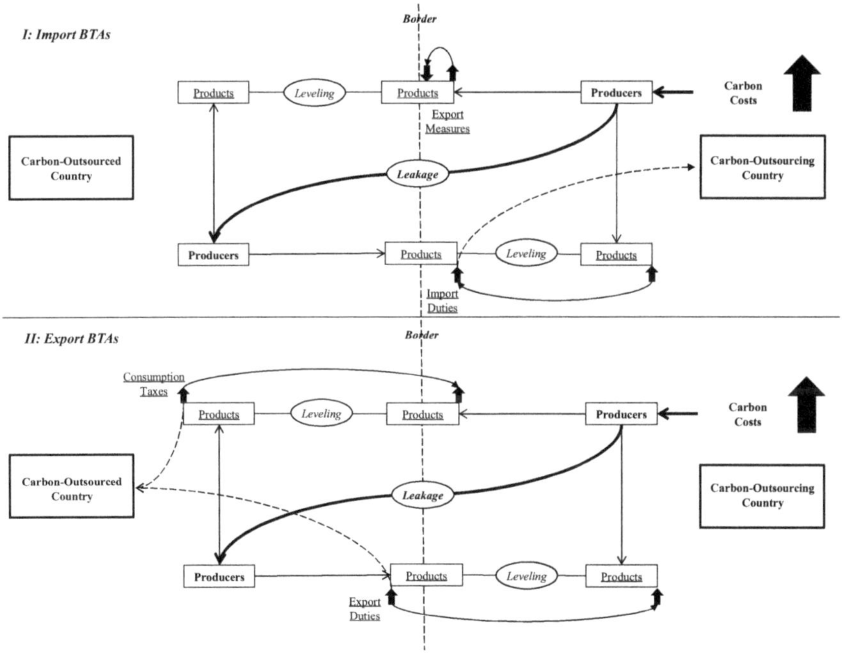

Figure 6.1 Export duties as an alternative to import BTAs

27 Robyn Eckersley, 'The Politics of Carbon Leakage and the Fairness of Border Measures', 24(4) *Ethics & International Affairs* (2010), at 367.
28 John Whalley and Simon J. Evenett, 'The G20 and Green Protectionism: Will We Pay the Price at Copenhagen?', No. 14 Policy Brief of the Centre for International Governance Innovation (2009).
29 Benito Müller and Anju Sharma, 'Trade Tactic Could Unlock Climate Negotiations', *SciDev.Net* (2005).

substantial duties on its lumber exports to the US. Thus, these export duties brought economic benefits for Canada in terms of the tax revenue that balanced out the import duties, whereas the US producers would be protected from high competition from Canada.

This same logic applies here. Since the rationale of import BTAs is to increase the carbon costs on energy-intensive imports from countries that have weak climate policies, alternatively, those carbon-outsourced countries may also impose duties on their energy-intensive exports by themselves in an effort to achieve the same objective. Compared with the import BTAs, export duties could assuage the concerns over the aforementioned unfairness since the revenue is collected by the carbon-outsourced countries, which are generally developing countries. For this reason, export duties have the potential to integrate developing countries into a global carbon-reduction scheme.

Such potential was recognised by the well-known Stern Review on the economics of climate change which referred to the use of export duties and incomplete value-added tax (VAT) rebates in China.[30] Its follow-up article in 2007 further compared China's export duties on such energy-intensive products as aluminium and cement with the EU ETS and concluded that the former one was more effective at some point.[31] A similar comparison was later made by two economists in 2009 who found that China's export duties on aluminium and steel were comparable to the EU ETS in terms of carbon price.[32] In this context, as proposed by a 2012 World Bank research paper, export duties could play a positive role in future negotiations aimed at reducing carbon leakage.[33] This, as suggested by a 2013 Peterson Institute for International Economics (PIIE) policy study, would address the competitive concerns of Western nations so that they would be better able to facilitate their political economy of raising carbon prices.[34]

30 'For example, after the abolition of a global quota system, China had offered to raise its export tariffs and reduce export tax rebate rates to help manage the entry of their textiles into the EU and US markets. Under this arrangement, the revenues would have been paid to the Chinese government, but EU and US producers would have been protected from high competition from abroad'. See Nicholas Stern, *The Economics of Climate Change: The Stern Review* (Cambridge, 2007), at 552.

31 Lorraine Hamid, Nicholas Stern and Chris Taylor, 'Reflections on the Stern Review (2): A Growing International Opportunity to Move Strongly on Climate Change', 8 (1) *World Economics* (2007), at 176. 'This compares well to the cost imposed by the EU ETS [emissions-trading scheme] on firms in these sectors. At allowance prices of €20/t CO2, the impact is estimated at 1% for integrated steel and 4% for aluminum, based on the increase in electricity prices. Current prices for EU ETS allowances are €2 to €5 euros, implying far smaller impacts'. Also see Pauwelyn (2013), above n 24, at 503.

32 Tancrede Voituriez and Xin Wang, 'Can Unilateral Trade Measures Significantly Reduce Leakage and Competitiveness Pressures on EU-ETS-Constrained Industries? The Case of China Export Taxes and VAT Rebates', Climate Strategies Working Paper (2009), at 28.

33 Brian R. Copeland, 'International Trade and Green Growth', No. 6235 World Bank Policy Research Working Paper (2012), at 41.

34 Aaditya Mattoo and Arvind Subramanian, 'Four Changes to Trade Rules to Facilitate Climate Change Action', No.10 PIIE Policy Brief (2013), https://www.piie.com/p

From a critical perspective, one may question the determination of China to impose export duties on a wide range of energy-intensive products at the cost of slowing down its economic growth. For instance, it has been argued that, if the problem of carbon leakage is to be tackled effectively, China needs to impose export duties on more higher value-added products including electronics and machinery which would lead to higher costs to the Chinese economy.[35] As long as the overarching policy goal of China is to maintain a steady growth rate of 10% annually, it is not likely to 'extend export taxes to major wealth-creating export sectors', a move that 'would be needed to make an export tax approach credible'.[36] The following section updates this old view by taking into account China's recent actions to combat climate change.

6.3. Chinese export duties as a credible climate policy tool

Although the framework legislation for export duties does not refer explicitly to carbon leakage, as introduced in the previous chapter, the State Council once issued the Plan for Energy Conservation and Emission Reduction for the Eleventh Five-Year Plan Period (2006–2010), a comprehensive environmental policy at the highest levels of government, mandates exploration of the potential of export duties to reduce carbon emissions.[37] Thus, the Customs Tariff Commission began to impose export duties on certain energy-intensive products in 2007 and 2008. As discussed above, this practice has been applauded by some commentators, who see the potential of export duties to combat carbon leakage.

Indeed, given the fact that China is the largest emitter and exporter of carbon dioxide emissions, export duties could effectively curb China's carbon leakage if the country were willing to target more energy-intensive products. There are at least three good reasons for China to develop a genuine climate policy despite the associated negative impact on its economic growth.

First, the short-run economic losses caused by targeting traditional energy-intensive industries could be justified by the long-run benefits through the development of new low-carbon technologies and sectors.[38] Even the authors with a critical view of China's export duties suggested that a credible climate policy would provide China with economic benefits over the longer term.[39] Despite the

ublications/policy-briefs/four-changes-trade-rules-facilitate-climate-change-action (visited on 4 September 2019).

35 Petersb, Guanc and Hubacekd (2008), above n 9, at 3576.

36 Susanne Dröge, 'Tackling Leakage in a World of Unequal Carbon Prices', Climate Strategies Working Paper (2009), at 67.

37 For further information, see Chapter 5.

38 Alexander Roth and Georg Zachmann, 'Learning for Decarbonisation', Bruegel Policy Brief, 8 November 2018, http://bruegel.org/2018/11/learning-for-decarbonisation/?utm_source=GDPR&utm_campaign=09e7baca4d-EMAIL_CAMPAIGN_2018_11_08_09_13&utm_medium=email&utm_term=0_7c51e322b7-09e7baca4d-278610661 (visited on 1 January 2019).

39 'If export taxes have induced modernisation of domestic production, this approach yields three benefits for the Chinese economy altogether'. See Dröge (2009), above n

potential negative impacts on traditional industries, climate action could also offer future economic opportunities for countries to develop new low-carbon industries.[40] Thus, boosting long-term economic growth and tackling climate change could go hand in hand. In particular, the imposition of export duties on a wide range of energy-intensive products could represent a way to advance in the global value chain. In an effort to improve its standing among world producers, China has long been promoting its high-tech industries, which generally produce much less carbon emissions than traditional low-end manufacturing. The existing strong energy-intensive sectors in China, however, could prevent other Chinese firms from developing green technologies.[41] Perhaps for this reason, export duties were considered part of the restrictions on the traditional energy-intensive industries in the subsector Five-Year Plans relevant to climate change (2006–2020).[42]

Second, the aforementioned doubts are based on the assumption that China needs to maintain 'a steady growth rate of 10% annually'.[43] This, however, does not fit today's reality.[44] One important reason is that the Chinese government needs to accommodate the public concerns over environmental protection. Given the fact that energy-intensive industries have created such environmental challenges as air pollution in China, the negative economic impacts caused by climate action could also be politically justified by an improved environment in China. Indeed, largely relying on coal-fired power, China's rapid economic development has come at the cost of environmental damage. Thus, in late 2016, Beijing issued two highest-level pollution alerts which advised residents to stay indoors;[45] for while the maximum safe level of fine particulate matter ($PM_{2.5}$), a key air pollutant, is 25 micrograms per cubic metre, the level in China's capital peaked at just below 300. Since long-term exposure to high levels of this pollutant are known to cause lung damage and other respiratory illnesses, there is widespread public anger over the state's inability to control it. As a fundamental part of the solution, China has no choice but to reduce the scale of its energy-intensive industries.

Third, if China makes export duties as a credible climate policy instrument, they could be used to counter BTAs involving carbon-outsourcing countries and thereby enhance international cooperation on climate change. For instance, the European Parliament in 2014 required the European Commission to examine the

36, at 67. 'However, over the longer term it is in the interest of both Western countries and China to lower the energy and carbon intensity of its production practices, as the advantages of producing in China are immense'. See Petersb, Guanc and Hubacekd (2008), above n 9, at 3576.

40 Ibid.

41 'Finally, we find that an existing strong sector can fail to develop new technologies (electric vehicles in Italy)'. See Roth and Zachmann (2018), above n 38, at 10.

42 See Chapter 5.

43 Dröge (2009), above n 36, at 67.

44 For instance, China's economy only grew by 6.9% in 2015. BBC, 'China economic growth slowest in 25 years', 19 January 2016, https://www.bbc.com/news/business-35349576 (visited on 15 June 2019).

45 BBC, 'China Smog: Beijing Issues Second Ever Pollution Red Alert', 8 December 2015.

feasibility of asking steel importers to purchase emission allowances for the purpose of 'eliminating the phenomenon of carbon leakage'.[46] Moreover, the more recent development shows that the EU may indeed have prepared to impose a carbon border tax.[47] Although China may respond by initiating WTO litigation or even a trade war, such approaches would inevitably be self-defeating and undermine international cooperation. A more favourable option in terms of tackling carbon leakage would be to exempt China from the BTAs by allowing it to voluntarily impose export duties on energy-intensive products.[48]

To accommodate the above considerations, China at the end of 2014 announced its plans to halt the increase in its carbon emissions around 2030.[49] This target was further confirmed in the Paris Agreement, which was ratified by China in 2016. As the first major developing country to set a total emissions peak target, China is committed to reducing its carbon emissions per unit of GDP by 60–65% compared to 2005 levels in order to meet the 2030 target date.[50] Moreover, China has recently promised to become carbon neutral before 2060.[51] If it is to achieve these ambitious goals, China must accelerate the transformation of its current development mode, which relies largely on energy-intensive industries. The country has thus, for the first time, incorporated a limit on energy consumption into its Guidelines for the Thirteenth Five-Year Plan (2016–2020). As discussed in the previous chapter, the relevant subsector Thirteenth Five-Year Plan considers export duties, as part of export control policy, an instrument to 'create a low carbon industry system'.

As an important part of its climate action, China has also developed emissions trading system. To date, 56 jurisdictions worldwide, 35 national and 21 subnational, have implemented emissions trading systems.[52] China became one of them in 2011 when the government began establishing carbon trading pilot

46 European Parliament, 'Post-2020 reform of the EU Emissions Trading System', http://www.europarl.europa.eu/RegData/etudes/BRIE/2016/579092/EPRS_BRI(2016)579092_EN.pdf. Moreover, environmental standards could also play a role under the new methodology of EU trade defence rules. European Commission, 'EU Puts in Place New Trade Defence Rules', 20 December 2017, available at http://trade.ec.europa.eu/doclib/press/index.cfm?id=1774 (visited on 23 July 2018).

47 Alan Beattie, 'Carbon Border Tax Sends Signals for Trade Deals', FT, 29 May 2019, https://www.ft.com/content/016adba8-82ed-11e9-b592-5fe435b57a3b (visited on 15 June 2019). Also see Von der Leyen (2019), above n 19.

48 For instance, 'any export tax on the exportation of carbon-intensive products (as China is reported doing) must be deducted from the US tax on imports'. See Pauwelyn (2013), above n 24, at 503.

49 White House, 'U.S.-China Joint Announcement on Climate Change', 11 November 2014.

50 Xinhuanet, 'China's Legislature Ratifies Paris Agreement on Climate Change', 3 September 2016.

51 Smriti Mallapaty, 'How China could be carbon neutral by mid-century', Nature, 19 October 2020, https://www.nature.com/articles/d41586-020-02927-9 (visited on 14 November 2020).

52 Jeff Swartz, 'China's National Emissions Trading System', No.6 ICTSD Series on Climate Change Architecture (2016), at 7.

programmes in seven provinces and cities as part of its Guidelines of the Twelfth Five-Year Plan (2011–2015).[53] These pilot programmes were transitioned into a national emissions trading system at the end of 2017. As the world's largest carbon trade market, this national emissions trading system will target some energy-intensive sectors, including power, petrochemicals, chemicals, iron and steel, non-ferrous metals, building production and materials, pulp and paper, and aviation.[54] Some sectors, including trade and services, however, are not included in this trading system owing to administrative difficulties; simply put, the targeted sectors are much easier for government officials to monitor.

As a result of these compromises, China's national emissions trading system will cover less than half of its total carbon emissions.[55] Carbon taxes have been proposed as a means to target the other half. In order to facilitate administration of these taxes, China may impose them on such upstream sectors as energy and mining. Given the emissions trading that takes place in some industries, however, it becomes difficult to distinguish the energy consumed by industries that are covered by national emissions trading system from the energy consumed by those that are not covered. China may therefore need to impose carbon taxes further downstream; but doing so again raises the spectre of administrative complexities.

Looking beyond such logistical challenges, China may also need to consider the significant economic impacts of such carbon pricing. Currently, only a few developed countries have enacted or proposed carbon taxes.[56] As an example of the difficulties involved, Australia in 2012 implemented detailed carbon taxes, only to have a new government repeal them in 2014.[57] Against this background, China's export duties may serve as an interim tool for combating carbon leakage until an economy-wide carbon tax is feasible in financial or practical terms. Thus even the author who once questioned the credibility of China's export duties as a climate policy tool suggested that export duties could be 'a first step to find agreements on carbon constraints with major EU trade partners from emerging economies'.[58]

6.4. Conclusions

Wrapping up the preliminary analysis offered in this book, this chapter discusses the potential of China's export duties to address carbon leakage. This problem is caused by variability in worldwide carbon prices, and it significantly undermines

53 Ibid., at 12.
54 Ibid., at 17.
55 Alvin Powell, 'Tackling Carbon Emissions in China', *Harvard Gazette* (2016).
56 Carbon Tax Center, 'Where Carbon Is Taxed', http://www.carbontax.org/where-carbon-is-taxed/ (visited on 21 June 2018).
57 BBC News, 'Australia Votes to Repeal Carbon Tax', 17 July 2014, https://www.bbc.com/news/world-asia-28339663 (visited on 21 June 2018).
58 'Nevertheless, as a first step to find agreements on carbon constraints with major EU trade partners from emerging economies, an export tax could be part of an emerging picture. From a political point of view, the benefit of this approach is its positive effect on the exporters' budget, making it a potential way to finance carbon policies in developing and emerging countries'. Dröge (2009), above n 36, at 67.

global efforts to combat climate change. While a worldwide agreement to equalise carbon costs is not realistic in the near future, support is growing for BTAs designed to address cross-border differences in carbon prices. From the perspective of carbon-outsourcing countries, a feasible BTA would target imports of energy-intensive products from countries with weak climate policies, which generally have less advanced economies. In the light of the principle of 'common but differentiated responsibility',[59] this approach may, however, be considered unfair to carbon-outsourced countries and could lead to a trade war.

Export duties have been proposed as an alternative in response to such concerns about BTAs. Using this approach, carbon-outsourced countries could achieve the same objectives as a BTA by targeting exports of energy-intensive products and generating tax revenue. Perhaps this was the thinking behind China's imposition of export duties on certain energy-intensive products in 2007 and 2008, a move that has been applauded by some commentators as a promising means to confront the country's carbon leakage problem. Admittedly, there remain doubts as to whether China would make export duties a credible climate policy tool by targeting more energy-intensive products because this move would have a negative impact on China's economic growth. Such negative impacts, however, could be justified by the long-run benefits through the development of new low-carbon technologies, an improved environment in China, and the potential to counter BTAs on China's exports, not to mention the urgency of delivering the global emissions reduction targets.

In theory, China could replace export duties with such alternative measures as carbon taxes or an emissions trading system, but the administrative and economic challenges associated with such steps are formidable. Thus, for example, China's emissions trading system covers less than half of its total carbon emissions, and, the adoption of an economy-wide carbon tax to address the other half of the emissions is still under discussion, carbon leakage continues. Under these circumstances, export duties could serve as an important tool for confronting the problem.

Based on the findings reported in Part II, the preliminary conclusion is offered that the WTO ban on China's export duties would constrain its policy space to fight climate change, especially on addressing the issue of carbon leakage. The *China—Raw Materials* and *China—Rare Earths* decisions have already made it clear that China cannot invoke the environmental exceptions under GATT Article XX to justify export duties. To provide the country with desirable policy space in this regard, a legal option that involves greening these decisions is needed. This issue is addressed in Part III; first, in Chapter 7, a determination is made concerning whether there is indeed a path for China to impose export duties for environmental reasons legally under WTO law. Next, in Chapter 8, China's policy space for adopting export duties as an environmental measure under Article XX is assessed.

59 Article 4(4) of the Paris Agreement.

Part III

Final analysis: Is there a way for China to use export duties legally in order to achieve environmental goals under WTO law?

7 Is there a legal path to a desirable policy space for China under WTO law?

Various legal solutions have been proposed to alter the World Trade Organization (WTO) ban on China's export duties.[1] In a judicial way, the Appellate Body (AB) could adopt a new interpretation to correct the *China—Raw Materials* and *China—Rare Earths* rulings. This approach, however, faces a preliminary issue of whether the AB could ever be convinced to depart from its previous decisions; the fact is that, in more than 20 years of jurisprudence, the AB has never explicitly reserved itself. Moreover, it is also challenging to develop a new substantive argument to prove China's right under Article XX after the previous two cases.

A political approach, on the other hand, would require China to request instead that the WTO's decision-making body issue an amendment, waiver, or authoritative interpretation establishing China's right to invoke Article XX. In pursuing this approach, a major challenge for China would be to garner sufficient support from other WTO members. For though not all political corrections of this sort necessarily require a consensus among members, the latter would presumably prefer not to break the general taboo against formal voting.[2] This is another important issue that has yet to be addressed in the literature.

This chapter thus provides a comprehensive assessment of those approaches in order to find the most feasible way to 'greening' the WTO ban. It begins with a consideration of the likelihood that the AB would reconsider the *China—Raw Materials* and *China—Rare Earths* decisions. This analysis includes a comparative perspective by taking into account the practices of tribunals at various levels, including the International Criminal Tribunal for the former Yugoslavia (ICTY), the International Court of Justice (ICJ), the European Court of Human Rights (ECtHR), the Court of Justice of the European Union (CJEU), and the selected domestic courts in both common and civil law systems, all of which offer references for the AB's departure from previous decisions. On this point, the

1 For further discussion, see Chapter 3.

2 An illustrative example in this regard is a 2009 call by the Egyptian ambassador for a vote to recognize Palestine as an observer; while many members supported the ambassador's effort in political terms, they valued more highly continued adherence to the general ban on voting. The Egyptian ambassador was thus persuaded to drop the matter. See Craig Van Grasstek, 'The History and Future of the World Trade Organization', *WTO Publications* (2013), at 219.

DOI: 10.4324/9781003162339-10

conclusion is reached that the AB could either overrule or (preferably) distinguish the harsh ban on China's export duties. The merits of substantive arguments in support of China's right under Article XX are then assessed in Sections 7.3 and 7.4, for determining which new interpretation would most likely be acceptable to the AB. All possible interpretative options based on both WTO norms and non-WTO norms in public international law are taken into account. Given the AB's membership crisis, it is probably not the best time to rely on a judicial approach. The next consideration is thus the likelihood that a political correction would loosen the ban on China's export duties in light of treaty provisions concerning the adoption of amendments, waivers, authoritative interpretations, or a more flexible alternative. The feasibility of these conceivable political corrections is further discussed in Section 7.6. The chapter is concluded with a comparison of the most feasible judicial and political corrections.

7.1. Possible ways to alter the WTO ban through a judicial correction

Various new interpretations of the relationship between China's export duty commitments and GATT Article XX have been proposed that would enable the use of the duties for environmental purposes. Such interpretations, however, would involve departing from the *China—Raw Materials* and *China—Rare Earths* decisions, something that the AB seems reluctantly to do given the apparent *de facto stare decisis* regime in WTO dispute settlement. To address this issue, possible legal options for the AB to depart from precedent in the context of WTO jurisprudence are considered in the following subsection. The advantages and disadvantages of those options are further assessed in the context of the practice of other selected tribunals at the international, regional, and national levels, based on which this section proposes the most feasible approach, relatively speaking, for the AB to reconsider the WTO ban on China's export duties.

7.1.1. Feasibility to depart from WTO jurisprudence

This part explores the potential options to depart from the previous AB reports supporting a harsh ban on China's export duties. First of all, given the fact that 'there is no rule of *stare decisis* in WTO dispute settlement',[3] one obvious way to get rid of the *China—Raw Materials* and *China—Rare Earths* decisions is to simply ask the AB to ignore them. But, as will be discussed below, this option is objectionable owing to its profoundly negative impacts on such important values as the legal certainty. This is why, as noted by former ICJ President Gilbert Guillaume, following precedents is very common in international jurisdictions even if these international tribunals are in fact not formally obliged to comply with precedent.[4] In support of a *jurisprudence constante* regime in the multilateral trading

3 WTO Secretariat, 'Legal Effect of Panel and AB Reports and DSB Recommendations and Rulings', available at https://www.wto.org/english/tratop_e/dispu_e/disp_settlement_cbt_e/c7s2p1_e.htm (visited on 18 June 2017).

system, this part discusses the other three options, namely explicit overruling, implicit overruling, and distinguishing, that could enable the AB to balance the precedential value and the flexibilities to loosen the grip of its settled jurisprudence.

7.1.1.1. Unwise to abandon the precedential value

WTO dispute settlement system is mandated to provide 'security and predictability to the multilateral trading system'.[5] Thus, for the purpose of creating 'legitimate expectations among WTO Members', the AB in *Japan—Alcoholic Beverages* suggested that its reports 'should be taken into account where they are relevant to any dispute'.[6] This raises the question of whether a panel or the AB itself may depart from an AB report in a relevant dispute.

In practice, the AB has never explicitly departed from its previous decisions.[7] In contrast, a panel had expressly challenged the AB's decisions in *US—Stainless Steel (Mexico)*. By acknowledging that the AB had reversed two panel decisions supporting the use of zeroing methodology in administrative review, the *US—Stainless Steel (Mexico)* panel still 'felt compelled to depart from' the AB's previous approach against the US's zeroing methodology.[8] For the AB, such departure from its 'well-established' jurisprudence had 'serious implications for the proper functioning of the WTO dispute settlement system'.[9] The AB thus in the same case required that subsequent panels should not be 'free to disregard the legal interpretations and the *ratio decidendi*' contained in previous AB reports unless 'cogent reasons' were presented for departing from them.[10]

The precedential value of AB reports, however, has drawn strong criticism from the US government. For instance, in its Trade Representative's 2018 Trade Policy Agenda and 2017 Annual Report, the US claimed that requiring panels to follow prior AB decisions absent 'cogent reasons' was inconsistent with WTO rules.[11] The US appeared to suggest that the only interpretation that panels should follow was the authoritative interpretation adopted by WTO members under Article IX:2 of the WTO Agreement though, in practice, the only one request made for an authoritative interpretation was rejected by the US itself.[12]

5 'The dispute settlement system of the WTO is a central element in providing security and predictability to the multilateral trading system'. Article 3,2 of the DSU.
6 AB Report, *Japan—Taxes on Alcoholic Beverages*, WT/DS8/AB/R, WT/DS10/AB/R, WT/DS11/AB/R, adopted 1 November 1996, at 14.
7 Implicitly, the AB seems to have changed its position on the so-called aim and effects test in the *EC—Asbestos*. For further discussion, see Section 7.1.3.4.
8 Panel Report, *US—Stainless Steel (Mexico)*, para 7.106.
9 AB Report, *US—Stainless Steel (Mexico)*, paras 161–162.
10 Ibid., paras 158–160.
11 Office of the United States Trade Representative, '2018 Trade Policy Agenda and 2017 Annual Report', at 28
12 Ibid. For further discussion about the use of authoritative interpretation to greening the ban on China's export duties, see Section 7.7.

This book argues that China should not support the US position even if the denial of the precedential value of AB reports could help China alter the WTO ban on its export duties. As correctly noted by the EU as a third participant in *US—Stainless Steel (Mexico)*, 'in practice most international tribunals do give certain weight to precedents when dealing with similar legal issues'.[13] The reason behind such common practice is rather self-evident which is for 'the maintenance of security and stability' as a primary function of law.[14]

That being said, however, '[t]he cult of the precedent is thus just as dangerous as the rejection of precedent'.[15] It is thus important to strike a balance between legal certainty and flexibility. The options to introduce flexibility into the WTO's precedent system are discussed as follows.

7.1.1.2. Option I: explicit overruling based on 'cogent reasons'

Within the framework of *jurisprudence constante*, a departure from precedent requires a tribunal to provide a good explanation in order to preserve the authority of precedent. That is to say, 'judicial precedents would only be devoid of authority if judges felt no need to offer reasons for their actions in those instances when they choose not to follow them'.[16] Thus the AB has introduced the concept of 'cogent reasons'.

The panel in the *US—Countervailing and Anti-Dumping Measures (China)* case defined the notion of 'cogent reasons' further in relation to four types of situations.[17] The first requires an authoritative interpretation under Article IX:2 of the WTO Agreement that departs from a prior AB interpretation, an option that is to be discussed in Section 7.6 of this chapter. The other three situations require demonstration that a prior AB interpretation proved to be either unworkable, in conflict with another provision of a covered agreement, or based on a factually incorrect premise. In view of these latter three criteria, it has been argued that there are indeed 'cogent reasons' for the AB to 'correct' the interpretation that it handed down in the *China—Raw Materials* and *China—Rare Earths* decisions.[18]

It is noteworthy that, although the notion of 'cogent reasons' has been clarified by a panel decision, there has been no successful attempt at offering 'cogent reasons' in front of the panels or the AB. Moreover, in the past 20 years, the AB has

13 Para 7.20. The EU referred to the practice of the European Court of Human Rights, the International Court of Justice, the International Tribunal for the Law of the Sea, the International Criminal Tribunal for the Former Yugoslavia, the International Criminal Tribunal for Rwanda, the International Criminal Court and the International Centre for Settlement of Investment Disputes. For further discussion about the practice of selected tribunals, see next subsection.

14 AB Report, *US—Stainless Steel (Mexico)*, footnote 313.

15 Guillaume (2011), see above n 4, at 23.

16 Neil Duxbury, 'Distinguishing, Overruling and the Problem of Self-reference', in *The Nature and Authority of Precedent* (Cambridge University Press, 2008), at 112.

17 Panel Report, *US—Countervailing and Anti-Dumping Measures (China)*, para 7.317.

18 Xuewei Feng, 'On the Feasibility of Self-Correction of the AB's Previous Decision: Lessons from China-Rare Earths', 2(1) *China and WTO Review* (2015), at 182.

never explicitly departed from its prior decisions. The very infrequency appears to suggest that express overruling based on 'cogent reasons' is not the first-best option in practice.

7.1.1.3. Option II: distinguishing

China may find a way that enable the AB to implicitly alter the *China—Raw Materials* and *China—Rare Earths* decisions by distinguishing them. Indeed, a common reason to not follow a precedent is that an earlier case does not apply to the instant one due to a distinction between them, which is often referred to as distinguishing. It is noteworthy that, in the more obvious form of distinguishing, if two cases are materially different, the earlier one is not really a precedent to the later one. In contrast, and more relevant to this chapter, is the more subtle form of distinguishing, namely 'where a court departs from a precedent by making a particular ruling depend on the presence of a more extensive range of material facts'.[19] For instance, assuming that a tribunal in an earlier case decided that facts A and B should lead to outcome X. In a later case when facts A and B are obtained, the tribunal may still choose to not follow the earlier case by distinguishing it and deciding that outcome X should be caused by facts A, B and C. Thus, by adding to the conditions necessary for applying a precedent, the restrictive distinguishing in effect amends an earlier case by narrowing its applicable scope.

An obvious example of distinguishing WTO precedents can be found in the *Indonesia—Import Licensing Regimes* case in which the AB expressly distinguished its long-established sequence of analysis under GATT Article XX. In this case, Indonesia requested the AB to the reverse the panel's findings under Article XX because the panel did not follow the 'well-established sequence of analysis under Article XX' by assessing the chapeau of Article XX without first examining the applicable paragraphs, namely paragraphs (a), (b), and (d) in the present case.[20] The sequence of analysis under Article XX was first set out in *US—Gasoline* in which the AB held that the analysis was two-tiered: first, provisional justification under the applicable paragraphs; second, further appraisal under the chapeau of Article XX.[21] This two-tiered sequence was highlighted in *US—Shrimp* as reflecting 'not inadvertence or random choice, but rather the fundamental structure and

19 Ibid., at 115.

20 AB Report, *Indonesia – Importation of Horticultural Products, Animals and Animal Products*, WT/DS477/AB/R, WT/DS478/AB/R, and Add.1, adopted 22 November 2017, para 5.86.

21 In *US—Gasoline*, the AB stated: 'In order that the justifying protection of Article XX may be extended to it, the measure at issue must not only come under one or another of the particular exceptions – paragraphs (a) to (j) – listed under Article XX; it must also satisfy the requirements imposed by the opening clauses of Article XX. The analysis is, in other words, two-tiered: first, provisional justification by reason of characterization of the measure under XX(g); second, further appraisal of the same measure under the introductory clauses of Article XX' at 20.

logic of Article XX'.[22] Thus, the panel in *Indonesia—Import Licensing Regimes*, choosing to only examine the measure under the chapeau of Article XX appears to be inconsistent with the AB's prior decisions.

However, rather than reversing the panel's findings, the AB held that, to first examine the applicable paragraphs, as the 'normal sequence', aimed to provide panels with the 'necessary tools to assess the requirements of the chapeau', namely to determine whether a discriminatory measure at issue was arbitrary or unjustifiable within the meaning of the chapeau and which 'conditions' prevailing in different countries are relevant in the context of the chapeau.[23] Thus, to distinguish between the normal circumstances and the 'particular circumstances' in which a panel might be able to analyse the elements under the applicable paragraphs that were relevant to assess the requirements of the chapeau 'even when the sequence of analysis under Article XX has not been followed',[24] the AB held that a panel might deviate from the 'normal sequence' in the 'particular circumstances of the case' provided that the panel had made findings under the applicable paragraphs in order to complete the analysis of the chapeau.[25] In this way, the AB effectively amended the sequence of analysis under Article XX by allowing a deviation under certain circumstances.

Compared with express overruling, however, the use of distinguishing has limitations. Although a tribunal could use distinguishing to amend a precedent by adding conditions, these conditions should be based on a material distinction between the precedent and the present one. After all, 'the judge who tries to distinguish cases on the basis of materially irrelevant facts is likely to be easily found out'.[26] Thus, when the important facts of two cases are identical, a tribunal may choose to overrule a precedent by 'declaring that, at least where the facts of a case are materially identical to those of the case at hand, a new ruling should be followed instead'.[27] In this way, the tribunal is *de facto* repealing a previous judgement rather than amending it.[28]

7.1.1.4. Option III: implicit overruling

It is noteworthy that the AB may have overruled its prior decisions in an implicit manner. Relevant here is the *EC—Asbestos* case in which the AB appeared to have implicitly overruled its prior decisions that rejected the 'aim and effect' test. This test was reinstated when the AB changed its established framework for analysing 'likeness' under GATT Article III in order to balance trade and non-trade values.

22 AB Report, United States – Import Prohibition of Certain Shrimp and Shrimp Products, WT/DS58/AB/R, adopted 6 November 1998, DSR 1998:VII, p. 2755, para. 119.
23 AB Report, *Indonesia – Import Licensing Regimes*, para 5.99.
24 Ibid., 5.100.
25 Ibid., 5.101.
26 Ibid., at 114.
27 Ibid., at 117.
28 Ibid., at 115.

Specifically, in examining the 'likeness' of chrysotile asbestos fibres, which are known to be highly carcinogenic, to other fibres,[29] the AB maintained the guise of the previous framework by 'squeezing health effects into its competition-oriented framework' rather than simply adopting a new framework.[30]

The framework for analysing 'likeness', which was first established in the Report of the Working party on *Border Tax Adjustments*, [31] consists of four general criteria: (i) the properties, nature, and quality of the products in question; (ii) the end uses of the products; (iii) consumers' tastes and habits; and (iv) the tariff classification of the products.[32] Since these four general criteria simply serve as tools for sorting and examining the relevant evidence,[33] the assessment of 'likeness' necessarily depends on the legal provision at issue.[34] In the case of GATT Article III, the competitive relationship between products is of particular importance in this regard.[35]

Following this competition-oriented framework, the panel in *EC—Asbestos* relied largely on the second criterion, which addressed the end uses of products, to conclude that chrysotile asbestos fibres and certain other fibres were 'like products' under Article III:4.[36] The AB, however, with one member dissenting, was concerned about the consequences of ruling that a product with enormous health and safety risks was 'like' certain much safer substitutes.[37] It then linked the health risks associated with the carcinogenic fibres to 'consumer preferences', another of the four general criteria for assessing 'likeness'. Approaching the case from this perspective, the AB reasoned that, because the ultimate consumer might cease to buy a product associated with serious health problems,[38] the relevant manufacturers would likely weigh the risks of including chrysotile asbestos fibres in their products. In this respect, the AB changed its previous competition-oriented framework by giving the priority to public health and thus reversed the panel's conclusion that the carcinogenic fibres and their safer substitutes were 'like products'.[39]

To sum up, three options are theoretically available for the AB to not follow the *China—Raw Materials* and *China—Rare Earths* decisions, namely explicit

29 WTO AB Report, *European Communities — Measures Affecting Asbestos and Products Containing Asbestos*, WT/DS135/AB/R, adopted on 12 March 2001.
30 Robert Howse, Comments on 'Interpretation and Institutional Choice at the WTO', *Opinio Juris* (2012), available at http://opiniojuris.org/2012/04/11/vjil-symposium-robert-howse-comments-on-interpretation-and-institutional-choice-at-the-wto/ (visited on 10 June 2018).
31 Working Party Report, *Border Tax Adjustments*, BISD 18S/97, adopted 2 December 1970.
32 AB Report, *EC—Asbestos*, para 101.
33 Ibid, para 102.
34 Ibid, para 103.
35 Ibid, para 117.
36 Panel Report, *EC—Asbestos*, para 84.
37 Howse (2012), above n 30.
38 AB Report, *EC—Asbestos*, para 122.
39 Ibid, para 126.

overruling based on 'cogent reasons', implicit overruling, and distinguishing. Given the fact that the AB is a relatively young tribunal, it could be beneficial to examine the practice of other more mature tribunals from which a most feasible option, relatively speaking, might be discerned. This analysis is discussed in the next subsection.

7.1.2. Moves by other tribunals to deviate from precedent: inspirations for the AB to reconsider the WTO ban on Chinese export duties

The problem of how to avoid undesirable precedents is not unique to the AB. Tribunals at the international, regional, and domestic levels have faced similar problems and have developed ways of dealing with them. This subsection provides a comparative analysis of these practices by the International Criminal Tribunal for the former Yugoslavia (ICTY), the International Court of Justice (ICJ), the European Court of Human Rights (ECtHR), the Court of Justice of the European Union (CJEU), and the highest courts of appeals in the United Kingdom (UK), Japan, and China. The aim here is to draw inspirations for the AB to reconsider the WTO ban on China's export duties.

7.1.2.1. The choice of tribunals at various levels

In general, the comparison with the select international or regional tribunals has often been made by either the AB itself or relevant literature.[40] With regard to select international and regional tribunals (an overview see Table 7.1 at the end of this subsection), an analysis of the practice of the ICJ and ICTY could provide the AB with references on how the other international tribunals departed from precedent. With regard to the CJEU, similar to the AB, many judgements of this regional court have trade-related aspects which could provide the former one with references on how to balance trade and non-trade interests. In contrast, although the ECtHR does not examine trade-related issues, its judgement may shed light on how the AB could accommodate environmental interests from a human rights perspective. Moreover, compared with international and regional tribunals, the national ones may have more experience with how to depart from precedent. In order to have an overview of the practice in both common law and civil law countries, this part examines the techniques of the highest appeal courts in the United Kingdom, Japan, and China to loosen the grip of their settled jurisprudence.

This comparison has its limitations because the select tribunals have different institutional features from the AB. According to certain criteria, the WTO dispute settlement is the least legalistic option.[41] The experience of the select tribunals thus may not be directly borrowed. That being said, however, the mandate of

40 See AB Report, *US—Stainless Steel (Mexico)* and Guillaume (2011), see above n 4.
41 Lisa L. Martin and Beth A. Simmons, *International Institutions: An International Organization Reader* (MIT Press, 2001), at 139.

Table 7.1 Moves by tribunals at the international and regional levels to deviate from precedent

Tribunals	*Moves to loosen the grip of their settled jurisprudence*		
International level			
		Overruling	
	Case	**Practice**	**Reasons**
International Criminal Tribunal for the Former Yugoslavia (ICTY)	*Kordić and Čerkez* Appeal Judgement (2004)	Explicitly overruled the *Krstić* Appeal Judgement (2004) and *Vasiljević* Appeal Judgement (2004) 'The Appeals Chamber considers that cogent reasons warrant a departure from this jurisprudence as an incorrect application of the *Čelebići* test to intra-Article 5 convictions' (para 1040).	The precedents incorrectly apply the legal test relating to cumulative convictions as set out in the *Čelebići* case. To 'ensuring that the convictions entered fully reflect his criminality' (para 1033).
	Žigić Appeal Decision (2005)	Explicitly overruled the *Čelebići* Appeal Judgement (2001) 'In light of these considerations, the Appeals Chamber has come to the view that cogent reasons in the interests of justice demand its departure from the majority opinion in the *Čelebići* Judgement on Sentence Appeal' (para 9).	The precedent is inconsistent with the ICTY Statute. To protect 'the interests of justice' to the victims or convicted person.
	Šainović et al. Appeal Judgement (2014)	Explicitly overruled the *Perišić* Appeal Judgement (2013) 'Consequently, the Appeals Chamber, Judge Tuzmukhamedov dissenting, unequivocally rejects the approach adopted in the Perišić Appeal Judgement as it is in direct and material conflict with the prevailing jurisprudence on the *actus reus* of aiding and abetting liability and with customary international law in this regard' (para 1650).	The precedent is inconsistent with prevailing jurisprudence and customary international law regarding the *actus reus* of aiding and abetting liability.

Tribunals	Moves to loosen the grip of their settled jurisprudence		
	Distinguishing		
	Case	**Practice**	**Reasons**
	Strugar Trial Judgement (2005)	Distinguished the *Čelebići* Appeal Judgement (2001) 'A strict application of the above mentioned Appeals Chamber test would allow cumulative convictions… …'(para 449); 'Counts 4 and 5 really add no materially distinct element, given the particular circumstances in which these offences were committed' (para 454).	Due to the 'particular circumstances' concerning the offences, some of the essential criminal conducts are 'directly and comprehensively reflected' in the others. Thus, the precedent should be amended in order to preserve the 'interests of justice and the purposes of punishment' (para 454).
International Court of Justice (ICJ)	**Overruling**		
	Case	**Practice**	**Reasons**
	Libya—Malta Judgement (1985)	Implicitly overruled the *North Sea Continental Shelf* Judgement (1969) 'However to rely on this jurisprudence would be to overlook the fact that where such jurisprudence appears to ascribe a role to geophysical or geological factors in delimitation, it finds warrant for doing so in a régime of the title itself which used to allot those factors a place which now belongs to the past, in so far as sea-bed areas less than 200 miles from the Coast are concerned' (para 40).	The 1969 Judgement, which stepped away from the equidistance method, appeared to cause uncertainties.
	NATO Judgement (2004)	Implicitly overruled the *Genocide* Judgement (2003)	Perhaps the majority had formed in 2004 within the ICJ wanted to use the 2004 case to 'sink' the 2003 judgment.
	Distinguishing		
	Case	**Practice**	**Reasons**
	Genocide Judgement (2008)	Distinguished the *NATO* Judgement (2004) The Court drew a distinction between the 2004 judgment and Croatia's case based on the fact that the FRY was the applicant in the former case but the respondent in the latter. The ICJ also relied on two further facts in reaching its conclusion.	There were certain situations in which realism and flexibility were called for to determine the jurisdiction.

Tribunals	Moves to loosen the grip of their settled jurisprudence		
Regional level			
European Court of Human Rights (ECtHR)	**Overruling**		
	Case	**Practice**	**Reasons**
	Huber v. Switzerland (1990)	Implicitly overruled *Schiesser v. Switzerland (1979)* 'Clearly the Convention does not rule out the possibility of the judicial officer who orders the detention carrying out other duties, but his impartiality is open to doubt … if he is entitled to intervene in the subsequent criminal proceedings as a representative of the prosecuting authority. Since that was the situation in the present case, there has been a breach of Article 5(3)', para 43.	The Court did not explain.
	Borgers v. Belgium (1993)	Implicitly overruled *Delcourt v. Belgium (1970)* 'In conclusion, having regard to the requirements of the rights of the defence and of the principle of the equality of arms and to the role of appearances in determining whether they have been complied with, the Court finds a violation of Article 6(1)', para 29.	The Court did not explain.
	Vilho Eskelinen and Others v. Finland (2007)	Explicitly overruled *Pellegrin v. France (1999)* 'The Court can only conclude that the functional criterion, as applied in practice, has not simplified the analysis of the applicability of Article 6 in proceedings to which a civil servant is a party or brought about a greater degree of certainty in this area as intended (see, mutatis mutandis, Perez v. France [GC], no. 47287/99, x 55, ECHR 2004-I)', para 55. 'It is against this background and for these reasons that the Court finds that the functional criterion adopted in the case of *Pellegrin* must be further developed', para 56.	The original approach was found unable to bring about 'a greater degree of certainty in this area as intended'.
	Kudla v. Poland (2002)	Explicitly overruled *Kamasinski v. Austria (1991)* 'In the Court's view, the time has come to review its case-law in the light of the continuing accumulation of applications before it in which the only, or principal, allegation is that of a failure to ensure a hearing within a reasonable time in breach of Article 6(1)', para 148.	The original approach was reconsidered 'forcing applicants to bring their Article 6 (1) unreasonable delay complaints to Strasbourg rather than having them resolved domestically'.

Tribunals — *Moves to loosen the grip of their settled jurisprudence*

Christine Goodwin—United Kingdom (2002)	Explicitly overruled the *Rees* Judgement (1986) and *Cossey* Judgement (1990). '… it should not depart, without good reason, from precedents laid down in previous cases (see, for example, Chapman v. the United Kingdom [GC], no. 27238/95, ECHR 2001-I, § 70). However, since the Convention is first and foremost a system for the protection of human rights, the Court must have regard to the changing conditions within the respondent State and within Contracting States generally and respond, for example, to any evolving convergence as to the standards to be achieved', para 74.	In order to take into account 'the changing conditions' within the contracting states and to ensure that the rights under the Conventions continued to be 'practical and effective', para 74.

Distinguishing

Case	**Practice**	**Reasons**
Kopecký (2003)	Distinguished the *Malhous* Grand Chamber Judgement (2000) and *Gratzinger and Gratzingerova* Grand Chamber Judgement (2002). 'In this respect the present case should be distinguished from the cases of *Malhous v. the Czech Republic* and *Gratzinger and Gratzingerova v. the Czech Republic* referred to above or the case of *Brezny & Brezny v. Slovakia* (application no. 23131/93, Commission decision of 4 March 1996, DR 85, pp. 65–83) in which the Court and the Commission respectively found that the applicants' claims for restitution of property did not amount to a legitimate expectation in the sense of the Court's case-law. In those cases the applicants were excluded from the very beginning from the possibility of having the property restored as it was obvious either that they failed to meet the relevant requirements or that their claim clearly fell outside the relevant law' (para 27).	In order to prevent the protection of the rights under the European Conventions on Human Rights and its protocols from being revealed as 'ineffective and illusory'.

Tribunals	*Moves to loosen the grip of their settled jurisprudence*		
Court of Justice of the European Union (CJEU)	**Overruling Case**	**Practice**	**Reasons**
	HAG II Judgement (1990)	Explicitly overruled the *HAG I* Judgement (1974) 'Bearing in mind the points outlined in the order for reference and in the discussions before the Court concerning the relevance of the Court's judgment in Case 192/73 *Van Zuylen v. HAG* [1974] ECR 731 to the reply to the question asked by the national court, it should be stated at the outset that the Court believes it necessary to reconsider the interpretation given in that judgment in the light of the case-law which has developed with regard to the relationship between industrial and commercial property and the general rules of the Treaty, particularly in the sphere of the free movement of goods' (para 10).	The precedent was out of step with subsequent developments in the case law on intellectual property rights and out of step with the evolving perception of the internal market. '… given in that judgment in the light of the case-law which has developed with regard to the relationship between industrial and commercial property and the general rules of the Treaty, particularly in the sphere of the free movement of goods' (para 10).
	Metock Judgement (2008)	Explicitly overruled the *Akrich* Judgement (2003) 'It is true that the Court held in paragraphs 50 and 51 of *Akrich* that, in order to benefit from the rights provided for in Article 10 of Regulation No 1612/68, the national of a non-member country who is the spouse of a Union citizen must be lawfully resident in a Member State when he moves to another Member State to which the citizen of the Union is migrating or has migrated. However, that conclusion must be reconsidered. The benefit of such rights cannot depend on the prior lawful residence of such a spouse in another Member State (see, to that effect, *MRAX*, paragraph 59, and Case C-157/03 *Commission v Spain*, paragraph 28)' (para 58).	In order to protect the right of EU citizens and their family members to move and reside freely within the EU. 'The benefit of such rights cannot depend on the prior lawful residence of such a spouse in another Member State' (para 28).
	Wouters Judgement (2002)	Implicitly overruled the *Métropole* Judgement (2001) by ignoring it.	The Court did not explain.

Tribunals	Moves to loosen the grip of their settled jurisprudence		
	Distinguishing		
	Case	**Practice**	**Reasons**
	Keck Judgement (1993)	Distinguished the *Dassonville* Judgement (1974) and *Cassis de Dijon* Judgement (1979) 'By contrast, contrary to what has previously been decided, the application to products from other Member States of national provisions restricting or prohibiting certain selling arrangements is not such as to hinder directly or indirectly, actually or potentially, trade between Member States within the meaning of the *Dassonville* judgment (Case 8/74 [1974] ECR 837), so long as those provisions apply to all relevant traders operating within the national territory and so long as they affect in the same manner, in law and in fact, the marketing of domestic products and of those from other Member States' (para 16).	In order to address concerns regarding potential abuse of Article 34. 'In view of the increasing tendency of traders to invoke Article 30 of the Treaty as a means of challenging any rules whose effect is to limit their commercial freedom even where such rules are not aimed at products from other Member States, the Court considers it necessary to re-examine and clarify its case-law on this matter' (para 14).
	Steenhorst-Neerings Judgement (1993), *Johnson* Judgement (1994), *and Fantask* Judgement (1997)	Distinguished the *Emmott* Judgement (1991) 'However, as was confirmed by the judgment in Case C-410/92 *Johnson v Chief Adjudication Officer* [1994] ECR 1–5483, at paragraph 26, it is clear from Case C-338/91 *Steenhorst-Neerings v Bestuur van de Bedrijfsvereniging voor Detailhandel, Ambachten en Huisvrouwen* [1993] ECR 1–5475 that the solution adopted in *Emmott* was justified by the particular circumstances of that case, in which the time-bar had the result of depriving the applicant of any opportunity whatever to rely on her right to equal treatment under a Community directive (see also *Haahr Petroleum*, cited above, paragraph 52, and Joined Cases C-114/95 and C-115/95 *Texaco and Olieselskabet Danmark* [1997] ECR 1–4263, paragraph 48)' (para 51).	Critics of the *Emmott* judgment seem to have prevailed over time, for the Court ended up distancing itself from this judgment.

Tribunals		*Moves to loosen the grip of their settled jurisprudence*	
	Alimanovic Judgement (2015)	Distinguished the *Brey* Judgement (2013) 'It must be stated in this connection that, although the Court has held that Directive 2004/38 requires a Member State to take account of the individual situation of the person concerned before it adopts an expulsion measure or finds that the residence of that person is placing an unreasonable burden on its social assistance system (judgment in Brey, C-140/12, EU:C:2013:565, paragraphs 64, 69 and 78), no such individual assessment is necessary in circumstances such as those at issue in the main proceedings' (para 59).	The Court did not explain.
	Altmark Judgement (2003)	Distinguished the *Ferring* Judgement (2001) 'It follows from those judgments that, where a State measure must be regarded as compensation for the services provided by the recipient undertakings in order to discharge public service obligations, so that those undertakings do not enjoy a real financial advantage and the measure thus does not have the effect of putting them in a more favourable competitive position than the undertakings competing with them, such a measure is not caught by Article 92(1) of the Treaty' (para 87).	In order to prevent Member States from abusing the *Ferring* formula.

those tribunals may not significantly differ from the one of the WTO, namely, to provide 'security and predictability'. Therefore, the practice in other jurisdiction may still provide the AB with inspirations to depart from *China—Raw Materials* and *China—Rare Earths.*

7.1.2.2. International Court of Justice (ICJ)

Although Article 59 of the Statute of the International Court of Justice states that the ICJ's judgments 'has no binding force except between the parties and in respect of that particular case', the ICJ has developed rules of *de facto stare decisis* by 'closely following its earlier judgements'.[42] Relevant in this context is the holding of the ICJ in the *Cameroon—Nigeria* case that it could depart from its own precedent if 'there is cause not to follow the reasoning and conclusions of earlier cases'.[43] It must be observed, however, that the ICJ has never explicitly departed from a prior judgment, having consistently chosen the options to implicitly overrule or distinguish precedent.

The practice of implicit overruling is observed in a series of ICJ judgments concerning alternative methods of maritime delimitation.[44] One, often referred to as the equidistance method, requires that maritime boundaries between states follow a median line, every point of which is equidistant from the nearest points on the respective coasts. In contrast, the second method, which is result-oriented, requires application of equitable principles in order to achieve equitable results. In other words, tribunals are not bound by the aforementioned equidistance method and thus enjoy 'a significant degree of discretion which, however, comes at the cost of consistency and predictability'.[45] In its 1969 *North Sea Continental Shelf* ruling, the ICJ imposed a delimitation on the continental shelf in accordance with the second approach by 'taking account of all relevant circumstances', including geological factors.[46] The choice of result-oriented approach seems to have caused uncertainty regarding maritime delimitation.[47]

42 August Reinisch, 'The Proliferation of International Dispute Settlement Mechanisms: The Threat of Fragmentation vs. the Promise of a More Effective System? Some Reflections From the Perspective of Investment Arbitration', in Isabelle Buffard, James Crawford, Alain Pellet and Stephan Wittich (eds), *International Law between Universalism and Fragmentation: Festschrift in Honour of Gerhard Hafner* (Brill, 2009), at 123.

43 ICJ Judgement, *Land and Maritime Boundary between Cameroon and Nigeria (Cameroon v. Nigeria: Equatorial Guinea intervening)*, adopted on 11 June 1998, para. 28.

44 Guillaume (2011), see above n 4, at 11.

45 Alina Kaczorowska-Ireland, '*Public International Law (5th Edition)*' (Routledge, 2015), at 325.

46 ICJ Judgement, *North Sea Continental Shelf (Federal Republic of Germany/Netherlands)*, adopted on 20 February 1969.

47 'The law appeared increasingly uncertain and even arbitrary'. See Guillaume (2011), see above n 4, at 11.

The ICJ became aware of the problems and implicitly 'reversed its jurisprudence'.[48] It began with the 1985 *Libya—Malta* case in which the ICJ considered the equidistance line as the starting point for marine delimitation.[49] The result of equidistance method could be adjusted if such a correction is justified by geographic or other circumstances in order to achieve equitable results.[50] The large discretion conferred by the result-oriented approach is thus constrained by the preliminary use of equidistance method. This implicit overruling was confirmed and further generalised in the 2001 *Bahrain—Qatar* and 2009 *Romania—Ukraine* cases.[51] As a result, the ICJ 'abandoned' the original approach adopted in 1969 by 'successive strokes without recognizing its original mistake'.[52]

The use of implicit overruling and distinguishing is also apparent in a series of judgments concerning access to the ICJ by the Federal Republic of Yugoslavia (FRY), later Serbia and Montenegro, during the special period from 27 April 1992, when the FRY declared independence, to 1 November 2000, when it was admitted to the United Nations. By implicitly overruling and distinguishing precedents, the ICJ in a series of cases involving genocide claims found its jurisdiction over the FRY as a respondent but reached an opposite conclusion when the FRY was an applicant.

The first of these cases was brought by Bosnia and Herzegovina in 1993 against the FRY for alleged violations of the Genocide Convention. The ICJ determined in its 1996 judgment that it had jurisdiction over the FRY.[53] The reason is that when the FRY had, in asserting its independence, declared that it would abide strictly by all of the international commitments that the former Yugoslavia had entered into, this commitment included the Genocide Convention, Article IX of which permits a party to the convention to bring a case 'relating to the interpretation, application or fulfilment of the present Convention' before the ICJ. It is noteworthy that the FRY did not challenge the jurisdiction by arguing that it was not a member of the United Nations because the ICJ 'shall be open to the states parties to the present Statute' pursuant to Article 35(1) of the Statute.[54] The

48 ICJ Judgement, *Continental Shelf (Libyan Arab Jamahiriya/Malta)*, adopted on 3 June 1985, para 40.
49 Ibid., para 42.
50 Kaczorowska-Ireland (2015), above n 45, at 326.
51 Guillaume (2011), see above n 4, at 12. ICJ Judgement, *Maritime Delimitation and Territorial Questions between Qatar and Bahrain (Qatar v. Bahrain)*, adopted on 16 March 2001; ICJ Judgement, *Maritime Delimitation in the Black Sea (Romania v. Ukraine)*, adopted on 3 February 2009.
52 Guillaume (2011), see above n 4, at 12.
53 ICJ Judgement, *Application of the Convention on the Prevention and Punishment of the Crime of Genocide (Bosnia and Herzegovina v. Serbia and Montenegro)*, adopted on 11 July 1996, para 17.
54 '1. The Court shall be open to the states parties to the present Statute. 2. The conditions under which the Court shall be open to other states shall, subject to the special provisions contained in treaties in force, be laid down by the Security Council, but in no case shall such conditions place the parties in a position of inequality before the Court. 3. When a state which is not a Member of the United Nations is a party to a case, the Court shall fix the amount which that party is to contribute towards the

reason behind this strategy seemed to be consistent with the political narrative of the Milošević regime.[55]

After the change of the Milošević regime in 2000, the new FRY government abandoned the insistence on the FRY as a continuation of the Socialist Federal Republic of Yugoslavia and applied for membership of the United Nations as a new state. When the FRY was admitted to the United Nations as a new member, thereby establishing that it had not been a United Nations member in 1993, it challenged the above 1996 judgement.[56] By referring to Article 35(1) of the Statute, the FRY argued that the ICJ could not have asserted jurisdiction the FRY were not a member of the United Nations. Based on this change of fact, the FRY filed an application for revision of the 1996 judgment according to Article 61(1) of the Statute, which permits an application for revision of a judgment based on the discovery of decisive new factors. The ICJ did not, however, consider the FRY's membership in the United Nations in 2000 a decisive factor regarding the question of personal jurisdiction over it in the 1996 judgment. From the ICJ's perspective, the period from 1992 to 2000 was for the FRY '*sui generis*', during which the FRY considered itself bound by the Genocide Convention.[57] Thus the ICJ in its 2003 judgment ruled that the FRY's admission to the United Nations in 2000 did not constitute a new fact relating to potential revision of the 1996 judgment. It is noteworthy that Article 35(2) of the Statute permits the ICJ's jurisdiction over a non-party to it 'subject to the special provisions contained in treaties in force'. In this context, the 2003 judgment appears to suggest that Article IX of the Genocide Convention meets the requirements under Article 35 (2) and thus extends the jurisdiction of the ICJ over the FRY as a non-member of the United Nations or a non-party to the Statute.[58]

A different approach involving the option of implicitly overruling was taken, however, in a later case, which this time was brought by the FRY against ten member States of NATO for the military bombing of the territory of Yugoslavia and other alleged violations of international law.[59] Following the 2003 judgment

expenses of the Court. This provision shall not apply if such state is bearing a share of the expenses of the Court'.

55 Vojin Dimitrijević and Marko Milanović, 'The Strange Story of the Bosnian Genocide Case', 21(1) *Leiden Journal of International Law* (2008), at 72.

56 UN Security Council, *3116th Meeting Resolution S/RES/777*, adopted on 16 September 1992; UN General Assembly, *Recommendation of the Security Council of 19 September 1992*, A/RES/47/1, adopted on 22 September 1992.

57 ICJ Judgement, *Application for Revision of the Judgment of 11 July 1996 in the Case concerning Application of the Convention on the Prevention and Punishment of the Crime of Genocide (Bosnia and Herzegovina v. Yugoslavia), Preliminary Objections (Yugoslavia v. Bosnia and Herzegovina)*, adopted on 3 February 2003, paras 54–64.

58 Ibid.

59 ICJ Judgements, *Legality of Use of Force (Serbia and Montenegro v. Belgium); Legality of Use of Force (Serbia and Montenegro v. Canada); Legality of Use of Force (Serbia and Montenegro v. France); Legality of Use of Force (Serbia and Montenegro v. Germany); Legality of Use of Force (Serbia and Montenegro v. Italy); Legality of Use of Force (Serbia and Montenegro v. Netherlands); Legality of Use of Force (Serbia and*

just described, although several respondents claimed that the FRY 'cannot rely on its acquiescence as respondent in one case in order to found jurisdiction as Applicant in this case',[60] the FRY argued that the ICJ should have personal jurisdiction over it as a party to Article IX of the Genocide Convention pursuant to Article 35 (2) of the Statute. Concerning this argument, the ICJ, with reference to the drafting history, interpreted the term 'treaties in force' under Article 35(2) restrictively and held that it only applied to the treaties in force by the date on which the ICJ Statute itself had entered into force (24 October 1945).[61] Accordingly, the Genocide Convention, which entered into force on 12 January 1951, was found to be irrelevant to this case. The ICJ thus in its 2004 judgment concluded that it had lacked jurisdiction over the case brought by the FRY (Serbia and Montenegro in 2004) because the latter did not, at the time of the institution of the present proceedings, namely 1999, have access to the ICJ under either Article 35(1) of the Statute, namely being a state party to the ICJ Statute, or Article 35(2), namely 'subject to the special provisions contained in treaties in force'. This 2004 judgment thus seemed to implicitly overrule the above 2003 case in which the ICJ found its jurisdiction over the FRY on the basis of Article IX of the Genocide Convention. According to a judge ad hoc in the 2003 case, a possible reason behind this overruling is that 'the Court which sat in 2004 was not the same Court which sat in 2003' and the majority had formed in 2004 within the ICJ wanted to use the 2004 case to 'sink' the 2003 judgement.[62]

This 2004 judgment was, however, distinguished in a third case, this one brought by Croatia against the FRY for alleged violations of the Genocide Convention in 1999. Croatia invoked Article IX of the Convention as the basis for the Court's jurisdiction. During the proceedings, with reference to the 2004 judgment, the FRY raised preliminary objections to the jurisdiction of the ICJ on the grounds that Croatia had filed its application before the FRY had been admitted to the United Nations, when it was not a party to the Statute, so that the conditions under Article 35(2) of the Statute were not met. While recognising that some of the facts and legal issues that had been dealt with in the previous cases were relevant to the present case, the ICJ considered that, since none of those decisions were given between the same parties of the present case, by virtue of Article 59 of the Statute, the previous judgments had no effect of *res judicata* on the present case.[63] Concerning the question of whether the conditions under Article 35(2) of the Statute were met, departing from its approach in the 2004 judgment, the ICJ did not emphasise the legal status of the FRY (then Serbia) in relation to the

Montenegro v. Portugal); Legality of Use of Force (Yugoslavia v. Spain); Legality of Use of Force (Yugoslavia v. United States of America), adopted on 15 December 2004.

60 ICJ Judgement, *Legality of Use of Force (Serbia and Montenegro v. Belgium)*, adopted on 15 December 2004, para 97.

61 Ibid., para 96.

62 Vojin Dimitrijević and Marko Milanović, 'The Strange Story of the Bosnian Genocide Case', 21(1) *Leiden Journal of International Law* (2008), at 82.

63 ICJ Judgement, Application of the Convention on the Prevention and Punishment of the Crime of Genocide (Croatia v. Serbia), adopted on 18 November 2008, para 53.

Statute at the time of the filing of the application.[64] Instead, the ICJ held that there were certain situations in which realism and flexibility were called for to determine the jurisdiction. Thus, because Croatia could have instituted a new proceeding to overcome the issue of access, the question of access should not be an obstacle to the ICJ's jurisdiction.[65] Subsequently, the ICJ drew a distinction between the 2004 judgment and Croatia's case based on the fact that the FRY was the applicant in the former case but the respondent in the latter. The ICJ also relied on two further facts in reaching its conclusion. First, Croatia had exercised care in instituting the proceedings, doing so at a time when the FRY had filed the cases against NATO countries. Apparently, the FRY considered that it had the capacity to participate in the Court's proceedings. Second, because Croatia had submitted its Memorial after 2000, the ICJ concluded that the conditions under Article 35(1) had been satisfied and that it thus had jurisdiction over the FRY.[66]

The above assessment shows that, like the AB, the ICJ has also never explicitly overruled a prior judgment. In order to introduce flexibilities, it chooses to implicitly overrule or distinguish precedent.

7.1.2.3. International Criminal Tribunal for the Former Yugoslavia (ICTY)

The ICTY Statute is silent on the issue of *stare decisis*. The ICTY Appeals Chamber in the *Aleksovski* case appeared to support the rules of *de facto stare decisis* by emphasising the 'interests of certainty and predictability' to follow its previous judgements.[67] In the same case, however, the Appeals Chamber also held that it should be free to depart from the previous judgements for 'cogent reasons in the interests of justice' which refers to two situations: first, a previous decision has been decided 'on the basis of a wrong legal principle', and, second, a previous decision 'has been given *per incuriam*, that is a judicial decision that has been "wrongly decided, usually because the judge or judges were ill-informed about the applicable law"'.[68] In practice, the Appeals Chamber has explicitly reversed previous holdings in several cases.

In *Kordić and Čerkez*, for instance, the Appeals Chamber explicitly overruled its judgements in *Vasiljević* and *Krstić* about the permissibility of cumulative convictions based on the same act.[69] In the latter cases, the Appeals Chamber held that the same conduct should not be convicted of both murder and persecution under

64 Ibid., para 58.
65 Ibid., paras 79–90.
66 Therefore, 'the Court's jurisprudence on the question of access in these cases with regard to Serbia's status cannot be deemed consistent and coherent'. See Hanqin Xue, 'Competent Parties—Jurisdiction ratione personae', in *Jurisdiction of the International Court of Justice* (Brill, 2009), at 152.
67 Appeals Chamber Judgement, *Prosecutor v. Zlatko Aleksovski*, adopted on 30 May 2001, paras 107–108.
68 Ibid.
69 Appeals Chamber Judgement, *Prosecutor v. Dario Kordić and Mario Čerkez*, adopted on 17 December 2004, para 1040.

Article 5 of the Rome Statute of the International Criminal Court (ICTY Statute) because the offence of murder is subsumed by that of persecution.[70] This finding was considered to incorrectly apply the legal test relating to cumulative convictions as set out in the *Čelebići* case which permitted multiple convictions on the basis of the same conduct provided that this conduct related to distinct crimes of which each one under a provision of the ICTY Statute contains 'a materially distinct element not contained in the other'.[71] Thus, through the correction of the *Vasiljević* and *Krstić* judgements, the Appeals Chamber further clarified the standards of *Čelebići* test emphasising the legal elements of each crime at issue rather than on the underlying conduct of the accused in order to ensure 'that the convictions entered fully reflect his criminality'.[72]

Similarly in *Žigić*, the Appeals Chamber explicitly overruled its *Čelebići* judgement that permitted a reconsideration of a final judgement.[73] In the Appeals Chamber's view, unlike the review proceedings that require a party to provide 'evidence of a new fact', the application for such reconsideration only requires a party to assert an Appeal Judgement is in error 'allowing in effect the submission of a second appeal'.[74] The right to such reconsideration could be easily abused as evident in the *Žigić* case in which Mr. *Žigić* makes 'no serious attempt to establish the existence of a clear error' but merely to file 'frivolous application'.[75] To protect the 'the interests of justice' to the victims or convicted person, the Appeals Chamber, thus, concluded that there was no mechanism to reconsider a final judgment other than the review process foreseen by the ICTY Statute.[76]

A more recent example is the 2013 *Perišić* case, in which the majority of the Appeals Chamber held that 'specific direction remains an element of the *actus reus* of aiding and abetting liability' and that 'no conviction for aiding and abetting may be entered if the element of specific direction is not established beyond reasonable doubt'.[77] Judge Liu offered a dissenting opinion and, one year later, as presiding judge joined with other judges in the 2014 *Šainović et al.* case to explicitly overrule the *Perišić* Appeal Judgement, stating that the finding, namely specific direction is an element of the *actus reus* of aiding and abetting liability, in the *Perišić* is 'in direct and material conflict with the prevailing jurisprudence on the

70 Appeals Chamber Judgement, *Prosecutor v. Mitar Vasiljevic*, adopted on 25 February 2004, para 146; Appeals Chamber Judgement, *Prosecutor v. Radislav Krstic*, adopted on 19 April 2004, para 231.

71 *Dario Kordi and Mario Cerkez*, above n 69.

72 Ibid., para 1033.

73 Appeals Chamber Decision on Zoran Žigić's Motion for Reconsideration of Appeals Chamber Judgement, adopted on 26 June 2006, para 9. 'In light of these considerations, the Appeals Chamber has come to the view that cogent reasons in the interests of justice demand its departure from the majority opinion in the *Čelebići* Judgement on Sentence Appeal'.

74 Ibid., para 8.

75 Ibid.

76 Ibid., para. 9.

77 Appeals Chamber Judgement, *Prosecutor v. Mom⊠ilo Perišić*, adopted on 28 February 2013, para 36.

actus reus of aiding and abetting liability and with customary international law in this regard'.[78]

The Trial Chambers, on the other hand, unlike the Appeals Chambers, tend to distinguish a precedent when compelled to depart from it.[79] For example, the Trial Chamber was required to examine whether the Yugoslav Peoples' Army artillery attack against the Old Town of Dubrovnik on 6 December 1991 should be convicted of the offences of (a) devastation not justified by military necessity, (b) unlawful attacks on civilian objects, and (c) destruction or wilful damage of cultural property.[80] After acknowledging that the Appeals Chamber case law, namely the abovementioned *Čelebići* test, 'on a theoretical basis', would support finding cumulative convictions for those three offences due to their materially distinct elements,[81] the Trial Chamber held that the 'essential criminal conduct' in the present case is 'directly and comprehensively reflected' in the third offence, namely destruction or wilful damage of cultural property.[82] Thus, by emphasizing the 'particular circumstances' concerning the offences at issue, the Trial Chamber, explicitly amending the *Čelebići* test, found that the conduct at issue would only lead to the conviction of destruction or wilful damage of cultural property for 'the interests of justice and the purpose of punishment'.[83]

The above practice of the Appeals Chambers shows that, when a judicial institution is compelled to depart from a prior decision, it may bravely admit that a previous ruling was flawed. This may provide the AB with support to adopt the option of explicit overruling. Moreover, given that both the Appeals Chambers and the AB are the highest appeal institutions, the different approaches between the Appeals Chambers and the Trial Chambers suggests that, if necessary, the AB could take a bolder step than a panel by explicitly correcting its prior decisions.

7.1.2.4. European Court of Human Rights (ECtHR)

Like the ICTY and the ICJ, the ECtHR has developed rules of *de facto stare decisis* for 'the interests of legal certainty', 'the orderly development of the Convention case-law' and 'foreseeability and equality before the law'.[84] It has been argued that 'the original Court was extremely reluctant to expressly overrule

78 Appeals Chamber Judgement, *Prosecutor v. Nikola Sainovic, Nebojsa Pavkovic, Vladimir Lazarevic and Sreten Lukic*, adopted on 23 January 2014, paras 1649–1651.

79 'As regards Trial Chambers, they have generally taken for granted the need to abide by Appeals Chambers' holdings'. See Guido Acquaviva, Fausto Pocar, 'Stare decisis', Max Planck Encyclopedias of International Law, https://opil.ouplaw.com/view/10.1093/law:epil/9780199231690/law-9780199231690-e1683?prd=EPIL (visited on 1 September 2019).

80 Trial Judgement, *Prosecutor v. Pavle Strugar*, adopted on 31 January 2005, para 452.

81 Ibid., para 452.

82 Ibid., para 454.

83 Ibid., para 455.

84 *Cossey v. the United Kingdom* [1991] 13 EHRR 622, ECHR 21, para 35.

established interpretations of the Convention'.[85] The option of implicit overruling is thus applied in a number of old cases. For instance, the Court in *Huber* held that to provide district attorneys with multifarious roles of investigator, authoriser of detention, and prosecutor was inconsistent with inconsistent with Article 5(3) of the Convention regarding the independence of judicial officer.[86] This conclusion is sharply contrary to a prior judgement, namely *Schiesser*, according to which another district attorney in a similar situation was found consistent with Article 5 (3).[87] The Court thus implicitly overruled *Schiesser* 'by not expressly acknowledging that they were overruling their earlier case law'. Another example is the *Borgers* case in which the participation of the Belgian avocat general in the deliberations of the Court of Cassation was found inconsistent with the fair trial commitments under Article 6(1) of the Convention,[88] despite that such practice was permitted according to the prior judgment of *Delcourt v. Belgium.* [89]

The contemporary Court appears more willing to adopt the option of explicit overruling. For instance, in order to increase legal certainty regarding the scope of 'civil rights and obligations' under Article 6(1) of the Convention, the Court in *Pellegrin v. France* explicitly overruled it case-law which 'contains a margin of uncertainty'.[90] The Court thus adopted a functional criterion approach based on which it 'wishes to put an end to the uncertainty which surrounds application of the guarantees of Article 6(1) to disputes between States and their servants'.[91] Eight years later in *Vilho Eskelinen and Others*, this functional criterion approach was, however, found unable to bring about 'a greater degree of certainty in this area as intended'.[92] The Court thus explicitly overruled the *Pellegrin* approach by introducing a new test to determine the applicability of Article 6(1) to civil servants.[93]

Another example is the *Kudla* case regarding unreasonable delays in the determination of judicial cases by national courts. Although both Article 6(1), right to 'a fair and public hearing within a reasonable time', and Article 13, right to 'an effective remedy before a national authority', of the Convention could potentially apply to such complaints, the Court previously declined to apply the latter provision which imposed less stringent requirements than Article 6(1).[94] This original approach was reconsidered 'forcing applicants to bring their Article 6(1)

85 Alastair Mowbray, 'An Examination of the European Court of Human Rights' Approach to Overruling its Previous Case Law', 9(2) *Human Rights Law Review* (2009), at 183.
86 *Huber v. Switzerland* [1990] A 188, para 43.
87 *Schiesser v. Switzerland* [1979] 2 EHRR 417.
88 *Borgers v. Belgium* [1993] 15 EHRR 92.
89 *Delcourt v. Belgium* [1970] 1 EHRR 355, para 29.
90 *Pellegrin v. France* [1999] 31 EHRR 26, para 60.
91 Ibid., para 61.
92 *Vilho Eskelinen and Others v. Finland* [2007] 45 EHRR 985, ECHR 2007-II, para 55.
93 Ibid., para 56.
94 *Kudla v. Poland* [2002] 35 EHRR 11, para 146. For instance, *Kamasinski v. Austria* [1991] 13 EHRR 36.

unreasonable delay complaints to Strasbourg rather than having them resolved domestically'.[95] Given 'the continuing accumulation of applications',[96] the Court thus in *Kudla v. Poland* explicitly overruled its prior judgements by recognising 'the need to examine the applicant's complaint under Article 13 taken separately, in addition to its earlier finding of a violation of Article 6(1)'.[97] In other words, the application of Article 13 would require 'States to establish effective domestic remedies to deal with complaints of unreasonable delay in court proceedings'.[98]

The Court may also explicitly overrule precedent 'to ensure that the interpretation of the Convention reflects societal changes and remains in line with present-day conditions'.[99] Illustrative in this context is the *Christine Goodwin* case, which concerned Article 8 of the Convention on respect for private life. The applicant in the case argued that the government of the United Kingdom had violated this provision by failing to recognise her gender reassignment.[100] The relevant precedents, such as the *Rees* judgement of 1986, suggested that the government's refusal to alter the register of births or to issue new birth certificates updating individuals' gender status could not be considered a prohibited interference with the right to respect for private life under Article 8.[101] However, after recognising that 'it should not depart, without good reason, from precedents laid down in previous cases', the Grand Chamber in 2002 held that its interpretation must also take into account 'the changing conditions' within the contracting states and to ensure that the rights under the Conventions continued to be 'practical and effective' by maintaining 'a dynamic and evolutive approach'.[102] Thus, by looking at the 'present-day conditions',[103] the Grand Chamber explicitly overruled its precedents by holding that the appropriate interpretation and application of the Conventions should favour the applicant in the present case and thus found that the respondent government was in violation of its obligation under Article 8.[104]

95 Mowbray (2009), above n 85, at 192.
96 *Kudla*, above n 582, para 148.
97 Ibid., para 149.
98 Mowbray (2009), above n 85, at 192.
99 *Goodwin and Liberty (intervening) v. United Kingdom* [2002] 35 EHRR 447, ECHR 2002-VI, para 60.
100 Ibid.
101 *Rees v. United Kingdom* [1987] 9 EHRR 56. *Cossey v. the United Kingdom* [1991] 13 EHRR 622, ECHR 21.
102 *Goodwin*, above n 99, para 74.
103 Ibid., para 75.
104 Ibid., para. 93. 'While the Court is not formally bound to follow its previous judgments, it is in the interests of legal certainty, foreseeability and equality before the law that it should not depart, without good reason, from precedents laid down in previous cases (see, for example, *Chapman v. the United Kingdom* [GC], no. 27238/95, ECHR 2001-I, § 70). However, since the Convention is first and foremost a system for the protection of human rights, the Court must have regard to the changing conditions within the respondent State and within Contracting States generally and respond, for example, to any evolving convergence as to the standards to be achieved' (para 74).

In addition to the above examples of explicitly and implicitly overruling, Chambers of the ECtHR once adopted the option of distinguishing in the *Kopecký* case which concerned an applicant's claim for the restitution of coins belonging to his father. The key issue in this case was whether the applicant had in his possession the coins under the meaning of Article 1 of Protocol No. 1 to the European Convention on Human Rights, which states that 'every natural or legal person is entitled to the peaceful enjoyment of his possessions'.[105] A Chamber of the ECtHR held that the 'present case should be distinguished from the case law' in which the applicants 'were excluded from the very beginning from the possibility of having the property restored' and on which the claims 'did not amount to a legitimate expectation'.[106] In the present case, however, a 'genuine dispute' was found to exist regarding whether the applicant could meet the requirements of the measure at issue, and thus the Court found that the applicant had a 'legitimate expectation' of obtaining effective enjoyment of the property right at issue.[107] In the view of the Chamber, the use of distinguishing in this case aimed to prevent the protection of the rights under the European Conventions on Human Rights and its protocols from being revealed 'ineffective and illusory'.[108] This judgement was, however, reversed by the Grand Chamber.[109]

Besides offering support to the option of overruling and distinguishing, the above practice also provides a useful observation of the interaction between the Grand Chamber and a Chamber. The former one does not only correct the decisions made by a Chamber, but also has no hesitation in departing from its own inappropriate judgements. In contrast, although the AB has explicitly reversed the panel reports in several occasions,[110] it has never explicitly departed from its prior

105 Article 1 of Protocol No. 1 to the European Convention on Human Rights.

106 *Kopecký v. Slovakia* [2005] 41 EHRR 43, ECHR 2004-IX, para 27.

107 Ibid., para 27. 'In this respect the present case should be distinguished from the cases of *Malhous v. the Czech Republic* and *Gratzinger and Gratzingerova v. the Czech Republic* referred to above or the case of Brezny & Brezny v. Slovakia (application no. 23131/93, Commission decision of 4 March 1996, DR 85, pp. 65–83) in which the Court and the Commission respectively found that the applicants' claims for restitution of property did not amount to a legitimate expectation in the sense of the Court's case-law. In those cases the applicants were excluded from the very beginning from the possibility of having the property restored as it was obvious either that they failed to meet the relevant requirements or that their claim clearly fell outside the relevant law'.

108 Ibid., para 29.

109 The Grand Chamber Judgement, *Kopecký v. Slovakia*, adopted on 28 September 2004, para 52.

'In the light of the foregoing it can be concluded that the Court's case-law does not contemplate the existence of a "genuine dispute" or an "arguable claim" as a criterion for determining whether there is a "legitimate expectation" protected by Article 1 of Protocol No. 1. The Court is therefore unable to follow the reasoning of the Chamber's majority on this point'.

110 For instance, the AB in the *US—Stainless Steel (Mexico)* case expressed deep concern over what it viewed as 'serious implications for the proper functioning of the WTO dispute settlement system' caused by the panel's decision to 'to depart from well-established AB jurisprudence clarifying the interpretation of the same legal issues'.

decisions. This reluctance to have any self-corrections might explain the extremist stance of the US to deny the precedential values of the AB reports. In this context, the AB may have additional reasons to consider the option of overruling in a future case.

7.1.2.5. Court of Justice of the European Union (CJEU)

The CJEU supports the rules of *de facto stare decisis* as 'there are passages in the judgements where the weights and the number of the previous decisions seen almost to be felt to be such as to make them binding in fact, if not in theory'.[111] In practice, the Court has explicitly overruled its previous decisions in several occasions. A good example is the change in the doctrine of common origin from the *HAG I* case to the *HAG II* case. *HAG I* concerned the 'Hag' trademark on decaffeinated coffee that was registered by the German firm Hag AG in both Germany and Belgium in the early twentieth century; a Belgian 'Hag' trademark was subsequently assigned to a Belgian subsidiary of the German firm, namely Hag S.A. After the Second World War, Hag S.A. was seized by the Belgian government, and the Belgian 'Hag' trademark was assigned by Hag S.A. to Van Zuylen Frères. When Hag AG began to export its German 'Hag' decaffeinated coffee to Luxembourg in 1972, Van Zuylen Frères, defending its Benelux 'Hag' trademark, brought a case in Luxembourg to stop the import of the German product. Seeking to promote the free movement of goods, the Court in *HAG I* held that a prohibition based solely on identical marks having a common origin would be incompatible with EU law, an approach often referred to as the doctrine of common origin.[112]

Years after the *HAG I* judgment, CNL-Sucal, the successor of Van Zuylen Frères, began to export its 'Hag' decaffeinated coffee from Belgium to Germany. In the *HAG II* case, Hag AG sought to exercise its German trademark rights in order to prohibit imports of Belgian 'Hag' decaffeinated coffee into Germany. This time, the Court held 'it necessary to reconsider the interpretation' in *HAG I* 'in the light of the case-law which has developed with regard to the relationship between industrial and commercial property and the general rules of the Treaty, particularly in the sphere of the free movement of goods'.[113] Subsequently, the Court found that the doctrine of common origin did not apply to situations in

111 Gunnar Beck, 'The Legal Reasoning of the ECJ II' in *The Legal Reasoning of the Court of Justice of the EU* (Hart Publishing, 2013), at 238.
112 ECJ, Case 192–73 *Van Zuylen fr`eres v. Hag ('HAG I')* [1974] ECR 731.
113 Case C-10/89 *S.A. CNL-Sucal NV v. Hag GF AG ('HAG II')* [1990] ECR 3711, para 10. 'Bearing in mind the points outlined in the order for reference and in the discussions before the Court concerning the relevance of the Court's judgment in Case 192/73 Van Zuylen v. HAG [1974] ECR 731 to the reply to the question asked by the national court, it should be stated at the outset that the Court believes it necessary to reconsider the interpretation given in that judgment in the light of the case-law which has developed with regard to the relationship between industrial and commercial property and the general rules of the Treaty, particularly in the sphere of the free movement of goods'.

which the event separated a trademark from its original owner without the owner's consent. Thus, the *HAG II* judgment explicitly repeals the *HAG I* judgment by replacing the doctrine of common origin with the doctrine of 'consensual' common origin.[114] A possible reason behind this overruling is that 'the ruling in *HAG I*, which had been delivered sixteen years earlier, was out of step with subsequent developments in the case law on intellectual property rights and out of step with the evolving perception of the internal market'.[115]

A more recent example of explicit overruling was the 2008 *Metock* case, which concerned the question whether Directive 2004/38 regarding the right of EU citizens and their family members to move and reside freely within the EU precluded member states from requiring that a non-EU citizen have had prior lawful residence in order to benefit from its provisions.[116] In the 2003 *Akrich* case regarding Regulation No. 1612/68, which was subsequently amended by Directive 2004/38, the Court held that, in order to benefit from Article 10 of the regulation concerning the right to join an EU citizen employed in a different member state, a non-EU citizen spouse must indeed have had prior lawful residence in a member state.[117] However, the Court in *Metock* held that the 2003 judgment 'must be reconsidered' and thus explicitly overruled itself by concluding that the benefit of the right under Directive 2004/38 'cannot depend on the prior lawful residence of such a spouse in another Member State'.[118] This explicit departure is further apparent in the subsequent *Sahin* case, in which the Court affirmed the conclusion in *Metock* and made no mention of *Akrich.* [119]

Aside from the above examples, the Court also adopted the option of explicit overruling in other cases such as *Brown v. Rentokil Ltd* [120] in which the Court

114 Robert S. Smith, 'The Unresolved Tension Between Trademark Protection and Free Movement of Goods in the European Community', 3 *Duke Journal of Comparative & International Law* (1992), at 122. 'Reviewing the case law of the ECJ and stressing the importance of the economic function of trademarks, Advocate General Jacobs proposed that the doctrine of common origin lacked any foundation in the EEC Treaty. Insofar as the facts of *Hag II* were concerned, the EC agreed', at 111.

115 Takis Tridimas, 'Precedent and the Court of Justice: A Jurisprudence of Doubt?', in Julie Dickson and Pavlos Eleftheriadis(eds.), *Philosophical Foundations of European Union Law* (Oxford University Press, 2008), at 317.

116 ECJ, Case 127/08 *Blaise Baheten Metock and ors v. Minister for Justice, Equality and Law Reform* [2008] ECR 6241.

117 ECJ, Case 109/01 *Secretary of State for the Home Department v. Hacene Akrich* [2003] ECR 9607, para 50.

118 Ibid., para 58. 'It is true that the Court held in paragraphs 50 and 51 of Akrich that, in order to benefit from the rights provided for in Article 10 of Regulation No 1612/68, the national of a non-member country who is the spouse of a Union citizen must be lawfully resident in a Member State when he moves to another Member State to which the citizen of the Union is migrating or has migrated. However, that conclusion must be reconsidered. The benefit of such rights cannot depend on the prior lawful residence of such a spouse in another Member State (see, to that effect, *MRAX*, paragraph 59, and Case C-157/03 *Commission v. Spain*, paragraph 28)'.

119 ECJ, Case 551/07 *Deniz Sahin v. Bundesminister fur Inneres* [2008] ECR I-10453.

120 ECJ, Case 394/96 *Brown v. Rentokil Ltd* [1998] ECR I-4185.

explicitly overruled *Larsson* [121] in order to interpret the Sex Equality Directive more favourably for pregnant employees.[122] However, it would be incorrect to say that the Court is quite willing to overrule its precedents as a former Advocate General once stated: 'express departures from earlier cases are "as few as they are celebrated"'.[123] Thus, for example, a survey demonstrated that none of the 52 Grand Chamber decisions of 2010, in which nearly 1,000 citations were made to previous cases, explicitly overruled its prior jurisprudence.[124] The following discussion introduces the practice of the Court to use the other two options to deviate from case law, namely implicit overruling and distinguishing.

As an example of implicit overruling,[125] the Court in *Wouters* simply ignored the *Métropole* judgment and reached an opposite conclusion.[126] In *Métropole*, the Court rejected to balance the pro and anti-competitive effects under Article 101 (1) TFEU and held that 'it would be wrong, when classifying ancillary restrictions, to interpret the requirement for objective necessity as implying a need to weigh the pro and anti-competitive effects of an agreement'.[127] In the Court's view, an analysis of the pro and anti-competitive effects 'can take place only in the specific framework' of Article 101(3) TFEU.[128] This refusal to balance the pro and anti-competitive effects under Article 101(1) was implicitly overruled in *Wouters* in which the Court accepted the pro and anti-competitive effects approach by holding that, in examining the application of Article 101(1) to a particular case,

> account must first of all be taken of the overall context in which the decision of the association of undertakings was taken or produces its effects' and 'it has then to be considered whether the consequential effects restrictive of competition are inherent in the pursuit of those objectives.[129]

This implicit overruling was confirmed in *Meca-Medina.* [130]

121 ECJ, Case 400/95 *Larsson v. Føtex Supermarked* [1997] ECR I-2757.
122 More examples of explicit overruling see Takis Tridimas, 'Precedent and the Court of Justice: A Jurisprudence of Doubt?', in Julie Dickson and Pavlos Eleftheriadis(eds.), *Philosophical Foundations of European Union Law* (Oxford University Press, 2008), at 316.
123 Marc Jacob, 'Avoiding ECJ precedents II', in *Precedents and Case-Based Reasoning in the European Court of Justice* (Cambridge University Press, 2014), at 159.
124 Ibid., at 160.
125 More examples of implicit overruling see Takis Tridimas, 'Precedent and the Court of Justice: A Jurisprudence of Doubt?', in Julie Dickson and Pavlos Eleftheriadis(eds.), *Philosophical Foundations of European Union Law* (Oxford University Press, 2008), at 320.
126 ECJ, Case 309/99 *Wouters and Others* [2002] ECR I-1577.
127 ECJ, Case T-112/99 *Métropole télévision (M6) v. Commission* [2001] ECR II-2459, para 107.
128 Ibid.
129 ECJ, Case 309/99 *Wouters and Others* [2002] ECR I-1577, para 97.
130 ECJ, T-313/02 *David Meca-Medina and Igor Majcen v. Commission* [2004] ECR II-3291 and Case 519/04 *David Meca-Medina and Igor Majcen v. Commission* [2006] I-6991, para 42. 'Not every agreement between undertakings or every decision of an

The option of distinguishing is also attractive for the Court because it 'does not challenge a previous decision outright'.[131] The Court thus in *Keck* chose to distinguish its earlier judgements in order to limit the scope of concerning measures equivalent to quantitative restrictions (MEQRs) under Article 34 TFEU. MEQRs are more difficult to define than quantitative restrictions,[132] but in the *Dassonville* case, the Court found them to refer broadly to all rules with the potential to hinder intra-community trade.[133] According to this definition, the key to proving that a MEQR is operative is its effect, so discriminatory intent is not required.[134] This broad view was affirmed by the Court in the *Cassis de Dijon* case, in which it further clarified the nature of MEQRs as national rules that inhibit trade and that thus differ from rules applicable within a country of origin, regardless of whether they discriminate against imported products.[135] Following the *Dassonville* and *Cassis de Dijon* judgments, an increasing number of traders began invoking Article 34 to challenge any rules perceived to limit their commercial freedom.[136]

This broad definition of MEQRs was narrowed in *Keck* in order to address concerns regarding potential abuse of Article 34.[137] This case involved two traders who, in an effort to increase their market share, sold coffee in France below cost, a type of transaction forbidden under French law. Their activity thus raised the question of whether the French rules governing such a selling arrangement fell within the scope of (now) Article 34 TFEU. Had the broad definition of MEQRs under the *Dassonville* and *Cassis de Dijon* judgments been followed, the French rules at issue would indeed have been subject to this article. The Court, however, decided to 're-examine and clarify its case-law' by explicitly distinguishing between

association of undertakings which restricts the freedom of action of the parties or of one of them necessarily falls within the prohibition laid down in Article 81(1) EC. For the purposes of application of that provision to a particular case, account must first of all be taken of the overall context in which the decision of the association of undertakings was taken or produces its effects and, more specifically, of its objectives. It has then to be considered whether the consequential effects restrictive of competition are inherent in the pursuit of those objectives (*Wouters and Others*, paragraph 97) and are proportionate to them'.

131 Jacob (2014), above n 123, at 127.

132 Paul Craig and Gráinne de Búrca, *EU Law – Text, Cases, and Materials*, Sixth Edition (Oxford University Press, 2011), at 639.

133 ECJ, Case 8/74 *Procureur du Roi v. Benoît and Gustave Dassonville* [1974] ECR 837, para 5.

134 Craig and de Búrca (2011), above n 132, at 640.

135 ECJ, Case 120/78 *Rewe-Zentral AG v. Bundesmonopolverwaltung für Branntwein* [1979] ECR 649, para 8.

136 ECJ, Joined Cases C-267/91 and C-268/91 *Criminal Proceedings against Bernard Keck and Daniel Mithouard* [1993] ECRI-6097, para 14.

137 'In view of the increasing tendency of traders to invoke Article 30 of the Treaty as a means of challenging any rules whose effect is to limit their commercial freedom even where such rules are not aimed at products from other Member States, the Court considers it necessary to re-examine and clarify its case-law on this matter'. Ibid.

MEQRs and selling arrangements from the perspective of burden-sharing.[138] It held that

> by contrast, contrary to what has previously been decided, the application to products from other Member States of national provisions restricting or prohibiting certain selling arrangements is not such as to hinder directly or indirectly, actually or potentially, trade between Member States within the meaning of the *Dassonville* judgment, so long as those provisions apply to all relevant traders operating within the national territory and so long as they affect in the same manner, in law and in fact, the marketing of domestic products and of those from other Member States.[139]

That is to say, MEQRs that apply to all goods would likely still impose an extra burden on imported goods, whereas rules concerning selling arrangements would impose a similar burden on all goods, provided that these rules affect domestic and imported goods.[140] Based on this distinction, then, the Court limited the scope of the *Dassonville* and *Cassis de Dijon* judgments.

A controversial example of the use of distinguishing, in a series of judgments regarding national procedural autonomy, shows that this technique can severely restrict the scope of a precedent. The case here is *Emmott*, in which the plaintiff, an Irish citizen, applied for a judicial review of her right to receive a retrospective social security payment under Directive 79/7/EEC for the period of time during which the directive had remained unimplemented. Her claim had been rejected because she had failed to apply for such a review 'within three months from the date when grounds for the application first arose'.[141] The Court, however, held that this time-limit requirement was inconsistent with EU law, reasoning that the national time-limits within which proceedings must be initiated by an individual against a defaulting member state for the purpose of protecting rights under a directive must run from the proper date on which the directive had been implemented.[142] Broadly speaking, the *Emmott* judgment could be considered to apply to all time-limit requirements that prevent individuals from enjoying the full extent of their rights under a directive owing to improper implementation of that directive by a member state.[143] Thus, the rationale behind this ruling could be that member states should not profit from their own failure to implement a directive by relying on time-limit requirements in national laws.[144]

138 Ibid., paras 15–17.
139 Ibid., para 16.
140 Ibid., paras 15–16.
141 Ibid., para 13.
142 ECJ, Case 208/90 *Theresa Emmott v. Minister for Social Welfare and Attorney General* [1991] ECR I-4269, para 23.
143 'Only the proper transposition of the directive will bring that state of uncertainty to an end and it is only upon that transposition that the legal certainty which must exist if individuals are to be required to assert their rights is created'. Ibid., para 22.
144 Nicola Notaro, 'Case C-188/95, *Fantask A/S and Others v. Industriministeriet (Erhvervsministeriet)*, Judgment of 2 December 1997, [1997] ECR I-6783', 35(6) *Common Market Law Review* (1998), at 1391.

However, critics of this judgment seem to have prevailed over time, for the Court ended up increasingly distancing itself from *Emmott.* [145] Thus the Court distinguished it in the subsequent *Steenhorst-Neerings* case with the argument that *Emmott* concerned 'the rule of domestic law fixing time-limits for bringing actions', but *Steenhorst-Neerings* concerned only the restriction of the retroactive effect of benefits claims to one year before they had been brought and imposed no restriction on the right of individuals to initiate a proceeding in order to protect the right under the directive.[146] The Court thereby limited the scope of the *Emmott* judgment to the time limit imposed on the initiation of judicial proceedings rather than that imposed on the retroactive effect of benefits claims while maintaining that the latter could also prevent an individual, at least in part, from enjoying his or her rights under a directive.[147]

The scope of *Emmott* was further restricted in the *Johnson* case, which shared similar facts with *Steenhorst-Neerings.* [148] Referring to the latter case, the Court held that the *Emmott* judgment could only apply to *Emmott*'s 'particular circumstances', which included a time limit that deprived the plaintiff of any opportunity to seek her right under the directive.[149] Like the time limit in *Steenhorst-Neerings*, the requirement in *Johnson* 'did not affect the right of individuals to rely on' the directive, which thus did not fall within the scope of the *Emmott* judgment.[150] The latter was thus limited to the restriction imposed on the initiation of judicial proceedings that absolutely prevented an individual from relying on a directive.

The *Fantask* case has been described as 'the final stage of what could be called the step-by-step overruling of the *Emmott* judgment'.[151] Unlike the time limit imposed on the retroactive effect of benefit claims in *Steenhorst-Neerings* and *Johnson*, the time limit in *Fantask* concerned the right to apply for refunding charges that had been levied erroneously under Directive 69/335/EEC of 17 July 1969 (amended by Council Directive 85/303/EEC of 10 June 1985), which imposed a harmonized duty on the raising of capital by companies and prohibited any other charge relating to the registration of companies. Relying on this directive, Fantask, a Danish firm, and several other companies in 1992 asked the Trade and Companies Office to refund certain charges that they had paid in the period from 1983 to that year. Under Danish law, however, a debt becomes statute-barred after five years running from the date on which it became payable.

Subsequently, the Court was asked to decide whether the time limit for the refund action could extend prior to the date on which Denmark actually implemented the directive. The applicants and the commission argued that a limitation

145 Jacob (2014), above n 123, at 140.

146 ECJ, Case 338/91 *H. Steenhorst-Neerings v. Bestuur van de Bedrijfsvereniging voor Detailhandel, Ambachten en Huisvrouwen* [1993] ECR I-5475, para 21.

147 Notaro (1998), above n 144, at 1392.

148 ECJ, Case 410/92 *Elsie Rita Johnson v. Chief Adjudication Officer* [1994] ECR I-5483, paras 26–27.

149 Ibid., para 26.

150 Ibid., paras 28 and 36.

151 Notaro (1998), above n 144, at 1390.

period under a national law should not have commenced until the Directive had been properly transposed; their reasoning was that the *Emmott* judgment indicated that a member state could not rely on a limitation period under a national law as long as the directive in question had not been properly transposed into national law.[152] The Court, however, with reference to the *Steenhorst-Neerings* and the *Johnson* judgments, held that, irrespective of the date of transposition, the time limit at issue commenced on the date on which charges became payable, provided that it was not discriminatory and did not interfere significantly with the exercise of EU rights.[153] Following this judgment, the applicants lost the right to claim a refund of charges that had erroneously been levied under the directive at issue because the time limit for some of the applications for repayment had expired.[154] Thus, by restricting the scope of the *Emmott* judgment to the 'particular circumstances', the Court arguably overruled the *Emmott* judgment 'in all but name' in an implicit manner.[155]

A more recent example of distinguishing is the *Alimanovic* case in which the Court narrowed the scope of the *Brey* judgement. In *Brey*, the Court had established the individual's personal situation test which required national authorities, in examining whether a person receiving social assistance had become an unreasonable burden on its social assistance system, to 'carrying out an overall assessment of the specific burden which granting that benefit would place on the national social assistance system as a whole, by reference to the personal circumstances characterising the individual situation of the person concerned'.[156] This test was amended by the *Alimanovic* case in which the Court, acknowledging the *Brey* judgement, held that 'no such individual assessment is necessary in circumstances such as those at issue in the main proceedings'.[157]

152 ECJ, Case 188/95, *Fantask A/S and Others v. Industriministeriet (Erhvervsministeriet)*[1997] ECR I-6783, para 45.

153 'It is true that the Court held in *Emmott*, at paragraph 23, that until such time as a directive has been properly transposed, a defaulting Member State may not rely on an individual's delay in initiating proceedings against it in order to protect rights conferred upon him by the provisions of the directive and that a period laid down by national law within which proceedings must be initiated cannot begin to run before that time' (para 50). 'However, as was confirmed by the judgment in Case C-410/92 *Johnson v. Chief Adjudication Officer* [1994] ECR 1–5483, at paragraph 26, it is clear from Case C-338/91 *Steenhorst-Neerings v. Bestuur van de Bedrijfsvereniging voor Detailhandel, Ambachten en Huisvrouwen* [1993] ECR 1–5475 that the solution adopted in *Emmott* was justified by the particular circumstances of that case, in which the time-bar had the result of depriving the applicant of any opportunity whatever to rely on her right to equal treatment under a Community directive (see also *Haahr Petroleum*, cited above, paragraph 52, and Joined Cases C-114/95 and C-115/95 *Texaco and Olieselskabet Danmark* [1997] ECR 1–4263, paragraph 48)'. Ibid., para 51.

154 Ibid., para 44.

155 Jacob (2014), above n 123, at 142.

156 ECJ, Case 140/12 *Brey* [2013] EU:C:2013:565, para 64.

157 ECJ, Case 67/14 *Alimanovic* [2015] EU:C:2015:597, para 59. 'It must be stated in this connection that, although the Court has held that Directive 2004/38 requires a

The above practice shows that the Court has adopted the options of explicit overruling, implicit overruling, and distinguishing to deviate from its previous judgments. Moreover, the series of judgments regarding national procedural autonomy shows that the use of distinguishing can severely restrict the scope of precedent.

7.1.2.6. Common law system: United Kingdom

In the United Kingdom, the House of Lords (HoL) had been absolutely bound to follow all of its previous decisions since its 1898 decision of *London Tramways Co Ltd v. London Country Council* which committed the HoL to the rule that they were irreversibly bound by their own prior decisions.[158] Under the constraint of this rule, the HoL needed to rely on the option of distinguishing to depart from precedent. For instance, in the case of *Quin v. Leatham*, Lord Shand explicitly distinguished between, on the one hand, the 1898 decision of *Allen v. Flood*, in which the defendant representing a group of ironworkers persuaded their employers to stop employing the plaintiff shipwrights, and, one the other hand, the present case in which the defendant aimed to injure the plaintiff 'as distinguished from the intention of legitimately advancing their own interests'.[159] Based on this 'vital distinction', the defendant's act in *Quin v. Leatham* thus was found to be prohibited.[160]

Although the rule of irreversible precedent was, by creating certainty in the law, made for the public interest, it was later on considered too rigid which may 'lead to injustice in a particular case and also unduly restrict the proper development of the law'.[161] Thus, the 1966 Lords' Practice Statement overruled the 1898 decision by proposing that the House of Lords could 'depart from a previous decision when it appears right to do so'.[162] The first example of the HoL to explicitly overrule its prior decision after the 1966 Statement is the 1968 case of *Conway v. Rimmer* in which the HoL unanimously overruled its 1942 judgement of *Duncan v. Cammell Laird and Co.* [163] In the latter case, the HoL held that a relevant document could be withheld during civil proceedings in order to protect the

Member State to take account of the individual situation of the person concerned before it adopts an expulsion measure or finds that the residence of that person is placing an unreasonable burden on its social assistance system (judgment in Brey, C-140/12, EU:C:2013:565, paragraphs 64, 69 and 78), no such individual assessment is necessary in circumstances such as those at issue in the main proceedings'.

158 John H. Langbein, 'Modern Jurisprudence in the House of Lords the Passing of London Tramways', 53(5) *Cornell Law Review* (1968). 'Although an attitude of sanctity toward precedent hovered over English law for most of the nineteenth century, not until London Tramways was the rule of irreversible precedent made absolute'.

159 House of Lords, *Quinn v. Leathem* [1901] UKHL 2, at 5.

160 Ibid., at 6.

161 Lord Chancellor's Practice Statement [1966] 3 All ER 77.

162 Ibid.

163 House of Lords, *Conway v. Rimmer* [1968] AC 910.

public interest including the situation in which the disclosure of a document would be damaging to the public interest or the public interest required certain information to be withheld from production.[164] Moreover, the same 1942 judgement also confirmed that ministers of the Crown could reject the production of a document in the form of affidavit stating that the production of the document would be against the public interest and this affidavit should be accepted by the Court as conclusive.[165] While the decision on the particular facts of *Duncan v. Cammell Laird and Co*, as a wartime case following the 'Thetis' submarine disaster, was not questioned,[166] it was criticised for allowing ministers of the Crown to be the 'sole arbiters of the public interest'.[167] Twenty years later, the HoL explicitly overruled the *Duncan v. Cammell Laird and Co* judgement in *Conway v. Rimmer* in which the HoL held that the issue of public interest protection should be decided conclusively by the Court rather than a minister's affidavit claiming public interest immunity in order to prevent the ministry from abusing the claim of public interest.[168]

As another example, *R v. Shivput* saw the first use of the 1966 Statement in criminal law. In this case, the HoL overruled its *Anderton v. Ryan* judgement in which the appellant, who believed that the video recorder at issue was stolen, was found to be not guilty of attempting dishonestly to handle a stolen good because there was no evidence to prove that the video recorder was stolen. This judgement was considered to be inconsistent with the Criminal Attempts Act 1981 which clearly stated that 'a person may be guilty of attempting to commit an offence to which this section applies even though the facts are such that the commission of the offence is impossible'. To correct this mistake, only one year after the *Anderton v. Ryan* judgement, the HoL explicitly overruled it in *R v. Shivput* in which the appellant, which thought his suitcase contained prohibited drugs, was held to be guilty of attempting to commit a drugs offence though the suitcase at issue only contained dried cabbage, snuff or some other harmless vegetable matter.[169]

Until 1 October 2009, when the role of the HoL as the highest appeal court in the United Kingdom was replaced by a new Supreme Court, the HoL explicitly applied its 1966 Statement in 21 cases.[170] Although the Supreme Court did not

164 House of Commons Library, 'Public Interest Immunity Research Paper 96/25', 22 February 1996, at 5.
165 House of Lords, *Duncan v. Cammell Laird & Co. Ltd* [1942] AC 624.
166 House of Commons Library (1996), above n 164, at 6.
167 Ibid.
168 Ibid., at 7. Lord Pearce: '"It is not surprising" it has been said (Professor Wade, Administrative Law (2nd edn.) at p. 285) "that the Crown, having been given a blank cheque, yielded to the temptation to overdraw"'.
169 *Criminal Attempts Act 1981.*
170 Louis Blom-Cooper, '1966 and All That: The Story of the Practice Statement', in Louis Blom-Cooper QC, Brice Dickson, and Gavin Drewry (eds.), *The Judicial House of Lords 1876–2009* (Oxford University Press, 2009), at 140. 'Thus it in the *R—G* case (2004) overruled its earlier decision on the meaning of recklessness in the *R—Caldwell* case (1982). Likewise, in *Horton—Sadler* (2006), the House of Lords decided to depart from the *Walkley—Precision Forgings Ltd* decision (1979)'.

re-issue the 1966 Statement, the Court in *Austin v. Mayor and Burgesses of the London Borough of Southwark* held that this Statement still applied to it as 'part of the established jurisprudence relating to the conduct of appeals', which was further confirmed in the Court's Practice Direction 3.[171] A recent illustration of the application of the 1966 Statement was seen in the 2016 judgement of *Knauer v. Ministry of Justice* in which the Court explicitly departed from two HoL judgements, namely the 1979 judgement of *Cookson v. Knowles* and the 1983 judgement of *Graham v. Dodds*, because of a material change in the legal landscape concerning damages for death. In the Court's view, the application of the reasoning in these judgements was 'illogical and their application also results in unfair outcomes'.[172] Moreover, these unsatisfactory decisions had encouraged courts to distinguish them on inadequate grounds which undermined the certainty and consistency of law.[173] To solve these problems, the Court had 'no hesitation in concluding' that it should overrule the two HoL judgements.[174]

7.1.2.7. Civil law system: Japan

As an example outside common law systems, the decisions adopted by the Japanese Supreme Court constitute a source of law, to which the principle of *stare decisis* thus applies.[175] A lower court's deviation from the existing case law of the Supreme Court constitutes grounds for appeal in both civil and criminal cases, though such deviation nevertheless occurs. In such cases, when a lower court is of the opinion that the underlying Supreme Court case law is, for example, out-dated and no longer appropriate, it will usually try to distinguish the facts at issue from that law, thereby making it easier for the higher court to affirm the lower's decision.[176]

This technique of distinguishing is also used by the Supreme Court to avoid its own precedents. For instance, the Supreme Court once in the *Niigata Prefecture*

171 The Supreme Court of the United Kingdom, 'Practice Direction 3: Applications for Permission to Appeal'. Lord Hope DPSC: 'So the question which we must consider is not whether the Court has power to depart from the previous decisions of the House of Lords which have been referred to, but whether in the circumstances of this case it would be right for it to do so'.

172 UKSC, *Knauer v. Ministry of Justice* [2016] AC 908, para 23.

173 Ibid.

174 Steve Wilson, Helen Rutherford, Tony Storey, and Natalie Wortley, *English Legal System* (Oxford University Press, 2017), in Chapter 5. 'An argument that such a change should be left to Parliament was rejected as the law under consideration had been made by judges and should be corrected by judges. The change did not have wider implications best left to Parliament to consider and it had been recognised by the Law Commission in a report that legislation was unnecessary and that there was room for judicial manoeuvre'.

175 Toshiaki Iimura, 'The Binding Nature of Court Decisions in Japan's Civil Law System', Stanford Law School China Guiding Cases project Commentary No. 14, available at https://cgc.law.stanford.edu/commentaries/14-Iimura-Takabayashi-Rademacher/ (visited on 10 June 2018).

176 Ibid.

Public Safety Ordinance case held that, unlike a general permit requirement, an advance notification requirement for a public demonstration was not against the freedom of expression because it could be justified for the purpose of public safety.[177] In a later case, however, by implicitly distinguishing its prior decision, the Supreme Court found that a measure setting out advance permit requirements could also be justified in order to prevent a danger to the public safety because this requirement was not 'much different' than the advance notification requirement.[178] In another example, the Supreme Court reinterpreted its precedent on the condition for the public to seek damages against an unconstitutional government action. In the *Voting at Home* case, the Supreme Court held that abolishing and failing to reinstate a voting system that enabled seriously disabled voters to cast votes at home did not violate the unequivocal language of the Constitution which is the condition to permit a recovery of damages against an unconstitutional government action.[179] This condition was considered too stringent to practically prevent the public from seeking damages.[180] Subsequently, the Supreme Court in the *Overseas Voters* case reinterpreted the condition to seek damages broadly in order to grant damage award to the overseas voters at issue against the exclusion of them from the proportional representation election before 1998 and their exclusion from district elections after 1998.[181]

When no such distinction has been made, the Supreme Court must decide whether to correct its own case law or to overrule the lower court's decision; the former option requires the Grand Bench of the Supreme Court to render a decision, something that rarely happens.[182] For instance, the Supreme Court once explicitly overruled its precedent which denied the right of the defendant to challenge the constitutionality of government action to confiscate property that was owned by a third party.[183] Such a right was subsequently conferred to the defendant by the Supreme Court in the *Confiscation of the Third Party Property* case because the court believed that the defendant in effect being held liable for damages caused by confiscation to the third party owing the property at issue should have the right to challenge the confiscation order.[184] As another example, the Supreme Court in the *Patricide* case explicitly overruled its prior decision that imposed a heavier penalty against parricide than regular homicide.[185] According to the Criminal Code, a defendant convicted of parricide must go to jail, whereas a defendant convicted of regular homicide may not be necessarily subject to

177 Shigenori Matsui, 'Constitutional Precedents in Japan: A Comment on the Role of Precedent', 88(6) *Washington University Law Review* (2011), at 1675.
178 Ibid.
179 Ibid., at 1676.
180 Ibid.
181 Ibid., at 1677.
182 A decision rendered by the Grand Bench is one issued by a majority of all 15 Supreme Court judges.
183 Ibid., at 1674.
184 Ibid.
185 Ibid.

imprisonment sentence. The constitutional challenge to the heavier penalty against parricide was rejected by the Supreme Court in an earlier case. Subsequently, in the *Parricide* case, recognising that the aim of heavier criminal punishment against parricide was to securing respect for parents which had been rejected by many countries, the majority of the Supreme Court held that the heavier penalty at issue that disallowed any chance to suspend the enforcement of the imprisonment sentence was unreasonable and thus explicitly overruled its precedent.[186] More recently, the Supreme Court in a 2008 decision found that its 1966 and 1992 decisions were contrary to the court's conclusion in the present case and therefore 'should be changed'.[187]

As an example to show that the use of distinguishing can severely restrict the scope of a precedent, the Supreme Court once implicitly overruled its prior decision on the rights of public workers to strike. The National Public Workers Act prohibits all types of public workers from striking though Article 28 of the Constitution provides them with the right to strike. In the *All Postal Workers, Tokyo Central Post Office* case, the Supreme Court held that the right of public workers to strike could be deprived only when it is necessary to protect the public.[188] As for the requirements to determining whether union leaders who solicited the illegal strike of public workers should be subject to criminal punishment, the Court held that criminal penalties could only be imposed to the union leaders if the strike at issue (a) was for an illegitimate purpose, (b) was accompanied with violence, or (c) was continued for an improperly long time.[189] Possibly due to the strong criticism from conservative politicians in the ruling party and the change in the composition of the Supreme Court, the Court's prior approach favouring the rights of public workers to strike was completely changed in the *All Forest and Agricultural Public Workers, Police Office Act Amendment Opposition* case in which the majority of the Supreme Court held that the strike by public workers was not only against the public nature of their positions but also undermined the principle of representative government due to the influence of strike to legislation.[190] By implicitly overruling *All Postal Workers, Tokyo Central Post Office* decision, the Court found that the leaders of a union of agriculture and forest in the present could be subject to criminal punishment.[191]

7.1.2.8. 'Socialist legal system with Chinese characteristics': Mainland China

Very different from the practice in the UK and Japan, the Supreme People's Court in China promulgates general judicial interpretations that elucidate statutory provisions. According to the Chinese Constitution and the Legislation Law, the

186 Ibid., at 1675.
187 Iimura, above n 175.
188 Shigenori Matsui, 'Constitutional Precedents in Japan: A Comment on the Role of Precedent', 88(6) *Washington University Law Review* (2011), at 1678.
189 Ibid.
190 Ibid.
191 Ibid., at 1679.

National People's Congress (NPC) and its Standing Committee are to enact and amend basic laws. The NPC has authorised the Court to interpret laws relating to their specific application at trial.[192] Over the years, the Court has promulgated numerous judicial interpretations pertaining to various areas of law that have legal effect and can be used by lower people's courts as the basis for a judgment.[193] It is noteworthy that, unlike the above-mentioned interpretations by other judges, the Supreme People's Court's judicial interpretations are not developed by adjudging cases but rather through such steps as placing an interpretation on the agenda, discussion, drafting, and revision. Thus the judicial interpretations have the characteristic of generality that is evident in their titles. As an example, one issued in 2015 concerning guidelines for granting remedies in environmental infringement cases was titled 'Supreme People's Court's Interpretation regarding Several Issues of the Application of Law in Adjudicating Environmental Infringement Liability Disputes'.

When necessary, the Court does not hesitate to 'overrule' its judicial interpretations by issuing decisions regarding their repeal. The most recent such decision, titled the 'Supreme People's Court's Decision regarding the Repeal of Some Judicial Interpretations and Judicial Interpretation-Type Documents (12th Batch)', was adopted in 2017 in order to abolish 15 judicial interpretations that had been issued in the period from 1988 to 2013.[194] According to this decision, the reasons to repeal 15 judicial interpretations range from these interpretations conflicting with new legislation to the changing conditions within China.[195] Thus, when it comes to loosening the grip of its own precedents, the Court has fewer incentives to rely on the technique of distinguishing. Similarly, the generality characteristic of judicial interpretations enables lower courts to get around these interpretations easily, even resulting in the problem of 'different adjudicatory outcomes for the same type of cases or different interpretations for the same law'.[196]

In an effort to address such threats to the credibility of the judiciary in China, the Supreme People's Court began in 2010 to establish a system of guiding cases.[197] Thus, whereas judicial interpretations that are formulated and promulgated by the Court provide lower people's courts with general guidance, the guiding cases demonstrate ways in which specific and concrete problems have been dealt with in the context of specific cases. The Office of Work on Guiding

192 *Resolution of the Standing Committee of the National People's Congress regarding Strengthening the Work of Statutory Interpretation*, National People's Congress Standing Committee, 10 June 1981.

193 Vai Io Lo, 'Towards the Rule of Law: Judicial Lawmaking in China', 28(2) *Bond Law Review* (2016), at 153.

194 Supreme People's Court's Decision regarding the Repeal of Some Judicial Interpretations and Judicial Interpretation-Type Documents (12th Batch), available at http://www.court.gov.cn/zixun-xiangqing-61462.html (visited on 10 June 2018).

195 Ibid.

196 Lo (2016), above n 193, at 155.

197 *Provisions of the Supreme People's Court Concerning Work on Case Guidance*, Discussed and Passed by the Adjudication Committee of the Supreme People's Court on 15 November 2010 and Issued on 26 November 2010.

Cases in the Court selects and recommends cases from across the judicial system that are to be decided further by the Adjudicatory Committee of the Court. A standard guiding case consists of eight components: a title, keywords, a summary of the judgment, relevant legal rules, basic facts, the adjudicatory outcome, the reasoning behind the judgment, and the names of the deciding judges.[198] During the period from January 2012 to November 2017, the Supreme Court of China issued 92 such guiding cases, which touched on topics including administrative law and procedure, civil procedure, company law, consumer protection, contract law, criminal law, intellectual property, labour and employment, maritime law, property law, torts, and unfair competition.

The lower courts, however, may not have the need to use the technique of distinguishing to avoid the guiding cases, one major reason being the insufficient number of guiding cases to follow owing to the slow pace of issuance: as of the end of 2015, a total of only 241 cases cited guiding cases, only 79 doing so explicitly by clearly citing the relevant guiding cases in their reasoning.[199] Moreover, guiding cases, unlike judicial interpretations, are not a source of law in China and thus have less authority. The 2010 Provisions regarding the Work of Guiding Cases requires only that the lower people's courts 'refer' to the guiding cases in their adjudication of similar cases and not that they use the guiding cases as the 'adjudicatory basis'.[200] The 2015 Detailed Rules on the Provisions regarding the Work of Guiding Cases, however, requires that, when the parties refer to a relevant guiding case, lower courts must indicate whether it has followed the guiding case and justify its approach in this regard.[201]

7.1.3. Suggestions to loosen the grip of China—Raw Materials and China—Rare Earths in light of the new facts of Chinese export duties

The above practices by tribunals at the international, regional, and national levels to deviate from precedent illustrate their efforts to strike a balance between legal certainty and flexibility in order to deal with important public policy issues or simply to keep up with the times.[202] The major techniques of deviation, namely explicit overruling, implicit overruling, and distinguishing, have been adopted in

198 *Detailed Implementing Rules on the "Provisions of the Supreme People's Court Concerning Work on Case Guidance"*, Discussed and Passed by the Adjudication Committee of the Supreme People's Court on April 27, 2015 and Issued on 13 May 2015, Article 3.

199 Lo (2016), above n 193, at 163. Citing guiding cases implicitly means that the adjudicatory outcomes are consistent with the relevant guiding cases though these cases are not cited in the reasoning part.

200 *Provisions of the Supreme People's Court Concerning Work on Case Guidance*, Article 7. *Detailed Implementing Rules on the "Provisions of the Supreme People's Court Concerning Work on Case Guidance"*, Article 10.

201 *Detailed Implementing Rules*, Article 11.

202 'Too much adherence to precedent and there is a risk of injustice and stagnation. Too little observance of it, and certainty, predictability, and fairness will suffer'. See Takis Tridimas, 'Precedent and the Court of Justice: A Jurisprudence of Doubt?', in Julie

different situations. Among the three options, it is very difficult to say which one is completely superior to the others because all of them have their advantages and limitations. Depends on the particular facts of a given case, however, there may exist an optimal option, relatively speaking, based on which positive impacts would be maximised. The following discussion seeks to find the optimal option for the AB to depart from the *China—Raw Materials* and *China—Rare Earths* decisions.

Compared with the other two options, an explicit overruling of earlier precedents may generate greater clarity in the existing body of case-law. A good example is the *Christine Goodwin* case where the ECtHR Grand Chamber explicitly overruled its precedents based on which Article 8 of the ECHR does not require a full legal recognition of gender re-assignment. After *Christine Goodwin*, it is quite clear that the old judgements, such as *Rees*, are no longer applicable owing to 'the changing conditions' within the contracting states. In other words, it leaves no room to doubt whether the precedents before *Christine Goodwin* might still be applicable, as in the case of implicit overruling, or to what extent those precedents would apply in the future, as in the case of distinguishing.

It is noteworthy that *Christine Goodwin* overruled the previous judgements that were made more than 15 years ago. This long period of time provides the Grand Chamber with good reasons to update its case-law in order to reflect 'societal changes'. In contrast, if a tribunal overrules a very recent decision, it may sometimes generate confusion and raises doubt about the direction and decisiveness of the tribunal. A classic example is the *Šainović et al.* case where the ICTY Appeals Chamber in 2014 found the *Perišić* Appeal Judgement, which was made by a different bench in 2013, was wrong and explicitly overruled it. Given this conflict between the different benches of the Appeals Chamber, it has been claimed that the ICTY jurisprudence on certain legal issues involved in these cases 'remains in a state of flux and fragmentation' based on which the result of a future case 'will very much depend on which judges get assigned to their Appeals Chamber'.[203]

The more recent WTO decision, namely *China—Rare Earths*, that banned China's export duties was made six years ago. Although this period is longer than the above ICTY example, it may not be long enough for the AB to adopt an evolutionary approach as the Grand Chamber did in *Christine Goodwin*. In *US—Shrimp*, the AB adopted an evolutionary interpretation to update the meaning of 'exhaustible natural resources', which, as particularly noted by the AB, was 'actually crafted more than 50 years ago'.[204] Thus, in order to explicitly overrule *China—Rare Earths*, the AB may need to admit its interpretive errors, which it never did, in both *China—Rare Earths* and *China—Raw Materials*. This seems to suggest that explicit overruling may only be a second-best option for the AB to depart from the ban on China's export duties.

Dickson and Pavlos Eleftheriadis(eds.), *Philosophical Foundations of European Union Law* (Oxford University Press, 2008), at 311.

203 Marko Milanovic, 'The Self-Fragmentation of the ICTY Appeals Chamber', EJIL: Talk!, at https://www.ejiltalk.org/the-self-fragmentation-of-the-icty-appeals-chamber/ (visited on 30 July 2019).

204 AB Report, *US—Shrimp*, para 129.

Compared with explicit overruling, implicit overruling does not require the AB to provide any reasons. This approach was preferred by the ECtHR at its early stage.[205] For instance, the original Court in *Huber v. Switzerland* completely reversed its *Schiesser v. Switzerland* judgment without acknowledging the practice of overruling.[206] The same approach was also adopted in *Borgers v. Belgium* where the Court made findings that were directly at odds with its *Delcourt* decision but again refused to speak of overruling.[207] This practice was criticised by one dissenting judge in *Borgers* for failing 'to do what a court that overrules an important judgment should do: it failed to state its reasons for doing so clearly and convincingly'.[208] Indeed, as the AB has repeatedly emphasised, its decisions should be followed unless 'cogent reasons' are presented. It is thus difficult to imagine how the AB would deliver a decision that is directly at odds with *China—Rare Earths* and *China—Raw Materials* without offering any good reasons. As a result, the option of implicit overruling seems to be the least feasible one for the AB to alter the ban on China's export duties.

Distinguishing would be the first-best option. This technique has been widely used by various tribunals including the AB itself. As discussed above, for instance, the AB in *Indonesia—Import Licensing Regimes* case expressly distinguished its long-established sequence of analysis under GATT Article XX with a distinction between the 'normal sequence' and the special one that could be adopted in the 'particular circumstances of the case'. Following this approach, the AB may also draw a line between the 'bad' export duties and those 'good' ones that would contribute to environmental protection based on the new facts of China's export duties as discussed in the previous chapters.[209]

It is noteworthy that the new facts of China's export duties may also provide the AB with sufficient incentives to adopt the options of distinguishing or overruling. The AB has in a few cases departed from its strict textual approach in order to accommodate environmental interests, in particular in the *US—Shrimp* decision just mentioned. In that case, the AB adopted an 'evolutionary' approach according to which it interpreted the phrase 'exhaustible natural resources' broadly to include not only 'non-living' resources but also living species, specifically turtles.[210] The *China—Raw Materials* and *China—Rare Earths* rulings suggest, however, that, in two significant respects, the AB was not convinced that the denial of China's right to invoke the GATT environmental exceptions would significantly hinder its environmental protection efforts. First, as the complainants

205 Mowbray (2009), above n 85.
206 For further information, see Section 7.1.2.4.
207 Ibid.
208 Dissenting Opinion of Judge Martens at para 1.
209 For further discussion, see Section 7.4.
210 AB Report, *United States – Import Prohibition of Certain Shrimp and Shrimp Products*, WT/DS58/AB/R, adopted 6 November 1998, para 130. 'From the perspective embodied in the preamble of the WTO Agreement, we note that the generic term "natural resources" in Article XX(g) is not "static" in its content or reference but is rather "by definition, evolutionary"'.

pointed out in *China—Rare Earths*, certain high-level Chinese documents, including the Guidelines of the Eleventh and Twelfth Five-Year Plans (for the period from 2006 to 2015), make clear that China's export duties were designed to increase the domestic production of high value-added downstream products that rely on the raw materials at issue. Second, export duties represent only the second-best option for protecting the environment.

However, as the preliminary analysis offered here shows, this reasoning has lost much of its persuasive force in light of changes in the factual context relating to China's export duties. Thus the Guidelines of the Thirteenth Five-Year Plan (for 2016–2020) explicitly prioritise the environmental purpose of export duties, and several subsector-level five-year plans appear to associate this environmental motivation with carbon leakage. Regarding the argument that China should always opt for the first-best option, it fails to take into account situations in which the ideal alternative is financially or practically unavailable.[211] In the case of China, as seen in Chapter 6, export duties could play an important role to tackle carbon leakage, an issue unaddressed in either *China—Raw Materials* or *China—Rare Earths.*

For these reasons, the AB may in the future find itself in the awkward situation of having to decide whether WTO law should prohibit China's use of export duties, even as part of a genuine climate policy, despite the fact that the country is the world's largest emitter of greenhouse gases. Such a position on the part of the AB is likely to meet with resistance from forces such as the major international environmental groups that united in opposition to the WTO decision that prohibited the US from adopting an extraterritorial measure to protect sea turtles.[212] Indeed, responding to the fact that global warming is accelerating even more rapidly than scientists had until recently anticipated, a recent and alarming IPCC report calls urgently for all nations to combat it through 'rapid, far-reaching and unprecedented' actions.[213] The WTO's refusal to allow China to impose export duties on energy-intensive products would thus be inconsistent with the pro-environmental stance that the organization has long been projected.[214]

The situation would become even more awkward should a future multilateral environmental agreement explicitly authorise the use of export duties by contracting parties for the purpose of combating climate change. This much is made clear in a suggestion in a World Bank research paper that it would be fruitful to

211 For more actual examples, see Chapter 4.

212 ICTSD, 'Shrimp-Turtle Ruling Gets Lukewarm Reaction from All Sides', 2 (40) Bridges (1998).

213 'Limiting global warming to 1.5°C would require rapid, far-reaching and unprecedented changes in all aspects of society'. See IPCC, 'Summary for Policymakers of IPCC Special Report on Global Warming of 1.5°C approved by governments', 8 October 2018, available at https://www.ipcc.ch/2018/10/08/summary-for-policymakers-of-ipcc-special-report-on-global-warming-of-1-5c-approved-by-governments/ (visited on 14 November 2018).

214 For instance, the broad statement, 'Under WTO rules, as confirmed by WTO jurisprudence, members can adopt trade-related measures aimed at protecting the environment, subject to certain specified conditions', is no longer valid. https://www.wto.org/english/tratop_e/envir_e/envir_e.htm (visited on 14 November 2018).

explore 'alternative possible negotiated agreements (such as export taxes aimed at neutralizing leakage effects)'.[215] In light of this evidence, the AB needs to address the explicit conflict between its decision and a multilateral environmental agreement.

Moreover, in the absence of such an agreement, the WTO ban on China's export duties also stands to undermine international cooperation on climate change by triggering further WTO disputes.[216] As a WTO working paper acknowledges, export duties 'may respond to threats of border tax adjustments abroad' by 'internalizing the amount of GHG tax their exports may otherwise pay in the importing country'.[217] This being the case, on the one hand, it would seem profoundly unfair were China to be prevented, owing to the two-tier membership structure of the WTO, from using export duties as a countermeasure. On the other hand, without access to export duties as a more acceptable alternative, China is likely to bring a case against any BTAs targeting its exports.

To conclude the arguments here, the change in the factual context of China's export duties—namely recognition of their potential to combat climate change—may provide the AB with sufficient new incentives to reconsider its prior decisions on the matter. In this respect at least, a new interpretation that allows China to use export duties for an environmental purpose remains a possibility. The best feasible option for the AB to depart from its *China—Raw Materials* and *China—Rare Earths* decisions would be to distinguish them; its second-best option would be to explicitly overrule them. With this standard in mind, specific feasibility tests for determining which new interpretation is mostly acceptable to the AB are offered in the following three sections.

7.2. Possible ways to develop a new substantive argument

The previous two sections have established that the AB could adjust the WTO ban by overruling or distinguishing its prior decisions, and the new facts of China's export duties would provide the AB with sufficient incentives to do so. Once the constraint of rule of precedent is loosened, a follow-up question is how to develop a *substantive* argument that provides China with policy space to use export duties to protect the environment. In other words, given the silence on the applicability

215 Brian R. Copeland, 'International Trade and Green Growth', No. 6235 World Bank Policy Research Working Paper (2012), at 41.

216 See Chapter 6.

217 'The GATT does not contain any discipline on export taxes or any price-based measures other than the most-favoured nation principle. It is not clear to what extent national climate change programmes will lead to action on exports. However, some authors have suggested that countries whose GHG emissions are related to products destined for export may respond to threats of border tax adjustments abroad with the adoption of their own export taxes, thus internalizing the amount of GHG tax their exports may otherwise pay in the importing country'. Patrick Low, Gabrielle Marceau, Julia Reinaud, 'The Interface between the Trade and Climate Change Regimes: Scoping the Issues', ERSD Staff Working Paper (2011), at 4.

of the environmental exceptions under Article XX to China's export duty commitments, a new argument should give meaning to that silence.

As noted by the AB, textual silence does not necessarily equal to negative intent of the treaty's drafters. In the past, the AB had no hesitation in giving meaning to the silence concerning several procedural issues, including the burden of proof, the interest required to bring a claim, the admissibility of *amicus curiae* briefs, and the principle of *res judicata*, doing so with reference to general principles of law or the practices of international tribunals.[218] No party protested such judicial act of formulating detailed rules of procedure and evidence.[219]

When it came to interpreting a substantive silence, the AB appeared to be more cautious and tended to largely reply on the context and the object and purpose of WTO agreements.[220] The *Canada—Autos* case, for instance, hinged on silence regarding the scope of SCM Agreement Article 3.1(b), specifically whether the article extended alike to subsidies contingent 'in law' and to subsidies contingent 'in fact' with respect to the use of domestic over imported goods. Taking into consideration the context and especially the object and purpose of Article 3.1(b), the AB found that this provision applied to subsidies contingent 'in law or in fact' because a narrow interpretation of the silence would 'make circumvention of obligations by Members too easy'.[221] By contrast, a negative example is the *EC—Bananas III* case in which the AB refused to give meaning to the silence on whether WTO members could deviate from GATT Article XIII in their commitments to market access and concessions on agricultural goods by stating that, if such deviation were intended, WTO members 'could, and presumably would, have done so'.[222]

A superficial look at the precedent of *EC—Bananas III* seems to support the harsh ban on China's export duties. As the panel noted in *China—Raw Materials*, 'if China and WTO Members wanted the defences of GATT Article XX to be available to violations of China's export duty commitments, they could have said so in Paragraph 11.3 or elsewhere in China's Accession Protocol'.[223] However, the nature of the silence in *EC—Bananas III* is fundamentally different from the one of the silence on the applicability of the environmental exceptions to China's export duty commitments.

218 Isabelle Van Damme, 'The Interpretation of Silence in the WTO Covered Agreements', in '*Treaty Interpretation by the WTO Appellate Body*' (Oxford University Press, 2009), at 136.
219 Georges Abi-Saab, 'The Appellate Body and treaty interpretation', in Giorgio Sacerdoti, Alan Yanovich, and Jan Bohanes (eds), *The WTO at Ten: The Contribution of the Dispute Settlement System* (Cambridge University Press, 2006), at 463.
220 Ibid., at 140.
221 Appellate Body Report, *Canada – Certain Measures Affecting the Automotive Industry*, WT/DS139/AB/R, WT/DS142/AB/R, adopted 19 June 2000, DSR 2000:VI, 2985, para 142.
222 Appellate Body Report, *European Communities – Regime for the Importation, Sale and Distribution of Bananas*, WT/DS27/AB/R, adopted 25 September 1997, DSR 1997:II, 59, para 157.
223 Panel Reports, *China—Raw Materials*, para 7.140.

In *EC—Bananas III*, the EU was seeking the right to allocate tariff quota shares on bananas in a discriminatory manner. WTO members have, however, given away such right concerning trade in goods under GATT Article XIII, entitled 'Non-discriminatory Administration of Quantitative Restrictions'. To reclaim such right concerning trade in agricultural goods, the EU referred to the Agreement on Agriculture (AoA) which is a separate agreement, to a degree, shelters agricultural policies from the full impact of GATT disciplines. However, the agricultural 'exceptions' provided in the AoA are silent on this issue of administration of quantitative restrictions. Thus, the AB correctly decided to not give meaning to that silence because there is a lack of textual support in the AoA to establish a right which has been given away in the GATT 1994.

In contrast, one can hardly disagree that China did have the right to use export duties for environmental purposes before entry into the WTO. Thus, the key issue in *China—Raw Materials* and *China—Rare Earths* was whether China had not silently negotiated away its right to invoke Article XX during its accession rather than reclaiming a right which had been generally prohibited by other WTO agreements. In this context, the dissenting panellist in *China—Rare Earths* correctly suggested that if the WTO members wanted China to abandon the right to invoke Article XX in Paragraph 11.3, 'they would have said so explicitly'.[224] Eventually, the AB seemed to find that China had implicitly waived its right to invoke Article XX in Paragraph 11.3 based on such textual support as a specific exception clause to China's export duty commitments.

The rationale behind a new substantive argument is thus to challenge the existence of China's 'acquiescence' to abandon its right to use export duties to protect the environment. This is likely to demand a lower burden of proof than reclaiming such right. Bearing in mind this distinction, there are two major approaches to develop a new substantive argument in favour of China's export duties as part of environmental policy: (i) there is textual support in China's accession documents to show that China has not acquiesced in giving away its right to use export duties for environmental purposes, or (ii) it is legally impossible for China to give away such important right in a silent way.

The first approach was largely adopted in *China—Raw Materials* and *China—Rare Earths* in which China spent much of its efforts on providing analyses of the relevant WTO provisions that indicate China's right to invoke Article XX. Although all of China's attempts to find textual support in WTO agreements were eventually dismissed by the AB, it does not necessarily mean that China would never find such support in a future case.

Alternatively, the second approach directly calls into question the assumption that China could legally negotiate away its right to use export duties to protect the environment in a silent manner. The starting point here is that, although WTO members have in practice required acceding members to make more stringent

224 Panel Reports, *China—Rare Earths*, para 7.137.

commitments as their 'entry fee',[225] the amount of the charges should not be unlimited. On the one hand, the 'entry fee' is subject to the legal constraints from public international law. For instance, a WTO-plus commitment that requires the acceding member to abandon its right to ban the import of slave-made goods is very likely to be prohibited by a peremptory norm.[226] As acknowledged by the panel in *China—Raw Materials*, the result of a harsh ban on China's export duties is apparently 'imbalanced' though it is not for the panel to 'recalibrate' it.[227] This raises the question of whether public international law would prevent such imbalance.

On the other hand, WTO law itself may also impose constraints on the 'entry fee'. As the panel suggested in *China—Raw Materials*, an interpretation that prevented China from enacting necessary environmental or public health measures 'would likely be inconsistent with the object and purpose of the WTO Agreement' though it subsequently found that the ban on China's export duties would not prevent China from protecting the environment.[228] However, as the preliminary analysis offered here shows, the WTO ban on China's export duties would indeed prevent it from adopting an important climate policy tool. Following these approaches, the next two sections explore the substantive arguments that provide China with policy space to use export duties to protect the environment.

7.3. Feasibility tests for interpretative options based on customary international law or non-WTO treaties

As acknowledged by the AB, WTO rules are not intended to be read in 'clinical isolation from public international law'.[229] In practice, all of the five major sources of international law, namely treaties between or among states, customary international law, general principles of law, judicial decisions, and the writings of 'the most highly qualified publicists', have been applied in settling WTO disputes.[230] Jurisprudence shows that general principles of law, judicial decisions, and the writings of 'the most highly qualified publicists' are not likely to play a significant role in giving a positive meaning to the silence on the relationship between Article XX and China's export duties commitment.[231] This section thus discusses the

225 Panel Reports, *China—Raw Materials*, para 7.112. 'Ultimately, the acceding Member and the WTO membership recognize that the intensively negotiated content of an accession package is the "entry fee" to the WTO system'.
226 Under Article 53 of the VCLT, any treaty that conflicts with a peremptory norm is void.
227 Panel Reports, *China—Raw Materials*, para 7.160 and footnote 192.
228 Ibid., para 7.111. para 7.117.
229 AB Report, *United States – Standards for Reformulated and Conventional Gasoline*, WT/DS2/AB/R, adopted 20 May 1996, DSR 1996:I, para 17.
230 The Statute of the International Court of Justice is annexed to the 1945 Charter of the United Nations.
231 General principles of law in practice is only used to clarify procedural issues whereas the other two are secondary source.

application of treaties and customary international law in settling disputes and explores the interpretive options based on them.

7.3.1. Possibilities and challenges to apply customary international law or non-WTO treaties in settling WTO disputes

7.3.1.1. The application of customary international law

Customary international law contains rules binding on all states that apply automatically to WTO agreements. The AB has at times understood 'general international law' to mean customary international law. In *US—Line Pipe*, for instance, the expressions 'customary international law rules on state responsibility' and 'general international law on state responsibility' were considered synonymous,[232] and in *EC—Hormones* the AB equated the two notions by referring to 'general or customary international law'.[233]

Another of the AB's expressions relating to customary international law is the 'general principle of international law'. This concept appears related to the definition of general principles of law, for the panel in *EC—Approval and Marketing of Biotech Products* stated that a 'general principle of international law' implies either customary international law, general principles of law, or both.[234] According to the definition in the Statute of the ICJ, however, general principles of law refer to norms in national legal systems that should be used differently from 'general principles of international law'.[235] Thus, in *US—Shrimp*, the AB described good faith as 'a general principle of law and a general principle of international law'. In this context, a general principle of international law could be seen as part of customary international law.

With a common intention, WTO members may contract out customary international law from WTO treaties. Thus the panel stated in *Korea—Government Procurement* that customary international law applied to the extent to which the WTO treaties did not 'contract out' from it.[236] This position was further confirmed by the AB in *US—Cotton Yarn*, in which it found that derogation from a general international principle of proportionality of countermeasures could be justified only if the drafters of the WTO rules had expressly

232 AB Report, *United States – Definitive Safeguard Measures on Imports of Circular Welded Carbon Quality Line Pipe from Korea*, WT/DS202/AB/R, adopted on 15 February 2002, para 259.

233 AB Reports, *European Communities – EC Measures Concerning Meat and Meat Products (Hormones)*, WT/DS26/AB/R, WT/DS48/AB/R, adopted on 16 January 1998, para 124.

234 Panel Report, *European Communities — Measures Affecting the Approval and Marketing of Biotech Products*, WT/DS291/R, WT/DS292/R, WT/DS293/R, adopted on 29 September 2006.

235 Christopher Greenwood, 'Sources of International Law: An Introduction', available at http://legal.un.org/avl/pdf/ls/greenwood_outline.pdf (visited on 18 June 2017).

236 Panel Report, *Korea—Measures Affecting Government Procurement*, WT/DS163/R, adopted on 19 June 2000, para. 7.96.

provided for it.[237] However, the derogation from customary international law should not include peremptory norms as the overriding principles of international law.[238]

The challenge of applying customary international law is that, being by nature an unwritten source, it requires panels and the AB to identify the norm at issue that has attained this status. Within its jurisprudence, the AB has found that several provisions in the Vienna Convention on the Law of Treaties (VCLT) contain rules of customary international law, including in *US—Offset Act*, [239]*Japan—Alcoholic Beverages II*, [240] and *Korea—Procurement*, [241] as well as in Articles 26, 32, and 48 of the VCLT. The AB has found other sources of customary international law as well. In *US—Line Pipe*, for example, it identified rules in Article 51 of the International Law Commission (ILC) Articles on State Responsibility as principles of customary international law.[242] So also in the *US—Shrimp* case, the AB referred to 'good faith' as such a principle.

Owing to the broad application of customary international law, panels and the AB are very careful about applying it. Thus, in *Guatemala—Cement II*, the panel refused to recognize the concept of 'harmless error', which required a party to show injury before obtaining the right to be compensated for a procedural error, as part of customary international law though Guatemala claimed that this concept, having been recognized by the ICJ, should also be applied in the present case to excuse its violation of procedural rules of the Anti-Dumping Agreement.[243] Moreover, the AB also in *EC—Hormones* and *US—Anti-Dumping and Countervailing Duties (China)* showed its reluctance to identify the status of customary international law. In the former example, the EU claimed that the precautionary principle, as a general principle of customary international environmental law, could allow it to act cautious 'when setting health standards in the face of conflicting scientific information and uncertainty'.[244] However,

237 AB Report, *United States—Transitional Safeguard Measure on Combed Cotton Yarn from Pakistan*, WT/DS192/AB/R, adopted on 8 October 2001, para 120.

238 Joost Pauwelyn, 'The Application of Non-WTO Rules of International Law in WTO Dispute Settlement', in *The World Trade Organization: Legal, Economic and Political Analysis*, Patrick F.J. Macrory, Arthur E. Appleton, Michael G. Plummer (eds.), Springer, 2005, at 1405–1425.

239 AB Report, *United States—Continued Dumping and Subsidy Offset Act of 2000*, WT/DS217/AB/R, WT/DS234/AB/R, adopted on 16 January 2003, footnote 247.

240 AB Report, *Japan—Taxes on Alcoholic Beverages*, WT/DS8/AB/R, WT/DS10/AB/R, WT/DS11/AB/R, adopted on 4 October 1996, footnote 17.

241 Panel Report, *Korea—Measures Affecting Government Procurement*, WT/DS163/R, adopted on 1 May 2000, para 7.123.

242 AB Report, *United States – Definitive Safeguard Measures on Imports of Circular Welded Carbon Quality Line Pipe from Korea*, WT/DS202/AB/R, adopted 8 March 2002, DSR 2002:IV, para 259.

243 Panel Report, *Guatemala—Definitive Anti-Dumping Measure on Grey Portland Cement from Mexico*, WT/DS156/R, adopted on 24 October 2000, para 8.22.

244 AB Report, *AB Report, EC Measures Concerning Meat and Meat Products (Hormones)*, WT/DS26/AB/R, WT/DS48/AB/R, adopted 13 February 1998, DSR 1998:I, para 16.

acknowledging that the status of the precautionary principle in international law was still debatable among 'academics, law practitioners, regulators and judges', the AB held that it is 'unnecessary, and probably imprudent' for it to address the question of whether the precautionary principle had attained this status because this principle still awaited 'authoritative formulation'.[245] In the latter case concerning whether Article 5 of the ILC Articles on Responsibility of States for Internationally Wrongful Acts reflects customary rules of international law, the AB found that it was not necessary for it to resolve this question because its legal analysis was not based on Article 5.[246]

Once a rule is found to attain the status of customary international law, the next step for a panel or the AB is to decide how to apply it. It is commonly accepted that customary international law can play a role in interpreting specific WTO terms. As discussed, Article 3.2 of the DSU requires that the panel and the AB clarify WTO regulations according to customary rules of interpretation. A typical example is the application of the aforementioned principle of good faith; although this principle can be found in neither the WTO Agreement nor the GATT 1994,[247] the AB in *US—Shrimp* linked the balance of rights and obligations under the chapeau of Article XX with it, based on which linkage the text of the chapeau had been interpreted as prohibiting the abusive exercise of a state's rights. In the AB's view, this principle, as customary international law, provided it with 'additional interpretative guidance'.[248]

Whereas the AB may apply customary international law in a complementary manner, namely providing 'additional interpretative guidance', in treaty interpretation, it appears to be reluctant to apply substantive customary international law independently in dispute settlement.[249] To be sure, a WTO member cannot bring a WTO complaint based solely on customary international law: according to Article 1.1 of the DSU, WTO dispute settlement only accepts a legal claim based on certain WTO agreements that are listed in its Appendix 1.

Thus, the independent use of customary international law here refers to the gap-filling role of these non-WTO norms. Unlike the common use of non-WTO norms to fill in the procedural gap in WTO agreements, the gap-filling role of substantive customary international law is very limited. For instance, in *India—Patents (US)*, the AB reversed a panel's finding regarding the principle of

245 Ibid., para 123.

246 AB Report, *US—Anti-Dumping and Countervailing Duties (China)*, para. 311.

247 Several agreements attached to the WTO Agreements refer to good faith. For instance, Articles 3.10 and 4.3 of the DSU and Articles 24, 48.2, and 58(c) of the TRIPS.

248 AB Report, *United States – Import Prohibition of Certain Shrimp and Shrimp Products*, WT/DS58/AB/R, adopted 6 November 1998, DSR 1998:VII, para 158.

249 Jan Wouters, Dominic Coppens, Dylan Geraets, 'The Influence of General Principles of Law', in *Liberalising Trade in the EU and the WTO A Legal Comparison*, Sanford E. Gaines, Birgitte Egelund Olsen, Karsten Engsig Sørensen (eds), Cambridge University Press, 2012, at 9. 'In other words, it seems that a claim cannot be based on customary international law and that it can also not be invoked as a defence to justify a violation of a WTO provision'.

'legitimate expectations', pointing out that an interpretation should not import unintended concepts into a treaty.[250] In other words, the principle of 'legitimate expectations' cannot impose an independent obligation on WTO members in the absence of a legal basis in the TRIPS Agreement.[251]

As an exceptional example concerning the application of substantive customary international law independent from WTO rules, in response to the argument of the US in *US—Offset Act* that

> no basis or justification in the WTO Agreement for a WTO dispute settlement panel to conclude that a Member has not acted in good faith, or to enforce a principle of good faith as a substantive obligation agreed to by WTO Members[252]

the AB held that 'Clearly, therefore, there is a basis for a dispute settlement panel to determine, in an appropriate case, whether a Member has not acted in good faith' by referring to its previous practice of using the principle of good faith.[253] Thus, it found a basis for applying the principle of good faith independently in order to assess the manner in which a WTO member had fulfilled its obligations but this ruling drew criticism from both WTO members and scholars.[254] One major reason behind this criticism is that, unlike to independently apply procedural non-WTO norms in disputes base on the AB's inherent jurisdiction, there is no legal basis for the AB to apply substantive customary international law to interpret provisions that do not specifically reflect such a rule.[255] It is noteworthy that, however, this exceptional decision has minimal practical relevance because the AB appeared to suggest that a violation of a WTO provision is a necessary condition to find a member to not act in good faith.[256] In other words, in the absence of a breach of a WTO treaty provision, a WTO member cannot be found to violate the principle of good faith.

250 AB Report, *India—Patent Protection for Pharmaceutical and Agricultural Chemical Products*, adopted on 16 January 1998, WT/DS50/AB/R, paras 42 and 45.
251 Wouters, Coppens, and Geraets (2012), above n 249.
252 AB Report, *United States – Continued Dumping and Subsidy Offset Act of 2000*, WT/DS217/AB/R, WT/DS234/AB/R, adopted 27 January 2003, DSR 2003:I, para 296.
253 Ibid., para 297.
254 Minutes of Meeting Held on 27 January 2003. Dispute Settlement Body, WT/DSB/M/142, 6 March 2003, para 57. Andrew D. Mitchell, '*Legal Principles in WTO Disputes*', Cambridge University Press, 2008, at 136. Wouters, Coppens, and Geraets (2012), above n 249, at 49.
255 Andrew D. Mitchell, 'Good Faith in WTO Dispute Settlement', 7(2) *Melbourne Journal of International Law* (2006), 'these provisions do not specifically reflect the principle of good faith beyond the general requirement that they be interpreted in good faith'.
256 AB Report, *United States – Continued Dumping and Subsidy Offset Act of 2000*, WT/DS217/AB/R, WT/DS234/AB/R, adopted 27 January 2003, DSR 2003:I, para 298.

7.3.1.2. The application of non-WTO treaties

Treaties, unlike customary international law, are binding only on the contracting parties. WTO jurisprudence, however, shows that non-WTO treaties can sometimes be applied in the process of interpreting specific WTO terms. For instance, in *US—Shrimp*, the AB interpreted the term 'exhaustible natural resources' in Article XX(g) by referring to several modern international conventions, including the United Nations Convention on the Law of the Sea (UNCLOS), the Convention on Biological Diversity, and the Convention on International Trade in Endangered Species.[257]

It is, however, unclear whether a WTO member could use non-WTO treaties to justify its violation of WTO rules. In the *Chile—Swordfish* case, the EU challenged Chilean legislation, which prohibited unloading of swordfish in its ports under Article 165 of its fisheries laws, before the WTO based on Articles V, providing for freedom of transit for goods through the territory of each contracting party on their way to or from other contracting parties, and XI, prohibiting quantitative restrictions on imports or exports, of the GATT 1994. Chile chose, with reference to the UNCLOS, the International Tribunal for the Law of the Sea (ITLOS) as an alternative forum to resolve the dispute and, having made various arrangements regarding the procedural suspension of WTO and UNCLOS provisions, settled with the EU in 2010.[258] However, if Chile had chosen to invoke several articles concerning conservation of environmental resources under UNCLOS, such as Article 64 calling for cooperation in ensuring conservation of highly migratory species and Articles 116 to 119 relating to conservation of the living resources of the high seas, in its defence in front of the AB, it is unclear whether the AB would allow it to do so.

In this context, Pauwelyn has argued that, if a non-WTO treaty binds the parties in a WTO dispute, this treaty then must be considered a potential defence.[259] To support his argument, he cites the AB's encouragement of the US in the *US—Shrimp* case to conclude treaties with other WTO members for the protection of sea turtles in order to avoid 'arbitrary or unjustifiable discrimination'. In his view, such a treaty, once concluded, could be used as a defence against a claim of 'arbitrary or unjustifiable discrimination'. To date, though, no WTO member has referred to a non-WTO treaty as part of a defence.

257 AB Report, *US—Shrimp*, paras 128–132.

258 WTO Secretariat, *Chile—Measures affecting the Transit and Importing of Swordfish*, available at https://www.wto.org/english/tratop_e/dispu_e/cases_e/ds193_e.htm (visited on 18 June 2017).

259 Joost Pauwelyn, 'The Application of Non-WTO Rules of International Law in WTO Dispute Settlement', in *The World Trade Organization: Legal, Economic and Political Analysis*, Patrick F.J. Macrory, Arthur E. Appleton, Michael G. Plummer (eds.), Springer, 2005, at 1416.

7.3.2. Options based on customary international law

At the oral hearing of the appeal of *China—Rare Earths*, China developed a new argument based on Article 30(3) of the VCLT.[260] Although the AB criticised China's failure to provide sufficient supporting evidence for this argument, China may develop it further in a future dispute. In keeping with the proposal of Qin,[261] the first issue to be examined is whether the application of VCLT Article 30 can lead to an interpretation in support of China's right to impose export duties. The next concern is the extent to which public international law does not support the *China—Raw Materials* and *China—Rare Earths* decisions, which touches on the feasibility of using the principle of sustainable development and the principle of abuse of rights as a defence against the denial of China's right under Article XX.

7.3.2.1. Paragraph 11.3 as a subsequent agreement or practice modifying WTO treaties

To further develop China's argument as mentioned above, Qin proposed considering China's Accession Protocol as a subsequent agreement as defined under VCLT Article 30(3), a provision that has been used as a basis for modifying WTO treaties.[262] Approached this way, China's export duty commitments under Paragraph 11.3 of its Accession Protocol have, in effect, modified GATT Article XI:1 so that this article essentially regulates them.[263] Thus, since GATT Article XX applies to Article XI:1, China is entitled to justify its use of export duties under the former unless the Accession Protocol explicitly states otherwise.

The interpretation of Paragraph 11.3 as a subsequent agreement, however, will face legal challenges. In particular, Article 30(3) only applies to the situation in which 'all the parties to the earlier treaty are parties also to the later treaty', that is to say in order to consider China's Accession Protocol as a subsequent agreement under VCLT Article 30(3), the parties to the Protocol should be the same as those to the earlier treaty, namely the GATT 1994. By contrast, however, China's Accession Protocol was signed between it and the WTO, while the GATT 1994 was signed by the original WTO members, of which China was not one. Therefore, Article 30(3) seems to be irrelevant to explain the relationship between Paragraph 11.3 and the GATT 1994.

In addressing this legal issue, Qin argued that China's Accession Protocol can be treated as a multilateral agreement signed by WTO members, on the grounds that it represented a consensus among them.[264] This argument is based on the approach, termed 'functionalism', to consider that international organizations are

260 The AB found in *US—Gasoline* that the general rule of interpretation in Article 31 of the VCLT was part of customary international law.
261 Julia Ya Qin, 'Conundrum of WTO Accession Protocols: In Search of Legality and Legitimacy', 55(2), *Virginia Journal of International Law* (2015), at 404.
262 Ibid. at 404–411.
263 Ibid.
264 Ibid.

mere functional vehicles for their member states.[265] In this sense, the parties to China's Accession Protocol, as a subsequent agreement, are in effect the same as the parties to the GATT 1994 in its capacity as an earlier treaty.

Regardless of the controversial nature of the 'functionalism' approach,[266] it is noteworthy that the conclusion of a treaty requires the approval of national decision-makers, however, and only China's parliament ratified its Accession Protocol.[267] Therefore, if the conclusion of China's Accession Protocol is considered a subsequent agreement that modifies the GATT 1994, the functionalist perspective fails to explain why the national decision-makers in other WTO member countries were excluded from the process of amendment. Furthermore, the form of China's Accession Protocol also lacks the rigor of treaty texts as a subsequent agreement to the GATT 1994.

As an alternative to the functionalist perspective, Qin proposes a bold solution by considering China's Accession Protocol subsequent practice for modifying WTO treaties. Yet while the parties to a subsequent practice need not necessarily to have been signatories to an earlier treaty, to consider China's Accession Protocol subsequent practice faces other legal challenges. It is in this respect important to note that the concept of a subsequent practice modifying treaties is not even mentioned in the VCLT; there was, during its drafting, a proposal of the ILC to include it as a means to modify a treaty by proposing that the 'treaty may be modified by subsequent practice in the application of the treaty establishing the agreement of the parties to modify its provisions',[268] but this was rejected owing to uncertainty regarding the effect of subsequent practice on the principle of consent and appeared to be the only proposed article of the ILC that was completely abandoned by the negotiator in 1966.[269]

In fact, the idea to amend or modify treaties by subsequent practice of the parties has still not been generally recognised by states nowadays according to the Fifth ILC Report (2018) on subsequent agreements and subsequent practice in relation to the interpretation of treaties.[270] Although, in practice, the ICJ has

265 Ibid.

266 Jan Klabbers, 'The Emergence of Functionalism in International Institutional Law: Colonial Inspirations', 25(3) *European Journal of International Law* (2014), at 645. 'It turns out that functionalism, as developed by Reinsch, was inspired by his familiarity with colonial administration: colonialism and international organization both manifested cooperation between states. While this is no reason to discard functionalism, it does provide an argument for viewing international organizations more critically than functionalism habitually does'.

267 WTO Secretariat, 'WTO Ministerial Conference approves China's accession', https://www.wto.org/english/news_e/pres01_e/pr252_e.htm (visited on 18 June 2017).

268 A/CN.4/SER.A/1966/Add.l YEARBOOK OF THE INTERNATIONAL LAW COMMISSION 1966, Volume II Documents of the second part of the seventeenth session and of the eighteenth session including the reports of the Commission to the General Assembly U N I T E D N A T I O N S, at 91.

269 Georg Nolte, *Treaties and Subsequent Practice*, Oxford University Press (2013), at 130.

270 Fifth ILC Report (2018) on subsequent agreements and subsequent practice in relation to the interpretation of treaties, para 66.

taken a decidedly liberal approach to recognising the role of subsequent practice in treaty modification,[271] WTO jurisprudence, to date, has only recognised the role of subsequent practice in treaty interpretation.[272] Considering the lack of consensus among the states on recognising subsequent practice as a way to change treaties, the AB is not likely to introduce the new role of subsequent practice in treaty interpretation. And even if the AB does so, it is noteworthy that subsequent practice requires the common intention of the WTO members. In both *China—Raw Materials* and *China—Rare Earths*, however, the differing opinions among the third-party participants that shared the legal position of China's Accession Protocol indicate a lack of common intention as required by subsequent practice. Thus, the argument that China's Accession Protocol modified the GATT 1994 is likely to be accepted by the AB.

Moreover, the argument based on subsequent practice, though aiming to favour China's export duties, may not be even accepted by the Chinese government itself, which just recently rejected the position to use subsequent practice 'as a tool to expand the scope of interpretation or to covertly amend the treaty' in the UN.[273]

Lastly, aside from all the above legal difficulties involved with interpreting China's Accession Protocol as either a subsequent agreement under VCLT Article 30(3) or subsequent practice, it is also uncertain whether the AB would view China's export duty commitments under Paragraph 11.3 of its Accession Protocol as a means to modify GATT Article XI:1; for in *China—Rare Earths*, the majority of the panel found that the commitment to eliminate export duties did not relate to GATT Article XI.[274] That is to say, even if China's Accession Protocol is generally considered a tool to modify the GATT 1994, the AB may still find that Article XI is not modified by Paragraph 11.3.

7.3.2.2. The principle of sustainable development

From *China—Raw Materials* to *China—Raw Materials II*, China has consistently argued that its export duties are intended to promote sustainable development. This claim in turn raises the question if sustainable development can, in the context of public international law, serve as an independent ground against the denial of China's right to impose export duties under Article XX.

As noted several times, the AB in the *US—Shrimp* case used sustainable development as a legitimising factor for an evolutionary interpretation by broadening the scope of the term 'exhaustible natural resources' to include sea turtles.[275] In that case, however, the AB referred to sustainable development as an objective in

271 Julia Ya Qin, 'Conundrum of WTO Accession Protocols: In Search of Legality and Legitimacy', 55(2), *Virginia Journal of International Law* (2015), at 408.
272 Ibid.
273 United Nations, General Assembly Seventy-first Session Official Records, 11 November 2016, para 70.
274 Panel Reports, *China—Rare Earths*, para 7.95.
275 AB Report, *US—Shrimp*, para 130.

the WTO Agreement rather than as a principle of customary international law. As a result, the legal implications of sustainable development have been 'drawn in a strictly conventional capacity' when it comes to settling WTO disputes.[276] For instance, the AB in *China—Raw Materials* held that the objective of sustainable development in the WTO Agreement does not provide 'specific guidance' clarifying the relationship between Paragraph 11.3 and GATT Article XX. Following this conventional approach, the AB would certainly not accept China's defence against the denial of its right under Article XX solely based on the objective of sustainable development.

Such a defence might be feasible, however, if the AB is willing to consider sustainable development as a norm of *jus cogens*. As peremptory norms of general international law, *jus cogens* norms, such as prohibitions of the slave trade, can invalidate conflicting rules, including WTO norms.[277] In other words, *jus cogens* norms enjoy absolute priority over other norms and permit of no derogation. It is accordingly doubtful that a panel or the AB would have the authority to nullify a WTO norm for a violation of *jus cogens*.[278] In this sense, were sustainable development to attain the status of a *jus cogens* norm, the strong presumption against violating such a norm would encourage an interpretation that allows China to use export duties for the purpose of sustainable development.[279]

However, sustainable development seems to have not yet attained this status. For while the existence of the category of *jus cogens* norms is recognised internationally, there is little international consensus as to which specific norms qualify.[280] A relevant notion in the literature might be the 'right to life', which is protected under every international human rights convention, but this right has not developed into a general prohibition against failing to avoid—or perhaps better, general permission to take measures to avoid—environmental damage that threatens the international community as a whole.[281] Moreover, tribunals have been, in practice, extremely cautious about recognising *jus cogens* status owing to uncertainty regarding the potential implications for a tribunal's legitimacy.[282] This

276 Virginie Barral, 'Sustainable Development in International Law: Nature and Operation of an Evolutive Legal Norm', 23(2) *European Journal of International Law* (2012), at 386.
277 Articles 53 and 64 of the VCLT.
278 The mandate of the panel and the AB is limited to recommending that a national measure be consistent with WTO laws. See Gabrielle Marceau, WTO Dispute Settlement and Human Rights, 13(4) *European Journal of International Law* (2002) at 756.
279 Ibid.
280 Possible norms of *jus cogens* include the prohibition on the use of force (e.g., an agreement between states to commit aggression against another state would be void), the prohibition on genocide and violations of other fundamental human rights.
281 Eva M. Kornicker Uhlmann, 'State Community Interests, Jus Cogens and Protection of the Global Environment: Developing Criteria for Peremptory Norms', 11 *Georgetown Environmental Law Review* (1998), at 135.
282 Matthew Saul, 'Identifying Jus Cogens Norms: The Interaction of Scholars and International Judges', 5(1) *Asian Journal of International Law* (2015) at 27.

being the case, it is also unrealistic to expect the AB, which once avoided addressing the question of whether the precautionary principle had attained the status of customary international law and proposed to wait for 'authoritative formulation', to find that sustainable development has attained the status of a *jus cogens* norm.

Alternatively, it can perhaps more easily be argued that sustainable development has attained the status of customary international law.[283] Thus, the AB would be required to rule in favour of China's export duties if China could prove, first, the notion of sustainable development conflicts with the WTO ban on China's export duties, and, second, sustainable development prevails over China's export duty commitments. However, it would be difficult for China to prove the existence of a conflict between the principle of sustainable development and the harsh ban on China's export duties. At least in theory, because customary international law is by nature less specific and explicit than a treaty provision, the latter is likely to prevail as *lex specialis* whenever a conflict arises between them.[284] Therefore, in a future case, even if the AB were to find the WTO ban on China's export duties to be in conflict with the principle of sustainable development, the prohibition would still likely to carry greater weight. Thus, considering the very cautious stance of the AB to identify customary international law and the vague nature of sustainable development, it is not feasible for China to rely on the principle of sustainable development as an independent ground against the denial of China's right under Article XX in a future case though this principle may help develop a more teleological approach prioritising the environmental objective under WTO law which is discussed in the next section.

7.3.2.3. The principle of good faith

In *US—Shrimp*, the AB referred to the principle of good faith for additional interpretative guidance in deciding whether the US passed the test under the *chapeau* of GATT Article XX.[285] In the view of the AB, in the application of the principle of good faith, the abuse of rights should be prohibited. Thus the doctrine of abuse of rights, for the AB, is one application of the principle of good faith, which requires that a state's right 'must be exercised *bona fide*, that is to say, reasonably'.[286]

The reception of the *China—Raw Materials* and *China—Rare Earths* decisions makes the stance of the complaining governments in seeking to prohibit China from using export duties appear extreme and unreasonable. Moreover, this book also shows that the WTO ban would in practice constrain China's policy space to

283 Virginie Barral, 'Sustainable Development in International Law: Nature and Operation of an Evolutive Legal Norm', 23(2) *European Journal of International Law* (2012), at 385.

284 Joost Pauwelyn, 'How to Win a WTO Dispute Based on Non-WTO Law? Questions of Jurisdiction and Merits', 37(6) *Journal of World Trade* (2003), at 1025.

285 AB Report, *United States—Import Prohibition of Certain Shrimp and Shrimp Products*, WT/DS58/AB/R, para. 158.

286 Ibid.

fight climate change, especially on addressing the issue of carbon leakage. Since the doctrine of abuse of rights 'prevents a Party to an agreement from exercising its rights in a way that is unreasonable in light of the spirit of the agreement',[287] the question arises whether the principle relating to the abuse of rights could serve to address what China views as the unreasonable acts of the complainants in the two cases.

Abuse of rights has expressly served as the basis of a claim before the ICJ, specifically in *Barcelona Traction, Light and Power Company, Limited (Belgium v. Spain) (New Application: 1962)*, in which the Spanish government invoked 'an abuse of the right of diplomatic protection'.[288] Although this principle has never been applied independently in WTO disputes, the AB in *US—Offset Act* found a basis for applying the principle of good faith independently in order to assess the manner in which a WTO member had fulfilled its obligations. In this context, China may argue that the principle of abuse of rights, as part of the principle of good faith, prohibits WTO members from assuming that China has implicitly signed away its valuable rights under Article XX. Indeed, as the panel held in *China—Rare Earths*, an interpretation of WTO law that in effect prevented WTO members from taking necessary measures to protect the environment could be considered inconsistent with the object and purpose of WTO law and thus 'manifestly absurd or unreasonable'.[289]

In *US—Offset Act*, however, the AB also appeared to suggest that a violation of a WTO provision is a necessary condition to find a member to not act in good faith. In this context, alternatively, China could claim that the attempt to deny its right to use export duties under Article XX constitutes an abuse of procedural rights under Article 3(10) of the Understanding on Rules and Procedures Governing the Settlement of Disputes (DSU), according to which all WTO members must engage in dispute settlement procedures in good faith. In view of the *US—Shrimp* case, the denial of China's right to impose export duties under Article XX could, then, constitute an unreasonable exercise of rights. This option is, however, less feasible than the above one because it requires the AB to adopt a very broad interpretation on procedural rights.

7.3.3. Options based on non-WTO treaties

As discussed above, after the *US—Shrimp* case, a treaty between the US and other WTO members designed to protect sea turtles could serve as a defence for the United States against a future claim of 'arbitrary or unjustifiable discrimination'. Thus, if China could conclude a treaty between it and the complaining

287 Thomas Cottier and Krista N. Schefer, 'Good Faith and the Protection of Legitimate Expectations' in Marco Bronckers and Reinhard Quick (eds.), *New Directions in International Economic Law, Essays: Essays in Honour of John H.Jackson* (Kluwer Law International, 2000), at 127.

288 Judgment of 5 February 1970 Second Phase Procedure(s): Preliminary objections, at 15.

289 Panel Reports, *China—Rare Earths*, para 7.111.

governments defining the legitimate use of export duties to protect the environment, this treaty could be used as defence against a claim of the violation of China's export duty commitments in a future case. However, this kind of agreement on the environmental role of China's export duties is not likely to be reached because, as evident in the *China—Raw Materials* and *China—Rare Earths* cases, the complaining governments, suggesting that China's export duties could be replaced by other better environmental instrument, rejected to recognise the importance of export duties in protecting the environment.

Aside from relying on a bilateral agreement, WTO members may also invoke a decision under the dispute settlement mechanism of a non-WTO treaty against a WTO complaint. Thus, by way of example, following the recommendations of the Resolution of the International Labour Conference (ILC) recommending action against Myanmar for breaching the International Labour Organization's Forced Labour Convention, a number of WTO members at one point imposed trade embargoes against Myanmar; had the latter complained to the WTO, the former would have been allowed to use the ILC recommendations, as the later and more specific norm, as a defence.[290] After all, the WTO may also expect other international organizations to respect an explicit WTO authorization.[291]

For instance, in the *EC—Bananas III* case, the Arbitrators found that Ecuador, pursuant to Article 22.2 of the DSU, may request authorization by the Dispute Settlement Body (DSB) to suspend certain TRIPS obligations as a countermeasure against a prior WTO violation by the EU's import regime for bananas.[292] To be sure, Ecuador never exercised its right to adopt such a countermeasure, but instead negotiated a settlement with the EU to improve market access for its bananas.[293] But if Ecuador did suspend intellectual property protection, the WTO would expect the WIPO to refuse finding a violation of the WIPO administered treaties.

This option is, however, not available to China because export duties have not been authorised under any organisation of non-WTO treaties. In the absence of such an authorisation, China may argue that export duties are instead authorised under a multilateral environmental agreement (MEA). Relevant in this context, the Montreal Protocol allows for trade restrictive measures that are inconsistent with the GATT 1994 against non-parties. To date, these authorised trade restrictive measures have never been challenged, though they are believed to be protected by GATT Article XX.[294] If, however, a measure such as an export ban

290 Pauwelyn (2003), above n 284, at 1022.
291 Ibid., at 1023.
292 Decision by the Arbitrator, *European Communities – Regime for the Importation, Sale and Distribution of Bananas – Recourse to Arbitration by the European Communities under Article 22.6 of the DSU*, WT/DS27/ARB/ECU, 24 March 2000, DSR 2000: V.
293 See Notification of Mutually Agreed Solution, EC – Bananas III, WT/DS27/58, 2 July 2001.
294 The Ozone Secretariat in 1999 issued a communication to the WTO Committee on Trade and Environment noting that the measures could be saved under Article XX.

authorised by the Montreal Protocol were to fail to pass the test under Article XX,[295] the Montreal Protocol could arguably be used as an independent defence. For instance, as discussed above, if Chile in the *Chile—Swordfish* case chose to invoke several articles concerning conservation of environmental resources under UNCLOS in its defence, the AB may allow it to do so.

In this context, China could refer to the Paris Agreement, which is within the United Nations Framework Convention on Climate Change (UNFCCC), as a defence against a WTO complaint prohibiting it from using export duties for fighting climate change. It is noteworthy that China in its second communication to the UNFCCC described its export duties as a type of instrument designed to 'effectively control greenhouse gas emissions'.[296] This assertion has also received support from some research reports, including a 2012 World Bank research paper suggesting that export duties could play a positive role in future negotiations aimed at reducing carbon leakage.[297]

However, unlike the Montreal Protocol, the Paris Agreement does not explicitly authorise China to impose export duties. So the AB needs to determine whether the Paris Agreement requires, or at least permits, China to adopt export duties as part of its climate policy, and this determination could also require China to prove the necessity of export duties to combat climate change. Therefore, although the Paris Agreement confirms China's target of halting the increase in its carbon emissions by around 2030, there remains enormous uncertainty regarding whether the AB would accept the Paris Agreement as a defence permitting a violation of China's export duty commitments. Moreover, one important assumption behind this option is that the Paris Agreement is binding on these WTO members which could potentially bring a case against China's export duties. This assumption is, however, challenged by the withdraw of the United States from the Paris Agreement.[298]

To conclude the present section, all potential interpretative options based on non-WTO norms appear to require the AB to overrule its prior decisions explicitly and therefore constitute second-best options. Among them, the argument that China's export duty commitments should be viewed as a subsequent agreement or practice modifying GATT Article XI is unlikely to be accepted by the AB.[299]

See Duncan Brack and Kevin Gray, 'Multilateral Environmental Agreements and the WTO', IISD Report (2003), at 20.

295 Ibid., at 21. The Director of the WTO Trade and Environment Division in 1996 suggested that the Protocol's trade measures would not pass the tests under GATT Article XX.

296 UNFCCC, 'Second National Communication on Climate Change of the People's Republic of China', October 2004, at 15, http://unfccc.int/resource/docs/natc/chnnc1exsum.pdf (visited on 1 January 2019).

297 Copeland (2012), above n 215, at 41.

298 The US keeps litigating against China's export duties in the *China—Raw Materials, China—Rare Earths* and *China—Raw Materials II* cases.

299 The reason is that, on the one hand, the parties to the China's Accession Protocol are not the same as those to the GATT 1994; and on the other hand, even China itself recently rejected considering subsequent practice as a tool to modify treaties.

Similarly, the AB can be expected to reject arguments based solely on the principles of sustainable development or of the Paris Agreement, though these non-WTO norms could bolster an interpretation favouring China's export duties. A more feasible second-best option appears to be founded on the principle of good faith which might be used against the assumption that China has implicitly signed away its valuable rights under Article XX. Alternatively, another less feasible option would be to argue that the denial of China's rights under Article XX is inconsistent with the principle of prohibition of abuse of rights under Article 3(10) of the DSU. The feasibility of various interpretative options under WTO law is assessed in the following section.

7.4. Feasibility tests for interpretative options based on WTO law

In this section, the feasibility of two major interpretative options under WTO law is assessed. The first is based largely on the major criticism of the WTO ban discussed in Chapter 3, namely that the AB, in adhering to a strict textual approach, ignored the environmental concerns raised in the Preamble to the WTO Agreement. The discussion begins by addressing the feasibility of the AB adopting a more teleological approach that gives greater weight to the environmental aims under WTO law than in the earlier cases. Since the AB has already found that the preamble does not provide 'specific guidance' that would clarify the relationship between Paragraph 11.3 and GATT Article XX, such an approach would likely require explicit departure from its previous decisions, a move that, as has been seen, constitutes a second-best approach. In an effort to find the most feasible solution, a second interpretative option is proposed that would enable the AB to distinguish the harsh ban on China's export duties.

7.4.1. A more teleological approach in light of the environmental context in the preamble of the WTO Agreement

The preamble to the WTO Agreement addresses several important environmental issues regarding 'sustainable development' and directives to 'preserve the environment'. This environmental context, as the AB held in the *US—Shrimp* case, 'must add colour, texture and shading' to its interpretation.[300] This jurisprudence, however, at least in the opinion of some scholars, was not followed in the *China—Raw Materials* and *China—Rare Earths* cases, and a group of interpretations has been proposed according to which the AB could take a relatively more holistic approach by emphasising the preamble's environmental context. The following discussion accordingly presents two ways in which the AB could adopt a new interpretation permitting China to use export duties under Article XX by relying on the environmental objective of WTO law.

300 AB Report, *US—Shrimp*, para 153.

7.4.1.1. Explicitly prioritising the object of environmental protection

If the object of environmental protection has some form of relative primacy in WTO law, the AB could rely on it to give meaning to the silence on the applicability of the environmental exceptions under Article XX to China's export duty commitments. There is, however, a lack of WTO jurisprudence about the prioritisation of a treaty's purpose and object. In order to provide the AB with a good example, this discussion refers to the ECJ's *Kadi I* judgment, which is concerned with the implementation of resolutions of the United Nations (UN) Security Council that imposed sanctions under Chapter VII of the UN Charter against individuals and entities alleged to be associated with terrorism. To give effect to these resolutions, the Council of the European Union adopted a regulation ordering the freezing of the funds and other assets of persons and entities appearing on a list annexed to the regulation. The appellants claimed that this regulation should be annulled because it infringed several of their fundamental rights, namely respect for property, to be heard before a court of law, and to effective judicial review.[301]

At first, this claim was rejected by the Court of First Instance because it lacked the jurisdiction to review the validity of the basis of regulation at issue, namely the relevant resolution adopted under Chapter VII of the UN Charter, which prevails over the obligations of member states under EU law by virtue of Article 103 of the UN Charter.[302] Subsequently, the claim of the appellants that the regulation violated their fundamental rights was supported by the ECJ, which held that, if it were to find a measure giving effect to a resolution of the UN Security Council to be inconsistent with 'a higher rule of law in the Community legal order', this finding would not change the 'primacy of that resolution in international law'.[303]

Relevant in the context of prioritising the object of environmental protection in WTO law is the practice of the ECJ in finding that the protection of fundamental rights at issue, as part of the 'very foundations' of the EU legal order,[304] forms 'the constitutional principles' of the EU law.[305] While the Court emphasised the importance of the protection of fundamental rights against 'the alleged absolute primacy of the resolutions of the Security Council', it also appeared to imply a 'hierarchy of norms' within EU primary law.[306] Thus, from a constitutional perspective, a finding by the AB that a hierarchy of norms exists in WTO law in

301 ECJ, Case C-402/05 P and C-415/05 P *Yassin Abdullah Kadi, Al Barakaat International Foundation v. Council of the European Union and Commission of the European Communities* (2008) ECRI-6351, para 59.
302 Except where these violate jus cogens. The CFI concluded that fundamental rights as protected by jus cogens have not been infringed. Kadi CFI judgment, paras 212–31, 233–91.
303 *Kadi* (2008), above n 301, para 288.
304 Ibid., para 304.
305 Ibid., para 285.
306 Ibid., para 305. Also see Armin Cuyvers, '"Give Me One Good Reason": The Unified Standard of Review for Sanctions after Kadi II' 51(6) *Common Market Law Review* (2014), footnote 14.

which the object of environmental protection has primacy would support the argument that China cannot legally sign away its right under Article XX during the accession negotiations, at least not in a silent manner.

The AB, however, has never established such a hierarchy of norms. Although the panel held in *China—Rare Earths* that an interpretation of WTO law according to which WTO members were legally prevented from taking measures necessary to protect the environment could be inconsistent with the object and purpose of WTO law, and that such a result could also be 'manifestly absurd or unreasonable',[307] which seems to suggest that environmental protection is one of the fundamental values under WTO law, this perspective has not been confirmed by the AB. On the contrary, the WTO has 'no constitutional court, no constitutional convention, and no constitutional drafting process',[308] and while scholars have articulated at least three approaches to WTO constitutionalism,[309] the use of constitutional analogies in analysing the WTO has not met with universal approval.[310] Thus, the AB is unlikely to prioritise the object of environmental protection in WTO law explicitly. Alternatively, the following discussion assesses the feasibility of the AB implicitly prioritising the object of environmental protection under WTO law as part of overriding principles.

7.4.1.2. Implicitly prioritising the object of environmental protection

Although the AB has not attempted to categorise various types of norms as constitutional or non-constitutional,[311] it does in practice treat certain norms differently from others in adopting a more teleological approach. Thus, to return to a useful example, it adopted in the *US—Shrimp* case an evolutionary interpretation that broadened the scope of 'natural resources' under Article XX(g) with reference to the environmental concerns articulated in the preamble.[312]

307 Panel Reports, *China – Measures Related to the Exportation of Rare Earths, Tungsten, and Molybdenum*, WT/DS431/R and Add.1 / WT/DS432/R and Add.1 / WT/DS433/R and Add.1, adopted 29 August 2014, upheld by AB Reports WT/DS431/AB/R / WT/DS432/AB/R / WT/DS433/AB/R, DSR 2014:IV, para 7.111.

308 Jeffrey L. Dunoff, 'Constitutional Conceits: The WTO's "Constitution" and the Discipline of International Law', 17(3) *European Journal of International Law* (2006), at 650.

309 Ibid., at 651. The three approaches include constitution as institutional architecture, constitution as normative commitment, and constitution as judicial mediation. The first approach highlights the institutional design of the WTO's constitution and posits that the constitution serves to efficiently resolve disputes between states. The second approach understands the constitution as a set of normative commitments to values such as individual freedom and the rule of law. The last approach focuses on the role of the judiciary in gradually constructing a package of constitutional norms through dispute resolution.

310 Ibid.

311 Isabelle Van Damme, 'Treaty Interpretation by the WTO AB', 21(3) *European Journal of International Law* (2010), at 644.

312 AB Report, *US—Shrimp*, paras 129–131.

Another example of a more teleological approach can be found in the AB's interpretation in the same case concerning the acceptance of *amicus curiae* briefs, which non-state actors have submitted in attempts to participate in WTO dispute settlement proceedings. According to Article 13 of the DSU, panels have the right to 'seek' information from any relevant source, including non-state actors; in *US—Shrimp*, the panel refused to consider several *amicus curiae* briefs on the grounds that it had not sought them.[313] On appeal, however, the AB explicitly rejected the panel's conclusion;[314] referring to the object and purpose of the panel's mandate under Article 11 of the DSU, the AB interpreted the term 'seek' to include accepting even briefs that had not been requested by the panel.[315] From a constitutional perspective, the AB chose an active fact-finding procedure in order to preserve the legitimacy of the WTO dispute-settlement proceedings.[316]

Compared with the two examples relating to *US—Shrimp*, however, the silence regarding the applicability of Article XX to China's export duty commitments would require the AB to give much greater weight to the environmental issues raised in the Preamble to the WTO Agreement if it were to support China's right. Such a teleological approach can in fact be discerned in a series of decisions by the AB regarding zeroing, a calculation methodology employed in the context of anti-dumping efforts that is not explicitly prohibited by the WTO.

Specifically, during an anti-dumping investigation, the level of anti-dumping duties is assessed based on the dumping margin, which refers to the gap between domestic and export prices. A positive dumping margin describes instances in which an export price exceeds a domestic price, and a negative dumping margin describes those in which the latter exceed the former. Since a product under investigation usually consists of various sub-products, its overall dumping margin is estimated as the sum of the dumping margins of the various individual sub-products, which may include both positive and negative margins. The zeroing methodology, however, ignores the negative dumping margin, in effect inflating the overall dumping margin for the product under investigation.

Thus, in *EC—Audio Cassettes*, Japan complained that the zeroing practice of the European Communities was inconsistent with 'fair comparison' under Article 2 of the Tokyo Round Anti-Dumping Code because it inflated dumping margins in this manner.[317] This argument was rejected by the panel, which opined that Article 2 concerned only those circumstances in which domestic prices exceed

313 Panel Report, *US—Shrimp*, para. 7.8.

314 AB Report, *US—Shrimp*, para 110.

315 But the panel still had the discretionary authority to reject them. AB Report, *US—Shrimp*, para 108.

316 Deborah Z. Cass, 'The "Constitutionalization" of International Trade Law: Judicial Norm-generation as the Engine of Constitutional Development in International Trade', 12(1) *European Journal of International Law* (2001), at 61. This interpretation is opposed by a large number of WTO members in a subsequent case and in practice the panel and the AB only address the amicus brief which is appended to a party's submission. Arguably, this undermines the constitutional arguments provided by Cass. See Dunoff (2006), above n 308, at 660.

317 Panel Report, *EC—Audio Cassettes*, para 115.

export prices and that nothing in it prevented the European Communities from adopting its own zeroing practice.[318] In other words, since Article 2 was silent on situations in which export prices exceed domestic prices, WTO members were free to exclude the negative dumping margin from anti-dumping investigations. Article 2 of the Tokyo Round Anti-Dumping Code now appears in Article 2 of the Agreement on Implementation of Article VI of the GATT 1994 (the 'Anti-Dumping Agreement').

Based on Article 2, the AB in the *EC–Bed Linen* case made a surprising departure from the *EC—Audio Cassettes* decision by holding that, because the zeroing methodology would indeed generate unfair results, it was therefore inconsistent with 'fair comparison' under the article,[319] which was exactly the position put forward by Japan and rejected by the panel in *EC—Audio Cassettes.* From a constitutional perspective, this hermeneutical shift reflects the AB's concern regarding the negative effects of the increasingly common practice of zeroing on 'the very *telos* of the WTO (free trade)'.[320]

In a series of subsequent cases, the AB held the zeroing methodology to be illegal in the context of, not only the original investigation, but also the administrative review process.[321] In the *US—Continued Zeroing* case, the AB faced a challenge in interpreting Article 17.6(ii) of the Anti-Dumping Agreement, a provision that regulates situations in which the panel has found that the agreement 'admits of more than one permissible interpretation'. According to this article, WTO members can choose 'one of those permissible interpretations', a strict textual analysis of which was likely to support the position of the US that 'dumping may be determined for individual export transactions'.[322] In order to avoid validating the zeroing methodology, the AB therefore employed a teleological interpretation that prioritised the first sentence of Article 17.6(ii).[323]

This zeroing jurisprudence, however, was met with harsh criticism on the grounds that it represented judicial activism. The US, for instance, at one point described the invalidation of zeroing as 'making up rules that the United States never negotiated'.[324] Several attempts to reach a compromise between the jurisprudence and the opposition of the US also failed in the WTO.[325] This being the case, when it comes to China's export duties, even if the AB were to understand environmental protection to be the very *telos* of the WTO, it would still be extremely cautious in employing an approach similar to that employed in the zeroing jurisprudence.

318 Ibid., para 350.
319 AB Report, *EC—Bed Linen*, para 59.
320 Sungjoon Cho, 'Global Constitutional Lawmaking', 31(3) *University of Pennsylvania Journal of International Law* (2014), at 23.
321 Ibid., at 13–18.
322 Panel Report, *US—Continued Zeroing*, para 7.162.
323 Cho (2014), above n 320, at 21.
324 Communication from the United States, 'Offsets for Non-Dumped Comparisons', 2, TN/RL/W/208, 5 June 2007.
325 Cho (2014), above n 320, at 23.

Further, a more teleological approach in light of the environmental context of the Preamble to the WTO Agreement would also require the AB to depart explicitly from its prior decisions, which, again, it has never done. As an alternative, the following discussion accordingly seeks an interpretation that would enable the AB to depart *implicitly* from the *China—Raw Materials* and *China—Rare Earths* decisions.

7.4.2. A new interpretation that distinguishes the China—Raw Materials and China—Rare Earths decisions

While various new interpretations have been proposed to repeal the *China—Raw Materials* and *China—Rare Earths* decisions, the feasibility for the AB to amend these decisions by employing the option of distinguishing has not been addressed.[326] In *Indonesia—Import Licensing Regimes*, the AB was requested to decide whether a panel should always follow the sequence of two-tiered analysis under Article XX. By distinguishing the normal situations and the 'particular circumstances' in which a panel might be able to analyse the elements under the applicable paragraphs that were relevant to assess the requirements of the chapeau without following the 'normal sequence', the AB narrowed the scope to apply the 'normal sequence' of two-tiered analysis that was established by the AB itself in *US—Gasoline*. This example raises the question of whether the scope to apply the *China—Raw Materials* and *China—Rare Earths* decisions could be limited to the extent that provides China with policy space to protect the environment.

As discussed in Chapter 4, the EU, one of the complainants in all three cases against China's export duties, once proposed a WTO agreement to restrict the use of export duties in the context of the Doha Development Agenda's negotiations on non-agricultural market access,[327] but in that instance it did not propose an absolute prohibition on export duties. Rather, the EU acknowledged their legitimate application in the context of 'financial crises, infant industry, environment (preservation of natural resources), and local short supply'.[328] In a broader context, then, when WTO members have sought to restrict the use of export duties through regional trade agreements, contracting parties have often been provided with exceptions under which their use is permitted.[329] By addressing the environmental issues associated with what China views as an extreme stance against its export duties, the AB could draw a clear line between protectionist export duties and those adopted for an environmental purpose.

326 See Chapter 3.

327 ICTSD, 'WTO Legal Status and Evolving Practice of Export Taxes', available at http://www.ictsd.org/bridges-news/bridges/news/wto-legal-status-and-evolving-practice-of-export-taxes (visited on 18 June 2017).

328 The European Communities, *Revised Submission on Export Taxes*, TN/MA/W/101, 17 January 2008, para 4(1).

329 Jane Korinek and Jessica Bartos, 'Multilateralising Regionalism: Disciplines on Export Restrictions in Regional Trade Agreements', No. 139 OECD Trade Policy Papers (2012).

In terms of its scope, Paragraph 11.3 regulates 'all taxes and charges applied to exports' except fees that are strictly related to the approximate costs of services rendered under GATT Article VIII. This broad notion is further defined in Paragraph 155 of China's Accession Working Party Report as 'taxes and charges applied exclusively to exports'. The term 'exclusively' here seems to suggest that Paragraph 11.3 excludes situations in which taxes and charges are not applied exclusively to exports. Such situations could, however, be regulated under Paragraph 170 of China's Accession Working Party Report, which states that 'China would ensure that its laws and regulations relating to all fees, charges or taxes levied on imports and exports would be in full conformity with its WTO obligations' under a section titled 'Taxes and Charges Levied on Imports and Exports'.

As the AB held in *China—Raw Materials*, Paragraph 170 is concerned with internal taxes that affect imports and exports, such as value-added taxes, which differ from the export duty commitments under Paragraph 155. Following this interpretation, China's commitments regarding taxes levied on exports can be classified into one or the other of two groups. The first includes taxes applied exclusively to exports, which are regulated by Paragraph 11.3 and, according to the AB's rulings in *China—Raw Materials* and *China—Rare Earths*, cannot be justified under GATT Article XX. The second group includes taxes that do not apply exclusively to exports, which are regulated by Paragraph 170, a provision concerned with internal taxes.

This distinction provides grounds for a new interpretation that departs implicitly from the prior decisions over China's export duties. The reason is that, since Paragraph 170 refers explicitly to Article III:2 of the GATT, which requires that internal taxes treat imported and domestic products equally, it can be argued that this national treatment requirement also applies to taxes on exported and domestically consumed products.

A violation of this extended requirement under Article III:2, however, could be justified under GATT Article XX. This distinction between export duties and internal taxes that affect exports is further supported by a report by the Havana Conference indicating that one of the criteria for making this distinction is whether 'they apply exclusively to imported products without being related in any way to similar charges collected internally on like domestic products',[330] language similar to that of Paragraph 155.

This distinction is important for providing China with policy space to use export duties for an environmental purpose. For from an economic perspective, export duties may encourage domestic sales, and this is 'an undesirable consequence for a policy designed to further environmental goals'.[331] In this context, taxes applied exclusively to exports, as absolutely prohibited by Paragraph 11.3, are by nature not likely to be helpful in the pursuit of an environmental goal, which is more likely to be achieved when export duties are adopted in conjunction with corresponding restrictions on domestic consumption. This being the case, it may be

330 Havana Report, para 42.
331 Panel Reports, *China—Rare Earths*, para 7.169.

wondered whether an export duty as defined in Paragraph 11.3 that had been adopted in conjunction with an internal tax, such as a consumption tax, would thereby constitute an internal tax under Paragraph 170.

A textual analysis of Paragraphs 155 and 170 suggests that export duties and internal taxes are closely related. The former, which regulate the use of export duties, fall under a section titled 'Customs Tariffs, Fees and Charges for Services Rendered, *Application of Internal Taxes to Exports*' (emphasis added). By contrast, Paragraph 170, which regulates the use of internal taxes affecting exports, falls under a section titled 'Taxes and Charges Levied on Imports and Exports'. The correlation between the titles of these two sections suggests that export duties may indeed be understood to constitute internal taxes that affect exports, at least under certain circumstances.

This interpretation is admittedly inconsistent with the traditional definition of internal taxes in the context of WTO jurisprudence. There are two decisive criteria for distinguishing import duties from internal taxes according to the AB's holding in the *China—Auto Parts* case. First, for a charge on a product to constitute an ordinary customs duty, the obligation to pay it must accrue the moment the product enters a particular customs territory (rather than when it is sold in a particular market).[332] Second, for a charge on a product to constitute an internal tax under GATT Article III:2, the obligation to pay must accrue owing to an internal factor (e.g., because the product was re-sold or used domestically).[333] Following these criteria, export duties do not constitute internal taxes, regardless of the existence of corresponding charges on domestic consumption, because the obligation to pay them accrues at the moment of export and because the motivation for the obligation is to enable the products at issue to leave a particular territory rather than to be sold within it.

This traditional definition of internal taxes, however, may ignore the distinction between those that affect imports and those that affect exports. To achieve a protectionist purpose with regard to imports, a country must impose higher charges on imported products than it does on like domestic products. Thus, for instance, a Korean tax on imported distilled alcoholic beverages that exceeded the tax on the traditional national drink, soju, was found to be inconsistent with GATT Article III:2.[334] In contrast, a country that seeks to achieve a protectionist purpose with regard to exports must impose higher charges on exported industrial inputs than on domestically consumed industrial inputs if it is to be successful. This protectionist purpose, however, cannot be achieved by means of internal taxes in the traditional sense because such taxes in practice fail to distinguish between products that are exported and those that are consumed domestically.

In this context, it would be pointless for China, by reading Paragraph 170 together with GATT Article III:2, to agree not to impose internal taxes that treat

332 AB Report, *China—Auto Parts*, para 158.
333 Ibid., paras 162–163.
334 AB Report, *Korea – Taxes on Alcoholic Beverages*, WT/DS75/AB/R, WT/DS84/AB/R, adopted 17 February 1999, DSR 1999:I.

exported and domestically consumed products differently. As the AB held in *Japan—Alcoholic Beverages II*, the aim of Article III:2 is to 'avoid protectionism in the application of internal tax'.[335] In order to make China's commitment under Paragraph 170 more meaningful, this provision could be used to regulate instances of protectionism in which export duties are adopted in conjunction with similar but lower charges on domestic consumption, in contrast with situations in which charges are 'applied *exclusively* to exports' (emphasis added) as regulated by Paragraph 155.

Following this interpretation, if China's export duties were adopted in isolation, they would be regulated by Paragraphs 155 and 11.3, a situation that could not be justified under GATT Article XX. Such an interpretation would not constrain China's policy space to protect the environment because the environmental purpose of the export duties would have to be achieved by imposing corresponding charges on domestic consumption, as described in Paragraph 170 and Article III:2, provisions requiring China to impose charges on exported and domestically consumed products in a non-discriminatory manner. If China's intent were to impose higher charges (by way of export duties) on exported than on domestically consumed products in the pursuit of an environmental goal, Article XX could be invoked to determine whether such discrimination would be justified.

This interpretation is of importance in combating carbon leakage, a problem caused by discrepancies in the climate policies that have been adopted in various countries. In order to equalise the prices of energy-intensive products from China with those from countries that have adopted stricter climate measures, duties could be applied to exports of Chinese products. Since many of the energy-intensive products are final products, an increase in prices on the former would not provide support for Chinese industry, such support having been a major concern of the complaining governments in the *China—Raw Materials* and *China—Rare Earths* cases. Admittedly, the imposition of export duties on energy-intensive raw materials, even in conjunction with similar charges on domestic consumption, could still provide Chinese industry with preferential access to these resources. Such discrimination could, however, be addressed by Article XX, which provides fairly strict tests for protectionist measures, as will be discussed in the next chapter.

Aside from preserving China's policy space for combating climate change, this new interpretation could also forestall future disputes regarding its export duties. For the fact is that, following the *China—Raw Materials* and *China—Rare Earths* decisions, China has nevertheless continued to impose export duties on certain products, behaviour that has led the EU and US to bring a third case, namely *China—Raw Materials II*, before the WTO. To some extent, China's persistence in this regard has been provoked by the extreme stance of the complaining governments and the contested outcomes of the *China—Raw Materials* and *China—Rare Earths* decisions. In this context, should the AB continue to support the complaining governments, China would still not be persuaded to abandon its export duties completely. Alternatively, the AB could send a clear message

335 AB Report, *Japan—Alcoholic Beverages II*, at 16.

regarding the proper use of export duties—that is, in a less protectionist manner. China would then need to counterbalance export duties with similar charges on domestic consumption in order to be compliant with Article XX, a provision that would make it difficult for the country to evade its export duty commitments, especially since it currently imposes consumption taxes on only 14 products apart from those at issue in *China—Raw Materials II.* [336]

In short, the analysis presented in this section shows that the AB is unlikely to accept a teleological approach informed by the environmental context in the Preamble to the WTO Agreement. It is instead more likely to accept an interpretation that draws a line between export duties of the sort at issue in the two previous cases, which exclusively restrict the exports, and 'export duties plus' that are adopted in combination with supplementary restrictions on domestic consumption. Following this line of reasoning, the AB would not need to depart from its prior decisions explicitly in order to accommodate both the trade values articulated in Paragraph 11.3 and the environmental values articulated in the Preamble to the WTO Agreement. Moreover, as in the case of the *Keck* proviso, this option would also provide guidance regarding a proper, which is to say less protectionist, way to impose export duties. Although this interpretation would still require the AB to go beyond its preferred strict textual approach, it represents the best among a number of unappealing paths by which the AB could surmount the difficulties created by the *China—Raw Materials* and *China—Rare Earths* decisions. Alternatively, the AB could also distinguish export duties from those enacted for the purpose of combating climate change, a move that would certainly provide China with the requisite policy space. Such a move would also, however, send the unwelcome message that China cannot use export duties to address domestic concerns until those concerns threaten the rest of the world. This distinction is, therefore, less desirable than the one between regular export duties and 'export duties plus'.

It is noteworthy that the options of distinguishing or overruling only constitute the judicial way to alter the ban on China's export duties. This outcome could also be achieved by political intervention. This approach has a broader scope of application than the judicial way because it could prevent not only the wrong outcomes caused by a bad precedent but also those caused by bad law. To solve the problem in the latter situation is usually beyond the power of a tribunal which thus tends to not rule against the text of law in order to avoid the charge of judicial lawmaking.[337] Moreover, given the AB's membership crisis, admittedly, it is probably not the best time to rely on a judicial approach. The next two sections explore the feasibility for a political solution.

336 *Regulation on Consumption Taxes*, the State Council, No.539.

337 One of the exceptional cases is the *Les Verts* in which the Court read into Article 173 EEC (the current Article 263 TFEU) a right to bring a case for annulment against binding acts of the European Parliament though the treaty text only refers to acts of the Council and the Commission. By contrast, the ECJ explicitly refused to de facto alter the text of 263 TFEU in the *Unión de Pequeños Agricultores v. Council* (UPA). Case 294/83 *'Les Verts' v. European Parliament* [1986] ECR 1339.

7.5. Possible ways to alter the WTO ban through a political correction

The WTO Agreement gives great power to the decision-making body, which consists of the Ministerial Conference and the General Council. The former, as the organisation's most authoritative body, has the power to settle all matters involving any of the multilateral trade agreements;[338] since it normally meets only every other year, however, day-to-day business is conducted by the latter.[339] As mentioned, various solutions have been proposed in which China would request that the decision-making body adopt an amendment, a waiver, or an authoritative interpretation reversing the *China—Raw Materials* and *China—Rare Earths* decisions. The theoretical possibilities of these solutions are examined in this section.

First, it is theoretically possible to change the outcome of the *China—Raw Materials* and *China—Rare Earths* decisions through an amendment of China's accession protocol by, for instance, incorporating GATT Article XX into Paragraph 11.3.[340] One may worry that there is no legal basis in the WTO Agreement for amending an accession protocol because neither Article XII, a provision dealing with accessions, nor Article X, a provision dealing with amendments, specifies the procedure to amend the terms agreed in a protocol.[341] It is noteworthy, however, Paragraph 1.2 in China's accession protocol clearly states that this protocol 'shall be *an integral part* of the WTO Agreement'.[342] Although there has been a considerable academic debate as to whether a protocol of accession can self-declare itself to be part of another agreement, i.e., the WTO Agreement,[343] such an objection has never been raised in practice. The disputes regarding China's accession protocol have been actually proceeded on the assumption that this protocol is part of the WTO Agreement based on the integration clause of Paragraph 1.2.[344] These facts seem to suggest that China's export duty

338 Article IV:1 of the WTO Agreement. Two plurilateral agreements set out in Annex 4 to the WTO Agreement are subject to different rules according to Article IV:8 of the WTO Agreement.

339 WTO Secretariat, 'The WTO General Council', https://www.wto.org/english/thewto_e/gcounc_e/gcounc_e.htm (visited on 18 June 2017).

340 Ying Liu, 'The Applicability of Environmental Protection Exceptions to WTO-Plus Obligations: In View of the *China – Raw Materials* and *China – Rare Earths* Cases', 27(1) *Leiden Journal of International Law* (2014).

341 This may explain why some authors did not even discuss the possibility of amending China' accession protocol while proposing a change of that protocol. They instead advocated the negotiation of a new plurilateral agreement. See Petros C. Mavroidis and André Sapir, 'China and the World Trade Organisation: Towards a Better Fit', Bruegel Working Paper Issue 6, 11 June 2019, https://bruegel.org/2019/06/china-and-the-world-trade-organisation-towards-a-better-fit/ (visited on 10 September 2019).

342 Paragraph 1.2 of China's Protocol of Accession.

343 For a more recent overview, see Dylan Geraets, *Accession to the World Trade Organization: A Legal Analysis* (Edward Elgar, 2018).

344 AB Report, *China—Rare Earths*, para 5.19, footnote 422. 'We note that this proposition has not been contested either in the present disputes or in any prior dispute involving China's Accession Protocol. In addition, we take note of the Panel's

commitments could be amended following the general procedural rules under Article X of the WTO Agreement.

Under these ordinary rules, 'any Member' may submit a proposal for an amendment to the Ministerial Conference, which then has 90 days to try to reach a consensus on it.[345] If no consensus is forthcoming, the Conference may decide, by a two-thirds majority vote, to submit the proposal to the WTO membership for acceptance. While an amendment takes effect once two-thirds of members have ratified it,[346] it is not binding on those that have not. The amendment process is thus complex and likely time-consuming.[347] To simplify this process, an alternative procedure has been suggested that consider China's accession protocol as a bilateral treaty between the acceding country and the WTO as an organisation.[348] A mutual consent of China and of the WTO is thus needed to amend China's accession protocol. The consent of the latter one generally takes decisions by consensus or, failing that, by simple majority.[349] Compared with the aforementioned ordinary procedure, this alternative option certainly looks more efficient because it does not require further acceptance by WTO members. On the other hand, it also allows the membership to take a decision with the least formality and a simple majority that possibly counts China. An obvious disadvantage of this alternative, however, is that the WTO membership at large may not accept this unusual legal construct.

Second, it is also theoretically possible to have a political correction through a waiver under Article IX:3 of the WTO Agreement. This may provide China with a legal defence to a claim for breach of its export duty commitments. The panel in *EC—Bananas III*, for instance, held that, although the tariff preferences at issue in the case were inconsistent with GATT Article I:1, the EU could use the Lomé Waiver as a defence to a claim that Article I:1 had been violated.[350] By analogy, China could request a waiver permitting it to impose export duties for environmental purposes.

In seeking a waiver of its export duty commitments, China must first request that the Council for Trade in Goods[351] consider its specific policy objectives and

statement that, in all prior cases involving China's Accession Protocol, panels and the Appellate Body "have proceeded on the assumption" that Paragraph 1.2 serves, inter alia, the function of making the obligations in China's Accession Protocol enforceable under the DSU'.

345 The Ministerial Conference must receive a proposal for an amendment by a Member or one of the three specialized Councils.

346 Article X:7 of the WTO Agreement.

347 It took almost 12 years after the proposal was adopted for the first amendment of a WTO agreement, TRIPS, to enter into force. For further information, see Section 7.6.

348 Julia Ya Qin, 'The Challenge of Interpreting 'WTO-PLUS' Provisions', 44 (1) *Journal of World Trade* (2010), at 134.

349 Article IX.1 of the WTO Agreement.

350 Panel Report, *European Communities – Regime for the Importation, Sale and Distribution of Bananas*, WT/DS27/R/ECU, WT/DS27/R/GTM/HND, WT/DS27/R/MEX, and WT/DS27/R/USA, paras 7.131–7.134.

351 Requests for waivers concerning the multilateral trade agreements in Annexes 1A, 1B and 1C must initially be submitted to the relevant sectoral Council.

its reasons for being unable to achieve them within the context of the commitments.[352] As Mongolia's request for a waiver of its export duty commitments regarding raw cashmere made clear,[353] the environmental purpose of preventing 'extensive environmental damages and desertification' constitutes legitimate justification for a member's deviation from its export duty commitments.[354] Thus, the purposes of China's export duties such as fighting climate change are also likely to be recognised as legitimate justification for China to deviate from its export duty commitments. In the next step in the process, the Council for Trade in Goods must, within a period not exceeding 90 days, submit a report to the Ministerial Conference or General Council.[355] The support of three-fourths of WTO members is required for approval.[356] Although a consensus is preferred as a statement about decision-making procedures by the Chairman of the General Council under Article IX of the WTO Agreement reveals,[357] the same statement also makes clear that the preference to a consensus 'does not preclude a Member from requesting a vote'.[358] China thus could demand a vote in the absence of a consensus. This move, however, would require the WTO members to break the general taboo against formal voting.[359]

Third, an authoritative interpretation may also alter the WTO ban on China's export duties. However, compared with an amendment or waiver, this option involves more uncertainties due to its limited legal effects. Although Article IX:2 of the WTO Agreement accords to the Ministerial Conference and General Council the 'exclusive authority to adopt interpretations' of WTO agreements, the final sentence of Article IX:2 requires that an authoritative interpretation 'shall not be used in a manner that would undermine the amendment provisions of Article

352 Paragraph 3 of the Understanding in Respect of Waivers of Obligations under the General Agreement on Tariffs and Trade 1994.

353 Communication from Mongolia, 'Request for a Waiver, G/C/W/571 and G/C/W/580, 26 January 2007.

354 Ibid. G/C/W/571, at 3. Footnote 3 'Goat heads 2002 accounted to 9,134 thousand. By 2005, they grew to 13,267 thousand, or by 1.5 times those in 2002. This rapid increase in the number of goat heads caused devaluation in the quality of cashmere'.

355 Article IX:3(a) of the WTO Agreement.

356 Article IX:3 of the WTO Agreement. But waivers for extensions of transition periods or periods of staged implementation require consensus as required by footnote 4 of the WTO Agreement.

357 Statement by the Chairman as Agreed by the General Council on 15 November 1995, Decision Making Procedures under Articles IX and XII of the WTO Agreement, WT/L/93, 24 November 1995.

358 James Harrison, 'Legal and Political Oversight of WTO Waivers', 11(2) *Journal of International Economic Law* (2008), at 413.

359 An illustrative example in this regard is a 2009 call by the Egyptian ambassador for a vote to recognize Palestine as an observer; while many members supported the ambassador's effort in political terms, they valued more highly continued adherence to the general ban on voting. The Egyptian ambassador was thus persuaded to drop the matter. See Craig Van Grasstek, 'The History and Future of the World Trade Organization', *WTO Publications* (2013), at 219.

X'. Thus, if a modification of the WTO ban on China's export duties is considered to fall exclusively within the scope of an amendment, the option of an authoritative interpretation will be unavailable for China.

Moreover, only one request has yet been made for an authoritative interpretation. The very infrequency appears to suggest that authoritative interpretations are not desirable in practice.[360] One possible reason is to avoid the discussion of the demarcation line with amendments. One may thus argue that the role of authoritative interpretations in practice has been taken over by those Ministerial Decisions or Declarations under Article IV:1 (Ministerial Conference) that constitute subsequent agreements on the interpretation of a provision of a WTO agreement within the meaning of VCLT Article 31(3)(a). In this sense, China may request the Ministerial Conference to take a decision updating its accession protocol regarding the use of export duties to protect the environment as a 'fudge'.[361] The feasibility of these political corrections is discussed below.

7.6. Feasibility tests for amendments, waivers, authoritative interpretations, or Ministerial Decisions

The previous section illustrates the challenges of various political corrections. This section assesses the feasibility for China to overcome these challenges in light of WTO practice regarding the adoption of amendments, waivers, authoritative interpretations, and Ministerial Decisions.

7.6.1. Article X:1: an amendment as a formal correction

7.6.1.1. Amendments in practice

On 23 January 2017, the WTO announced an amendment to its Trade-Related Aspects of Intellectual Property Rights (TRIPS) Agreement, the first to a core WTO agreement since the organization's establishment in 1995.[362] This amendment was based on a protocol unanimously adopted by WTO members in 2005, the aim of which was to improve the access of less-affluent member states to

360 Other factors to explain the non-use of Article IX:2 of the WTO Agreement see Claus-Dieter Ehlermann and Lothar Ehring, 'The Authoritative Interpretation Under Article IX:2 of the Agreement Establishing the World Trade Organization: Current Law, Practice and Possible Improvements', 8(4) *Journal of International Economic Law* (2005), at 818.

361 For general discussion of the decision-making in the WTO, see Pieter Jan Kuijper, 'WTO Institutional Aspects', in Daniel Bethlehem, Isabelle Van Damme, Donald McRae, and Rodney Neufeld (eds.), *The Oxford Handbook of International Trade Law* (Oxford, 2009). Mary Footer, 'Principal Rule-making', in *An Institutional and Normative Analysis of the World Trade Organization* (Martinus Nijhoff, 2006).

362 WTO Secretariat, 'WTO IP Rules Amended to Ease Poor Countries' Access to Affordable Medicines', https://www.wto.org/english/news_e/news17_e/trip_23jan17_e.htm (visited on 18 June 2017). The Protocol (2001) Amending the Annex to the Agreement on Trade in Civil Aircraft amended a plurilateral agreement.

affordable generic medicines produced in other countries by creating a system of compulsory licensing for pharmaceutical products produced solely for export.[363]

Under the TRIPS Agreement, WTO members can issue compulsory licences that permit companies to make a patented product or to use a patented process under licence without the consent of the patent owner when the reason for doing so is to protect public health. This flexibility, however, extends only to the domestic market in the country in which the drugs are produced, leaving countries without the capacity to produce generic drugs unable procure them at affordable prices. In order to address this issue, WTO members in 2003 decided to waive the restriction that limited these compulsory licences to local markets.[364] Since the waivers were designed to function as temporary instruments under the WTO Agreement, the amendment to the TRIPS Agreement in effect created a permanent legal basis for dealing with issues concerning compulsory licences.

However, the permanent legal effect of the amendment comes with a price, in that, compared with the adoption of a waiver, amendment procedures are more cumbersome. For unlike waivers, amendments take legal effect only if at least two-thirds of WTO members have deposited formal instruments of acceptance with the Director-General, a process that can result in considerable delays;[365] thus it took almost 12 years for the amendment to the TRIPS Agreement to enter into force. This problem could be solved, though, if WTO members were willing to take the necessary steps. A good parallel is the process for accepting the Protocol of Amendment to insert the WTO Trade Facilitation Agreement into Annex 1A of the WTO Agreement, which the General Council completed on 27 November 2014, marking the first multilateral deal in the WTO's 21-year history; in this case, two years elapsed before the amendment received the necessary two-thirds acceptance (specifically by 110 of the 164 WTO members).[366]

Another disadvantage of amendments is that, even after one enters into force, WTO members that have not accepted it retain their rights under the agreements as originally drafted. The result is a two-tier system that undermines the effectiveness of an amendment by making it depend largely on the consent of a few key members. Thus, for example, a protocol amending Part I of the GATT 1947 was abandoned after 10 years because one contracting party was unable to obtain parliamentary approval.[367] Moreover, even if all members were eventually to accept the amendment for incorporating the new agreement, a two-tier system

363 The Protocol is attached to the General Council Decision on Amendment of the TRIPS Agreement, WT/L/641, adopted on 6 December 2005. The TRIPS Amendment itself is annexed to the Protocol.

364 General Council Decision on Implementation of Paragraph 6 of the Doha Declaration on the TRIPS Agreement and Public Health, WT/L/540 and Corr.1, adopted on 30 August 2003.

365 Article X:7 of the WTO Agreement.

366 WTO Secretariat, 'WTO's Trade Facilitation Agreement enters into force', available at https://www.wto.org/english/news_e/news17_e/fac_31jan17_e.htm (visited on 10 June).

367 BISD 15S/65.

would still exist, at least temporarily, because the length of time required for the domestic ratification process varies considerably among WTO members. For these reasons, an amendment would not serve to address an urgent issue in practice.

7.6.1.2. Feasibility to amending China's export duty commitments

The above practice of amendments shows that to amend China's export duty commitments is not an ideal option if China needs these duties to address urgent environmental issues. Alternatively, it has been argued that China's accession protocol could be seen as a bilateral treaty between China and the WTO.[368]

In this scenario, Article IX (Decision-Making) or Article XII (Accession) should apply. Either way, once the WTO as a contracting party agrees to amend China's export duty commitments, no such further formal acceptance as ratification by individual WTO members would be required. This would allow the membership to take a decision with the least formality and thus increase efficiency. More importantly, if a consensus is not achieved, a majority of the votes cast under Article IX or a two-thirds majority for approval under Article XII would be sufficient to amend China's export duty commitments. Such a decision would be binding on all WTO members.[369] The challenge is, however, that WTO members may prefer not to break the general taboo against formal voting. Moreover, this alternative reading of the existing relationship between China's accession protocol and the WTO Agreement also comes with a considerable degree of uncertainty because neither Article X (Amendments) nor Article XII specifies the procedure for amendments to an accession protocol.[370]

A much more conventional view would perhaps treat China's accession protocol as part of the WTO Agreement. Article X thus should apply. As discussed in the previous section, the effectiveness of any amendment designed to create a desirable policy space for China under this provision would be undermined if China could not get the support from all WTO members. The reason is that an amendment only takes effect on those that have ratified it. Thus, China would be unable to invoke Article XX to justify its export duties during any litigation with the members that are unwilling to ratify it.

As revealed in the *China—Raw Materials*, *China—Rare Earths*, and *China—Raw Materials II* cases, the extreme stance of the complaining governments in denying China's right to use export duties under Article XX shows that these members are accordingly unlikely to support an amendment that contradicts their claims in the three cases. Moreover, several third parties that had supported the claims of the complainants in the earlier cases would be similarly unlikely to agree to any such amendment. Since the unfriendly members number among China's

368 Qin (2010), above n 348, at 134.
369 Ibid.
370 Qin thus proposed to add a special procedure to Article X. See Julia Ya Qin, 'The Conundrum of WTO Accession Protocols: In Search of Legality and Legitimacy', 55 (2), *Virginia Journal of International Law* (2015).

major export destinations,[371] the effectiveness of an amendment option would be greatly undermined.

The issue concerning the effectiveness of the amendment could alternatively be addressed through a waiver releasing WTO members from certain legal obligations under the WTO agreements.[372] In the aforementioned case of the amendment to the TRIPS Agreement, members that have not accepted the amendment can refer to the 2003 waiver decision regarding access to affordable medicines from a third country. The following discussion explores the feasibility of a waiver as a stopgap measure that would allow China to use export duties under certain circumstances.

7.6.2. Article IX:3: a waiver as a stopgap measure

7.6.2.1. Waivers in practice

WTO members rely more heavily on waivers than amendments as a means to deviate from agreed-upon trade disciplines. Thus, while only two amendments have been approved since the organization's establishment in 1995,[373] in 2017 alone the General Council granted eight waivers.[374] An individual WTO member may request suspension of its obligations in this way for two main reasons.[375] One is to address capacity problems in complying with WTO commitments, examples being waivers that extended transitional periods for implementing obligations under the Customs Valuation Agreement, the Individual Harmonized System waiver decisions, and the waivers of Cuba's obligation under GATT Article XV:6, which required any contracting party that ceased to be a member of the International Monetary Fund (IMF) to enter into a special exchange agreement with the WTO.[376]

Another major reason is to accommodate policy conflicts, that is, to retain a WTO-inconsistent measure in the furtherance of specific policy objectives. Rather than addressing the incapacity of a WTO member, this type of waiver relieves a

371 In 2015, the top export destinations of China are the United States ($457B), Hong Kong ($273B), Japan ($152B), Germany ($97.4B) and South Korea ($90.1B).

372 ACWL, 'Giving Legal Effect to the Results of the Doha Round: An Analysis of the Methods of Changing WTO Law', Background Paper for ACWL Members and LDCs (2006), at 9.

373 Introduction of Harmonized System 2002 changes to WTO schedules of tariff concessions; Introduction of Harmonized System 2007 changes to WTO schedules of tariff concessions; Introduction of Harmonized System 2012 changes into WTO schedules of tariff concessions; Introduction of Harmonized System 2017 changes to WTO schedules of tariff concessions; Former Trust Territory of the Pacific Islands; Trade Preferences granted to Nepal; Application of autonomous preferential treatment to the Western Balkans; Article XV:6 – Extension of waiver.

374 WTO Secretariat, The WTO 2018 Annual Report, 31 May 2018.

375 Isabel Feichtner, *The Law and Politics of WTO Waivers: Stability and Flexibility in Public International Law* (Cambridge University Press, 2012), at 52.

376 Request for an extension of the waiver concerning Article XV:6 of the GATT 1994, WT/L/100, 12 December 2016.

member of an obligation that has impeded the achievement of certain objectives, examples being waivers that permit trade-related investment measures, that render compliance with specific commitments unnecessary, and that allow for protectionist measures, residual quantitative restrictions, tariff surcharges, and market integration. Relevant in the context of China's export duties is Mongolia's request in 2007 for a five-year waiver of its export duty commitments regarding raw cashmere.[377] For Mongolia, export duties could contribute to improve the competitiveness of local cashmere industry and to address 'environmental concerns as the increase in exports of raw cashmere has encouraged the growth of goat herds that now surpass the sustainability of the country's pasture lands'.[378] In the same year, the Council for Trade in Goods approved Mongolia's request.

Waivers can be adopted for the benefit of groups of members as well, in which case they are referred to as 'collective waivers'.[379] WTO members have generally adopted such waivers in the pursuit of three major objectives. One is to defer compliance with WTO obligation, a good example being the 2002 suspension of the obligations of least developed country members with respect to pharmaceutical products under Article 70.9 of the TRIPS Agreement until 1 January 2016.[380] The waiver of this obligation was part of a package of measures intended to mitigate the obligations that the TRIPS Agreement impose on developing countries and that affect their capacity to ensure affordable healthcare for their populations.

The second major objective of collective waivers is to modify existing WTO rules. For instance, unlike the 2002 TRIPS waiver decision just discussed, the 2003 TRIPS waiver released any least developed country member and any other WTO member that had notified the TRIPS Council from the requirements that normally restrict the use of compulsory licensing with respect to pharmaceutical products. Another example of this type of waiver is the GATT practice of permitting preferential tariff treatment in accordance with the General System of Preferences as agreed upon in UNCTAD as well as preferential trade arrangements among developing countries, which were later replaced by the Enabling Clause and now form a permanent part of the GATT 1994.[381]

A third major objective in adopting collective waivers is to coordinate WTO rules with other international legal regimes. Thus, for instance, the collective Harmonized System (HS) waivers mentioned above have been adopted in order to suspend GATT Article II for WTO members that have implemented changes to

377 Communication from Mongolia, 'Request for a Waiver, G/C/W/571 and G/C/W/580, 26 January 2007.
378 WTO Secretariat, 'Goods Council approves waivers for Mongolia, US', available at https://www.wto.org/english/news_e/news07_e/good_counc_9july07_e.htm (visited on 10 June 2018).
379 Feichtner (2012), above n 375, at 124.
380 Article 70.9 of the TRIPS Agreement: to grant exclusive marketing rights to pharmaceutical products.
381 Generalized System of Preferences, Decision of 25 June 1971, L/3545, 28 June 1971. Trade Negotiations Among Developing Countries, Decision of 26 November 1971, L/3636, 30 November 1971.

the Harmonized Commodity Description and Coding System in their domestic tariffs but require additional time to adapt their GATT schedules of concessions accordingly.[382] More specifically, most WTO members cannot completely adapt these schedules to HS changes before those changes are able to take effect on account of the administrative complexity involved and the need for tariff renegotiations.[383] An HS collective waiver can, then, legalise the domestic implementation of HS changes before those changes have been made to the schedules of concessions; otherwise, the changes could be inconsistent with the prohibition under GATT Article II of a change in a domestic tariff that negatively impacts tariff reduction commitments.

Instructive here as well is the collective waiver legalising trade measures that were mandated under the 2002 Kimberley Process Certification Scheme for Rough Diamonds, the aim of which was to suppress trade in so-called blood diamonds. The measure at issue, under which participants in the scheme could neither import rough diamonds from nor export them to non-participants, had the potential to violate several WTO obligations, including the obligation to grant most-favoured-nation treatment under GATT Article I:1, the prohibition on quantitative restrictions under Article XI:1, and the requirement that quantitative restrictions be non-discriminatory under Article XIII:1. To avoid the norm conflict, a waiver was granted by the General Council on 15 May 2003 that suspended Articles I:1, XI:1, and XIII:1 retroactively from the date on which the scheme was launched until 31 December 2006.[384]

Waivers, admittedly, have one major disadvantage that amendments do not, namely that they are granted only on a time-bound basis and can be modified or terminated by a simple majority of WTO members during annual reviews. For this reason, WTO members seeking a permanent and definitive reduction of their obligations cannot rely on waivers alone. It is noteworthy, however, that the 2003 TRIPS waiver decision did not specify a termination date as required by Article IX:4 of the WTO Agreement but rather stated that the waiver would terminate for each member when the amendment replacing the decision took effect. This practice speaks to the role of waivers as an interim instrument in the pursuit of a permanent suspension of obligations through the adoption of an amendment, which might shed light on how to permanently allow China to use export duties for environmental purposes under WTO law.

382 Up to the end of 2010, 26 collective Harmonized System waivers (including extension decisions) have been adopted by the WTO General Council. Collective waivers see the Secretariat, Committee on Market Access, Situation of Schedules of WTO Members, G/MA/W/23/Rev. 6, 19 March 2009.

383 Feichtner (2012), above n 375, at 149.

384 General Council, Decision of 15 May 2003, WT/L/518, 27 May 2003. The waiver decision was extended until 31 December 2012 by a second decision of 15 December 2006. General Council, Waiver Concerning Kimberley Process Certification Scheme for Rough Diamonds, Decision of 15 December 2006, WT/L/676, 19 December 2006.

7.6.2.2. Feasibility to waive China's export duty commitments

The above practice of waivers shows that this instrument could be a feasible option for China to address urgent environmental issues. Moreover, since a waiver is a more temporary exception than an amendment, the consensus requirement, as discussed in the previous section, may be met more easily than is the case with the approval of an amendment for reasons as follows.

Articles IX:3 and IX:4 of the WTO Agreement stipulate that a waiver should be granted in exceptional circumstances and that any such decision should specify the conditions to which it applies and the date on which it is to expire. WTO members could, then, in order to prevent China from misusing Article XX for an industrial purpose, set conditions stricter than the article itself by permitting export duties to be imposed only in conjunction with identical or at least similar restrictions on domestic consumption. In this way, China's domestic industry is less likely to receive preferable access to raw materials, an outcome that has been a major concern in regard to the three cases challenging its export duties.

More importantly, any waiver granted for a period of more than a year is, as alluded to earlier, subject to annual review, in the context of which WTO members have the opportunity to determine whether the exceptional circumstances justifying it persist. Thus, if a simple majority of members were to conclude that a prohibition on export duties has not been or is no longer a cause of environmental concern in China, any relevant waiver could be modified or allowed to expire.[385] These procedures regarding the approval and monitoring of waivers may help China to convince other members to allow the use of export duties in exceptional circumstances, such as for the purpose of tackling carbon leakage.

Alternatively, China could offer a political package deal in which export duties and other, unrelated items are combined in a manner sufficiently attractive to members who have opposed its imposition of the duties. In this context, the waiver at issue could function as an enforcement mechanism to ensure China's compliance with the other commitments are included in the package deal. As a further alternative means to obtain recognition of its right the use of export duties to combat climate change, China could request a collective waiver allowing for the adoption of WTO-inconsistent measures with reference to the exceptional circumstances created by climate change.[386] One the one hand, an import border tax adjustment on carbon-intensive products, for instance, especially those varying in terms of the carbon intensity of their production, could violate GATT Article I (regarding the most favoured nation), Article II (non-tariff duties or charges), or Article III (national treatment).[387] On the other hand, an export rebate that returns any carbon taxes paid in connection with domestic production could

385 Article IX:4 of the WTO Agreement.

386 James Bacchus, 'The Case for a WTO Climate Waiver', Centre for International Governance Innovation Special Report, 2 November 2017.

387 Joel P. Trachtman, 'WTO Law Constraints on Border Tax Adjustment and Tax Credit Mechanisms to Reduce the Competitive Effects of Carbon Taxes', RFF Discussion Paper 16–3 (2016).

render it an export subsidy, something prohibited under the SCM Agreement. The export rebates, unlike import BTAs, if found to be inconsistent with the SCM Agreement, may not be justified under Article XX, which pertains to violations of the SCM prohibitions on export subsidies. In exchange for China's agreement to waive those obligations, WTO members could allow it to use the prohibited export duties as a climate policy instrument.

7.6.3. Article IX:2: an authoritative interpretation as a flexible correction

An authoritative interpretation, which was not part of the GATT 1947, would appear to be a necessary instrument amid the checks and balances of judicial interpretation adopted by the AB.[388] The space for judicial interpretations has increased owing to the differing systems of checks and balances that distinguish the GATT from the WTO.[389] To begin with, under the GATT dispute settlement system, individual members can veto the adoption of a judicial interpretation. Thus, for instance, the US has blocked the adoption of judicial interpretation that made what it considered to be inappropriate claims.[390] Under the current WTO dispute settlement system, by contrast, a consensus is required to block the adoption of such an interpretation. The formation of this sort of consensus is unlikely, however, because the victorious party in a dispute at least can be expected to refuse to join in blocking a report favourable to itself. In this context, an authoritative interpretation could have been widely used to correct judicial interpretation because Article IX:2 of the WTO Agreement only requires a three-fourths supermajority of members for the adoption of an authoritative interpretation that binds all of them, including those who voted in opposition.

However, only one request has yet been made for an authoritative interpretation. This single request, by the EU, was for a clarification of the relationship between Articles 21.5 and 22 of the DSU.[391] The US, however, objected that the requested interpretation would have contradicted the final sentence of Article IX:2 of the WTO Agreement, which states that an authoritative interpretation 'shall not be used in a manner that would undermine the amendment provisions of Article X'.[392] This argument, however, fails to take into account the divergence of views

388 Claus-Dieter Ehlermann and Lothar Ehring, 'The Authoritative Interpretation Under Article IX:2 of the Agreement Establishing the World Trade Organization: Current Law, Practice and Possible Improvements', 8(4) *Journal of International Economic Law* (2005), at 812.

389 Richard H. Steinberg, 'Judicial Lawmaking at the WTO: Discursive, Constitutional, and Political Constraints', 98(2) *The American Journal of International Law* (2004), at 263.

390 Ibid.

391 Request of an Authoritative Interpretation pursuant to Article IX:2 of the Treaty Establishing the WTO, 25 January 1999, WT/GC/W/133.

392 Claus-Dieter Ehlermann and Lothar Ehring, 'The Authoritative Interpretation Under Article IX:2 of the Agreement Establishing the World Trade Organization: Current Law, Practice and Possible Improvements', 8(4) *Journal of International Economic Law* (2005), at 814.

among WTO members regarding the correct application of the DSU rules at issue, which divergence itself suggests that the rules lack sufficient clarity and that an authoritative interpretation represents a better solution than an amendment.[393]

Unconvincing though it may be, this argument could also be extended to the interpretation of the silence on the relationship between Article XX and China's export duty commitments. As has been seen, the AB held in the *China—Raw Materials* and *China—Rare Earths* cases that this silence does not justify China's use of export duties under Article XX. From China's perspective, since the AB's interpretation was in error, it would be reasonable to request an authoritative interpretation that would clarify the relationship at issue. The members that had prevailed in the disputed cases, and perhaps others, conversely, would almost certainly block China's request by arguing that granting it would amount to an amendment and therefore be beyond the scope of an authoritative interpretation. In theory, China does not necessarily have to win the support of all members because Article IX:2 only requires a three-fourths supermajority of members for the adoption of an authoritative interpretation that binds all of them. In practice, however, WTO members may prefer not to break the general taboo against formal voting.

7.6.4. Article IV:1: a more flexible alternative

The very infrequency appears to suggest that authoritative interpretations are not desirable in practice.[394] One possible reason is to avoid the discussion of the demarcation line with amendments. As an alternative, China may thus request the Ministerial Conference to take a decision under Article IV:1 of the WTO Agreement updating its accession protocol regarding the use of export duties to protect the environment. This decision may constitute a subsequent agreement on the interpretation of a provision of a WTO agreement within the meaning of VCLT Article 31(3)(a).

In practice, Ministerial Decisions or Declarations have been found to qualify as subsequent agreements in *US—Clove Cigarettes* and *Australia – Tobacco Plain Packaging*. In the former case, the AB found that Paragraph 5.2 of the Doha Ministerial Decision on Implementation-Related Issues and Concerns constitutes a 'subsequent agreement between the parties' within the meaning of VCLT Art. 31 (3)(a). The AB thus held that the measure allowing only three months between the publication and the entry into force of the technical regulation at issue was inconsistent with TBT Article 2.12 because Paragraph 5.2 required a minimum of six months in that situation.[395] In the AB's view, a Ministerial Decision may qualify as a 'subsequent agreement between the parties' if

393 Ibid.
394 Ehlermann and Ehring (2005), above n 392.
395 AB Report, *US—Clove Cigarettes*, paras 241–275.

> (i) the decision is, in a temporal sense, adopted subsequent to the relevant covered agreement; and (ii) the terms and content of the decision express an agreement between Members on the interpretation or application of a provision of WTO law.[396]

In a more recent example of *Australia – Tobacco Plain Packaging*, the panel qualified the Public Health Declaration, which 'was adopted by a consensus decision of WTO Members, at the highest level, on 14 November 2001 on the occasion of the Fourth Ministerial Conference of the WTO', as a 'subsequent agreement between the parties'.[397] To support its analysis, the panel referred to the *US – Clove Cigarettes* AB report.[398]

The idea that Ministerial Decisions or Declarations may substitute for authoritative interpretations to clarify WTO rules seems to gain support from *EC—Bananas III (Article 21.5 – Ecuador II) / EC—Bananas III (Article 21.5 – US)*. In these cases, the AB stated that 'in the WTO context, multilateral interpretations adopted pursuant to Article IX:2 of the WTO Agreement are most akin to subsequent agreements within the meaning of Article 31(3)(a) of the Vienna Convention'.[399] In other words, once Ministerial Decisions or Declarations are found to constitute subsequent agreements, they may function as authoritative interpretations.

The challenge here is that such a Ministerial Decision or Declaration as a subsequent agreement may not legally correct the absolute ban on China's export duties. As the AB emphasised in *US—Clove Cigarettes*, authoritative interpretations under Article IX:2 and subsequent agreements within the meaning of VCLT Article 31(3)(a) 'serve different functions and have different legal effects under WTO law'.[400] A strict reading of the AB's reasoning seems to suggest that subsequent agreements cannot take over the role of authoritative interpretations to correct an AB interpretation.

This problem could be solved by introducing an update that does not explicitly contradict the *China—Raw Materials* and *China—Rare Earths* decisions. As discussed in Section 7.4, the AB is likely to accept an implicit correction that draws a line between export duties of the sort at issue in the two previous cases, which exclusively restrict the exports, and 'export duties plus' that are adopted in combination with supplementary restrictions on domestic consumption. For the same reason, WTO members, especially the victorious parties in the two cases, may find it easier to accept a ministerial update that does not explicitly alter the WTO ban on China's export duties. Moreover, in order to make such updates more attractive, such updates could also include a redefinition of other commitments in China's accession protocol such as subsidies or technology transfer, which are of the interest to the rest of the WTO membership.

396 Ibid., para 262.
397 Panel Report, *Australia – Tobacco Plain Packaging*, para 7.2409.
398 Ibid., footnote 5010.
399 AB Report, *EC—Bananas III*, para 390.
400 AB Report, *US—Clove Cigarettes*, para 257.

To sum up, all political options are constrained in practice by the organisation's *de facto* consensus requirement. China might find it easier to seek a consensus for a waiver as a stopgap measure, the legal effects of which would be conditional and temporary, rather than an amendment or an authoritative interpretation. This much is suggested by Mongolia's successful request for a waiver of its export duty commitments on raw cashmere and by the fact that waivers have been adopted much more often than amendments (of which there have been only two) or authoritative interpretations (which to date have not been used at all). In terms of a long-term solution, an authoritative interpretation is more flexible than an amendment which generally requires formal acceptance.[401] Given the unpopularity of authoritative interpretations in practice, China may request the Ministerial Conference to take a decision updating its accession protocol regarding the use of export duties to protect the environment. To make such updates more attractive, they may not need to explicitly contradict the *China—Raw Materials* and *China—Rare Earths* decisions but rather to distinguish them by drawing a line between export duties and 'export duties plus'.

7.7. Conclusions

This chapter has offered a thorough analysis of the judicial and political options for creating desirable policy space for China's export duties. Thus, to begin with, the AB could adopt a new interpretation that allows China to adopt export duties for environmental purposes. On the one hand, the evolving context of China's export duties could provide the AB with good reasons to reconsider its prior decisions in this regard. As the survey of the practice of selected tribunals at various levels in this chapter suggests, the AB could choose either to distinguish (the most feasible option) or to explicitly overrule (the second-best) the *China—Raw Materials* and *China—Rare Earths* rulings.[402]

There remain, on the other hand, substantive and feasible arguments regarding the applicability of Article XX to China's export duty commitments. China could argue from the perspective of non-WTO norms that the assumption that it has signed away its rights under Article XX is inconsistent with the principle of good faith or that the denial of its rights under Article XX is inconsistent with the

401 As discussed in Section 7.6.1, it has been argued that China's accession protocol could be seen as a bilateral treaty between China and the WTO. In this scenario, once the WTO as a contracting party agrees to amend China's export duty commitments, no such further formal acceptance as ratification by individual WTO members would be required. This alternative reading, however, comes with a considerable degree of uncertainty because neither Article X (Amendments) nor Article XII specifies the procedure for amendments to an accession protocol.

402 Unlike the option of overruling which in effect repeals an earlier judgement, the technique of distinguishing aims to amend a previous judgement, by adding to conditions necessary for applying such a judgement, which is considered less judicially radical and more commonly used by international, regional, and domestic tribunals when avoiding an awkward situation that is to be caused by a prior decision. See Duxbury (2008), above n 16, at 115.

prohibition of abuse of rights under Article 3(10) of the DSU. However, both of these interpretative options would require the AB to overrule its prior decisions explicitly and for this reason constitute second-best choices. A more feasible interpretative option, and one based on WTO norms, has been proposed in this chapter. This new interpretation involves drawing a line between regular export duties applied exclusively to exports on the one hand and 'export duties plus'—those adopted in conjunction with corresponding restrictions on domestic consumption—on the other. This interpretation would provide China with the right to justify 'export duties plus' under Article XX without reversing the *China—Raw Materials* and *China—Rare Earths* decisions.

Turning now from judicial to political options, the simplest approach for China might be to seek a consensus for an individual waiver, as Mongolia was able to do in 2007. Alternatively, a collective waiver could be sought covering all of the climate change measures that have been considered inconsistent with WTO law. Using this approach, China might be able to garner support from the US and EU, which might themselves wish to impose BTAs on carbon-intensive products at some point in the future.

While waivers could be useful as a stopgap measure, China may request amendments or authoritative interpretations as a long-term solution in order to better accommodate the climate considerations.[403] Given the rigidity of amendment processes and the deep unpopularity of authoritative interpretations in practice, this chapter has proposed a more flexible alternative based on Article IX:2 of the WTO Agreement.[404] China thus may request the Ministerial Conference to take decisions updating its accession protocol under which 'export duties plus' could be adopted in a manner consistent with Article XX. In order to make such updates even more attractive to the WTO's membership at large, they could also include a redefinition of other commitments in China's accession protocol such as subsidies or technology transfer.

Should the environmental exceptions under Article XX become available with respect to China's export duty commitments, its policy space to use these duties to protect the environment would be subject to the fairly strict tests specified in Article XX. A practical question for China therefore concerns the manner in which its export duties could be justified under these exceptions. This issue is taken up in the following chapter, which concludes with some policy recommendations.

403 'Thus without a commitment or fall-back mechanism (like an import border adjustment), export taxes cannot be regarded as an equivalent tool to the long-term EU carbon pricing'. Susanne Dröge, 'Tackling Leakage in a World of Unequal Carbon Prices', Climate Strategies Working Paper (2009), at 68.

404 These decisions may constitute subsequent agreements on the interpretation of a provision of a WTO agreement within the meaning of VCLT Article 31(3)(a).

8 China's policy space for adopting 'export duties plus' under GATT Article XX

Following the judicial or political options as suggested in the previous chapter, while export duties, which exclusively restrict exports, should be prohibited outright, 'export duties plus' that are adopted in combination with supplementary restrictions on domestic consumption would be allowed for pursuing environmental purposes subject to the scrutiny of Article XX. An important follow-up question concerning China's policy space for adopting 'export duties plus' is whether Article XX requires 'export duties plus' to always treat domestic and foreign consumers in an identical manner. In other words, if differential 'export duties plus' are proved to reduce pollution, would these duties necessarily be prohibited under Article XX.

It has been argued that China should impose equivalent charges on products destined for domestic consumption in order to justify its export duties under Article XX.[1] At least from an economic point of view, the price of targeted products under 'export duties plus' should be the same for both Chinese and foreign consumers in order to allocate those products to the most efficient consumers.[2] Moreover, identical 'export duties plus' would also dismiss the suspicion that 'export duties plus' are actually adopted to provide Chinese downstream industries with favourable access to raw materials.

This book generally subscribes to the above view and suggests that 'export duties plus' should be adopted identically in most cases. One exception, however, might be found in the climate change regime where the parties listed in Annex I of the United Nations Framework Convention on Climate Change (UNFCCC)

1 Eric W. Bond and Joel P. Trachtman, '*China–Rare Earths*: Export Restrictions and the Limits of Textual Interpretation', 15(2) *World Trade Review* (2016), at 199. 'Economic efficiency suggests a simple solution, which is that the price of Chinese products should be the same for both Chinese and foreign consumers. The reduced output under the conservation policy should be allocated to its most productive uses, which requires consumers in all locations facing the same price'.

2 When a large proportion of products is exported, one may argue that the efficiency cost of export duties is relatively low because there are not many consumers in China anyway. Given that export duties have less administrative cost than identical 'export duties plus' or production taxes, when the increase of administrative efficiency outweighs the loss of economic efficiency, export duties might make economic sense. But this is an exceptional case for export duties rather than differential 'export duties plus'.

DOI: 10.4324/9781003162339-11

have explicitly committed to take a greater mitigation role than non-Annex I countries like China in light of the principle of 'common but differentiated responsibilities'.[3]

The requirement of identical 'export duties plus' seems to be at odds with the *differentiated* obligations of Annex I and non-Annex I countries because it may in effect require China to adopt the *same* climate measures as those in place in Annex I countries. The reason is that, when it comes to combating climate change, identical 'export duties plus' constitute a *de facto* economy-wide carbon tax. Thus, for instance, when 'export duties plus' are used to counter border tax adjustments (BTAs) involving carbon-outsourcing countries, which are most likely listed in Annex I, the requirement of identical restrictions in effect would impose upon China a mitigation policy as stringent as that in place in Annex I countries. This result may be inconsistent with the principle of 'common but differentiated responsibilities'.[4]

Alternatively, China may impose identical 'export duties plus' in a less stringent manner. This, however, may not solve the problem of carbon leakage because the carbon cost of Chinese exports remains lower compared with those from Annex I countries. Such an outcome contradicts the fundamental goal of deploying 'export duties plus' as a more feasible alternative to address the concern of carbon leakage.[5]

This dilemma shows the unique features of the climate change problem. On the one hand, compared with other global environmental problems, cutting carbon emissions is more costly and complicated. For instance, while countries can achieve the goal of protecting ozone layer under the Montreal Protocol by 'switching one set of chemicals for another', there are currently no straightforward solutions to replace fossil fuels with low carbon energy sources.[6] This appears to

3 For instance, all parties have committed to take general actions under UNFCCC Article 4(1), whereas only Annex I parties have agreed to follow more stringent rules under Article 4(2). For a comprehensive analysis of this issue, see Jutta Brunnée and Charlotte Streck, 'The UNFCCC as a Negotiation Forum: Towards Common but More Differentiated Responsibilities', 13(5) *Climate Policy* (2013).

4 For instance, Hertel has argued that BTAs requiring non-Annex I countries to adopt mitigation policies that are 'comparable in effect to those' adopted by Annex I countries are inconsistent with the principle of 'common but differentiated responsibilities' and thus cannot be justified under Article XX. See Michael Hertel, 'Climate-Change-Related Trade Measures and Article XX: Defining Discrimination in Light of the Principle of Common but Differentiated Responsibilities', 45(3) *Journal of World Trade* (2011). Annex I countries are thus generally advised to adopt BTAs that distinguish countries in light of the principle of 'common but differentiated responsibilities'. See Michael A. Mehling, Harro van Asselt, Kasturi Das, Susanne Droege and Cleo Verkuijl, 'Designing Border Carbon Adjustments for Enhanced Climate Action', 113(3) *American Journal of International Law* (2019), at 469. Fabio C. Morosini, 'Trade and Climate Change: Unveiling the Principle of Common But Differentiated Responsibilities from the WTO Agreements', 42 *George Washington International Law Review* (2010), at 747.

5 See Chapter 6.

6 'That makes persuading people to act on climate change a lot harder than simply switching one set of chemicals for another'. Carbon Brief, 'Why we may never get a Montreal protocol for climate change', 12 September 2014, https://www.carbon

be the rationale behind the legal distinction between Annex I and non-Annex I countries under the UNFCCC.[7] On the other hand, China's position as both a non-Annex I party as well as the largest emitter and exporter of carbon dioxide emissions adds another layer of complexity. Any ambitious climate action taken by Annex I countries may fail to effectively tackle carbon leakage if China is exempted from adequately targeting its carbon-intensive exports.

The present chapter takes up the question of whether Article XX is flexible enough to accommodate the unique characteristics of the climate change issue. Given that neither Articles XX(b) or XX(g) requires identical treatment, Section 8.1 focuses on the comparison of different policy spaces for adopting 'export duties plus' under these subparagraphs. In Section 8.2 and 8.3, the issue of whether differential 'export duties plus' would necessarily constitute 'arbitrary or unjustifiable discrimination' or 'disguised restriction on international trade' under the chapeau is addressed. These findings are applied to China's current environmental policy in Section 8.4. This analysis serves in turn as the basis for a series of policy recommendations.

8.1. Tests under Articles XX(b) and XX(g)

Articles XX(b) and XX(g) do not necessarily prohibit differential 'export duties plus' because the tests under these subparagraphs examine the measures as a whole, not merely their discriminatory aspects.[8] Thus at least two discriminatory measures in the past have been successfully justified under Articles XX(b) or XX (g). In the *Brazil—Retreaded Tyres* case, an import prohibition on retreaded tyres together with exemption of retreaded tyres imported from MERCOSUR countries was found consistent with Article XX(b). In the *US—Gasoline* case, a gasoline rule that applied different methods to domestic and imported gasoline was justified under Article XX(g). That being said, however, differential treatment may undermine the effectiveness of 'export duties plus' in terms of reducing pollution because they could incentivise the manufacture of targeted products for Chinese consumers. This section thus examines the challenges of justifying differential 'export duties plus' under Articles XX(b) and XX(g). The findings serve in turn as the basis for a comparison of different policy spaces for adopting 'export duties plus' under these subparagraphs.

8.1.1. Article XX(b): Local pollution

Article XX(b) permits World Trade Organization (WTO) members to adopt measures that are 'necessary to protect human, animal or plant life or health', a

brief.org/why-we-may-never-get-a-montreal-protocol-for-climate-change (visited on 13 August 2019).

7 There is no such a distinction, for instance, under the Montreal Protocol.

8 Patrick Low, Gabrielle Marceau, Julia Reinaud, 'The Interface between the Trade and Climate Change Regimes: Scoping the Issues', 46(3) *Journal of World Trade* (2012), at 509.

provision easily connected to the goal of reducing local pollution associated with the manufacture of high-polluting products.[9] To succeed in a claim under Article XX(b), China must first show that the challenged 'export duties plus' are specifically designed to protect the environment or public health. This purpose test, as shown in the *China—Rare Earths* case, requires the text of the challenged measures to demonstrate a link between 'export duties plus' and the avowed environmental purpose.[10] One such link is to show that export duties may reduce various negative environmental impacts associated with the manufacture of the targeted products. Thus, for instance, as the panel in *China—Rare Earths* recognised, environmental harm caused by the manufacture of high-polluting products can take the form of water pollution.[11]

Once the harm arising from the manufacture of high-polluting products has been proved, China needs to demonstrate that 'export duties plus' are designed and structured to reduce their manufacture, a fact relevant to domestic and foreign demand alike. Export duties, however, can only decrease foreign demand. Therefore, their potential to reduce the production of the targeted products is proportional to the extent to which they are consumed outside China. One essential aspect of proving the environmental purpose of 'export duties plus' is accordingly the proportion of the targeted products destined for export.

Also essential to proving the environmental purpose of 'export duties plus' is the restriction on domestic consumption. Absent an identical restriction, the price differential between foreign markets and the Chinese market could generate an increase in domestic consumption that would undermine the capacity of 'export duties plus' to reduce the manufacture of the targeted products in China.[12] In this case, the adverse effect would reduce the ability to prove the environmental purpose of differential 'export duties plus'.

Analysis of the purpose test would be complicated if the targeted products include industrial inputs. In this situation, a lower price on products destined for domestic consumption than on those for exports could provide industry in China with preferential access to these industrial inputs. Thus, in the *China—Rare Earths* case, the panel suspected China of having adopted the challenged export duties in order to incentivise the domestic use of the targeted raw materials, thereby raising the question of whether these duties would still pass the purpose test if they in effect offered advantages to domestic industry.

The answer appears to be affirmative, at least according to the *Brazil—Retreaded Tyres* case, in which the panel, while recognising that the import of used tyres through court injunction (which in effect benefitted the domestic retreaded tyres industry which needs used tyres as industrial inputs) could undermine the effectiveness of the import ban in terms of reducing waste tyres in Brazil,[13] nevertheless

9 Ibid. at 512.
10 Panel Reports, *China—Rare Earths*, para 7.165.
11 Ibid. para 7.152 and 7.156.
12 Ibid. para 7.169.
13 The import ban on retreaded tyres (which are produced by using used tyre casings) in dispute aims to reduce waste tyres in Brazil. However, the court injunctions at issue

found that the ban at issue had been adopted for an environmental purpose under Article XX(b).[14] In light of this ruling, differential 'export duties plus' on industrial inputs may stand a chance of passing the purpose test.

If 'export duties plus' are found to have been adopted for an environmental purpose, the necessity test under Article XX(b) requires China as a first step to prove that the environmental interests at stake are significant. Significant interests could include the nation's public health, as claimed in *China—Raw Materials* and *China—Rare Earths*. Relevant in this context is the AB's statement in *Brazil—Retreaded Tyres* that 'few interests are more vital and important than protecting human beings from health risks, and ... protecting the environment is no less important'.[15] China's 'export duties plus' on high-polluting products seem likely to meet this requirement.

Another requirement under the necessity test is the demonstration that 'export duties plus' have made or are likely to 'make a material contribution' to the furtherance of reducing local pollution, which represents a higher threshold than the aforementioned purpose test. To estimate such a contribution, an analysis could rely on either quantitative projections into the future or on qualitative reasoning based on a set of hypotheses that are tested and supported by sufficient evidence.[16] In either of these methods for assessing the material contribution of 'export duties plus', the two essential elements mentioned above in the context of the purpose test, namely export proportions and restrictions on domestic consumption, also play important roles. One may argue that the more the targeted products are consumed abroad, the more policy space for China to adopt 'export duties plus'. It is noteworthy that the requirement of material contribution does not necessarily prohibit differential 'export duties plus'. In the *Brazil—Retreaded Tyres* case, a discriminatory measure was nevertheless found to make a material contribution to the protection of public health.

The necessity test would further examine the trade restrictiveness of 'export duties plus', assessing whether they are necessary to protect the alleged environmental interests. The *China—Raw Materials* case shows that the trade-restrictive effects depend in part on the market size of the exporting country.[17] Since China, as the world's largest exporter, has a large export share for many products, its export duties might be found to have a large trade-restrictive impact. The analysis of trade restrictiveness is, however, irrelevant to the discriminatory aspects of differential 'export duties plus'.

leads to imports of used tyres, which thus could undermine the effectiveness of the former measure. Panel Report, *Brazil—Retreaded Tyres*, para 7.107 For instance, 'The European Communities argues that this discriminates in favour of domestic retreaded tyres made from imported used tyres, which generate the same waste as that arising from imported retreads'. Panel Report, *Brazil—Retreaded Tyres*, para 7.241.

14 Ibid., para 7.215.
15 AB Report, *Brazil—Retreaded Tyres*, paras 144 and 179.
16 Low, Marceau and Reinaud (2012), above n 8, at 509.
17 Panel Reports, *China—Raw Materials*, para 7.563.

If 'export duties plus', be it identical or differential, are found to be necessary on a preliminary basis, it is for the complaining governments to show, in the first instance, that there are no reasonably available alternatives.[18] Thus the complainants need to prove, first, that the proposed alternatives are financially or practically within China's reach and, second, that these alternatives are capable of achieving at least the same level of environmental protection as the 'export duties plus' at issue.[19]

For the purpose of reducing local pollution, the complainants in *China—Raw Materials* and *China—Rare Earths* identified various alternative measures such as a pollution tax that restrict the production in general. In response to China's argument that many of these measures had already been implemented, the panel suggested that they could be strengthened.[20] Indeed, China after the *China—Rare Earths* decision, for instance in 2015, replaced the export duties with increased environmental protection taxes on the production of the minerals in dispute.[21] In a future case, it would accordingly be difficult for China to explain why it could not likewise increase environmental protection taxes instead of imposing 'export duties plus'. One possible argument might be that, compared with such demand-side measures as environmental protection taxes, 'export duties plus' as a type of demand-side control measure could enable lifestyle and behavioural change. When it comes to differential 'export duties plus', however, it seems to be very difficult for China to explain why this discriminatory measure could not be replaced by identical 'export duties plus'.

In short, compared with identical 'export duties plus', differential 'export duties plus' could undermine their effectiveness in reducing local pollution and, thus, reduce their chance of being justified under Article XX(b). The biggest challenge here seems to be the necessity test, which requires proof that alternative measures consistent with the WTO not be reasonably available. In contrast, there is no such a test under Article XX(g) as discussed below.

8.1.2. *Article XX(g): Global pollution*

Article XX(g) permits WTO members to adopt measures relating to 'the conservation of exhaustible natural resources'. The *US—Gasoline* decision shows that clean air, which naturally falls under the 'natural resources' category, could be affected by pollutants, for which reason regulation of pollutant-emitting gasoline combustion was justifiable. Following this line of reasoning, Article XX(g) could be relevant to 'export duties plus' that reduce global pollution such as carbon emissions; for preserving the global climate could be considered analogous to the preservation of clean air or to addressing potentially dangerous levels of carbon

18 AB Reports, *US—Gambling*, para 309.
19 Low, Marceau and Reinaud (2012), above n 8, at 514.
20 Panel Reports, *China—Rare Earths*, para 7.186.
21 Notice on Imposing Resources Taxes in 2015, the Ministry of Finance, Cai Shui [2015] No.52.

and other greenhouse gases in the atmosphere.[22] Alternatively, the loss of biodiversity as a result of climate change may also qualify as the exhaustion of a natural resource.[23]

In a manner similar to the purpose test under Article XX(b), the term 'relate to' under Article XX(g) also requires 'a close and genuine relationship' between 'export duties plus' and their purpose of reducing global pollution.[24] As the AB held in the *US—Gasoline* case, 'a close and genuine relationship' requires that a measure should be directed primarily at the conservation of such resources.[25] Thus 'export duties plus', be it identical or differential, would fall within the scope of Article XX(g) if they were adopted primarily for reducing global pollution.

The feasibility of passing the purpose test largely depends on the contribution of 'export duties plus' to reduce the manufacture of targeted products, such as those energy-intensive ones, in China. Again, as discussed above, this contribution is closely related to the export proportion of the targeted products and to the restriction on their domestic consumption. Therefore, although the purpose test does not require 'export duties plus' to be identical, different treatment would decrease the feasibility of justifying 'export duties plus' under Article XX(g). It is noteworthy that, according to the panel report in the 1987 *Herring and Salmon* case, which was referred to by the panel in *US—Gasoline*, 'primarily aimed at the conservation of an exhaustible natural resource' does not require a measure to be 'necessary or essential' to the conservation purpose.[26] This ruling appears to suggest that the purpose test under paragraph XX(g) sets a lower threshold than the 'necessity test' under paragraph XX(b).

Although Article XX(g) does not include a 'necessity test', this paragraph requires explicitly that China should prove 'export duties plus' to have been 'made effective in conjunction with domestic restrictions on production or consumption'. As the AB noted in *US—Gasoline*, a meaningful parallel domestic restriction needs to be imposed in an even-handed manner.[27] This so-called 'even-handedness' requirement, however, does not necessarily prohibit differential 'export duties plus'.

The *China—Raw Materials* decision shows that a complementary measure that restricts domestic production alone is not even-handed because such a restriction affects both foreign and domestic consumers, whereas export duties affect foreign consumers exclusively.[28] In this context, 'export duties plus' may include a parallel restriction on domestic consumption, which can be fiscal in nature (e.g. consumption taxes) or quantitative (e.g. consumption quotas). Such a restriction on

22 Bradly J. Condon, 'Climate Change and Unresolved Issues in WTO Law', 12(4) *Journal of International Economic Law* (2009), at 911–12.
23 Jochem Wiers, 'French Ideas on Climate and Trade Policies', 2(1) *Carbon & Climate Law Review* (2008), at 25.
24 AB Report, *US—Shrimp*, para 136.
25 AB Report, *US—Gasoline*, at 17.
26 Panel Report, *US—Gasoline*, at 15.
27 AB Report, *US—Gasoline*, at 20–21.
28 Panel Reports, *China—Raw Materials*, para 7.465.

domestic consumption does not, however, need to be identical with export duties. In the *US—Gasoline* case, a measure that imposed greater costs on foreign producers than domestic producers (thereby favouring the latter over the former) was still found to meet the requirement of even-handedness despite having failed to pass the tests under the chapeau of Article XX. Indeed, as the AB stated in *China—Rare Earths*, the so-called 'even-handedness' requirement merely prohibits 'a significantly more onerous burden on foreign consumers or producers'.[29]

8.1.3. Comparing different policy spaces under Articles XX(b) and XX(g)

The above analysis shows that, compared with Article XX(b), Article XX(g) generally provides more policy space for adopting 'export duties plus'. In terms of identical 'export duties plus', they would certainly meet the 'even-handedness' requirement under Article XX(g). In contrast, even if 'export duties plus' treat domestic and foreign consumers in an identical manner, they might still be found to fail the necessity test under Article XX(b). In other words, Article XX provides China with more policy space to adopt identical 'export duties plus' for reducing global pollution.

This result makes economic sense because global negative environmental externalities are more difficult to solve than local ones. Local environmental problems, such as water or soil pollution, arguably improve after a sufficient level of income has been reached.[30] In other words, the negative impacts on local environments caused by trade may be outweighed by the benefits of trade in the long run. In contrast, global negative environmental externalities may worsen as a consequence of international trade at any given level of income;[31] for, unlike local pollution, which can be tackled at the national level, such pressing issues as ozone depletion, air pollution, and carbon emissions cannot be addressed effectively on a country-by-country basis because of the free rider problem.[32] It is thus reasonable to provide China with more policy space to tackle global environmental problems.

When it comes to differential 'export duties plus', Article XX(g) seems to provide more policy space in most cases. The 'even-handedness' test requires 'export duties plus' to not impose 'a significantly more onerous burden on foreign consumers or producers'.[33] According to this standard, one could argue that a 1/4 difference between export duties (20%) and domestic charges (15%) might be permitted under Article XX(g), whereas a 1/2 difference (20% export duties plus 10% domestic charges) might be prohibited. The former one, however, might still be found to fail the necessity test under Article XX(b). In this case, Article XX(g) provides more policy space for adopting differential 'export duties plus' to reduce

29 AB Report, *China—Rare Earths*, para 5.134.
30 Jeffrey A. Frankel, 'The Natural Resource Curse: A Survey of Diagnoses and Some Prescriptions', RWP12–014 HKS Faculty Research Working Paper Series (2012), at 25.
31 Ibid.
32 Ibid.
33 Ibid.

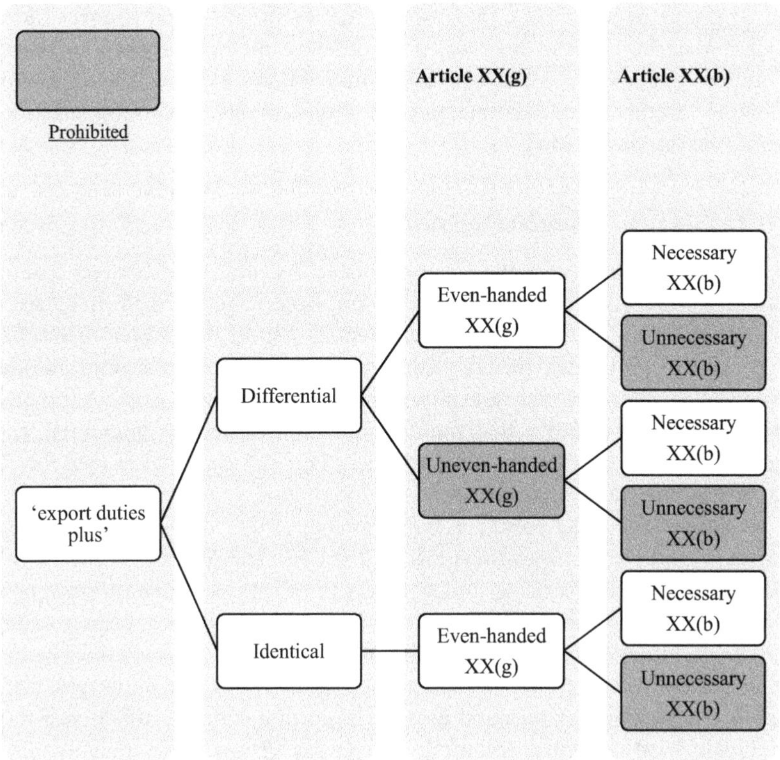

Figure 8.1 Different policy space under Articles XX(b) and XX(g)

global pollution. In exceptional cases where the products at issue are primarily consumed abroad, the 'export duties plus' that are not even-handed under Article XX(g) might nevertheless be found necessary under Article XX(b) (see Figure 8.1).

Compared with identical 'export duties plus', differential 'export duties plus' that are provisionally justified under Articles XX(b) or XX(g) need to be further assessed under the chapeau of Article XX. The next two sections discuss whether those differential 'export duties plus' would necessarily constitute 'arbitrary or unjustifiable discrimination' or 'disguised restriction on international trade'.

8.2. First condition of the chapeau: 'arbitrary or unjustifiable discrimination between countries where the same conditions prevail'

After differential 'export duties plus' have been provisionally justified under Articles XX(b) or XX(g), they must further meet the requirements under the chapeau, the aim of which is to prevent abuse of the exceptions described in Article XX. These requirements have proven decisive in justifying a measure with a discriminatory aspect, an example being the *US—Gasoline* case, in which, although the US was permitted to impose certain standards on gasoline in order to protect clean air under Article XX(g), the gasoline rule eventually failed to meet the conditions under the chapeau because of its different methods applied to domestic and imported gasoline.[34] The discussion that follows explores the feasibility of differential 'export duties plus' meeting the requirements concerning 'arbitrary or unjustifiable discrimination'.

8.2.1. Do 'the same conditions' prevail?

The chapeau prohibits 'arbitrary or unjustifiable discrimination between countries where the same conditions prevail'; this language suggests that there are two separate conditions that could justify differential 'export duties plus'. First, China would need to prove that the 'the same conditions' that prevail domestically do not prevail in countries that are importing the products at issue. Alternatively, China would need to prove that the discrimination caused by differential 'export duties plus' is not 'arbitrary or unjustifiable'. This subsection examines the feasibility of meeting the first condition.

That differences in the prevailing conditions in various countries are relevant to the analysis under the chapeau was made clear when the AB held in the *EC—Seal Products* case that the particular policy objective of the applicable subparagraph of Article XX provided 'pertinent context'.[35] This interpretation appears to suggest that the conditions in China and the importing countries at issue could be examined in the context of the environmental purposes of 'export duties plus'. If the conditions prevailing in China and in these importing countries differ with respect to reducing local or global pollution, differential 'export duties plus' would not constitute discrimination within the meaning of the chapeau.

The panel in *China—Rare Earths* assumed that the same conditions indeed prevailed across China and the complaining countries in terms of the use of export restrictions to reduce local pollution. As a result, China's export duties were found to constitute discrimination under the chapeau solely based on the difference in treatment accorded to products destined for domestic consumption and those destined for exports.[36]

Possible support for this assumption could be that the specific goal of reducing pollution generated by the production of certain products is served irrespective of where the products are consumed. Thus, for instance, the consumption of high-polluting products manufactured in China by either a Chinese consumer or a consumer abroad would generate the same amount of pollution associated with the manufacture of these products. In other words, at least for the purpose of reducing pollution, the conditions prevailing in China and in importing countries seem to be the same.

One exception, however, might be found in the climate change regime where the parties listed in Annex I of the UNFCCC have explicitly committed to take a

34 Another example is the *Brazil—Retreaded Tyres* case.
35 AB Report, *EC—Seal Products*, para 5.300.
36 Panel Reports, *China—Rare Earths*, para 7.190.

greater mitigation role than non-Annex I parties like China in light of the principle of 'common but differentiated responsibilities'. Unlike the vague and thus controversial distinction between developing and developed countries under WTO law,[37] the distinction between Annex I and non-Annex I parties is clearly recorded in the UNFCCC.[38] In terms of substantial commitments, for instance, all parties have committed to take general actions under Article 4(1) of that convention, whereas only Annex I parties have agreed to follow more stringent rules under Article 4(2).[39] Given the important position of the UNFCCC as a framework treaty for fighting climate change, it may provide 'pertinent context' to assess the conditions in China and the importing countries.[40] In other words, for the purpose of fighting climate change, the conditions prevailing in China and in Annex I parties might not be the same.

That being the case, differential 'export duties plus' for fighting climate change would not constitute discrimination within the meaning of the chapeau. Indeed, as the AB recognised in *US—Shrimp*, differing conditions may call for different approaches.[41] If, however, the conditions in China and the importing countries were found to be the same, China would need to prove that the national treatment-type discrimination associated with differential 'export duties plus' is not 'arbitrary or unjustifiable' under the chapeau, as is discussed as follows.

8.2.2. Is such discrimination 'arbitrary or unjustifiable'?

Once a measure is found to constitute discrimination within the meaning of the chapeau, it is very challenging to prove such discrimination is not 'arbitrary or unjustifiable'. At least six GATT-inconsistent measures have been provisionally justified under Article XX,[42] but only two were found not to constitute 'arbitrary or unjustifiable discrimination' under the chapeau, namely the ban on asbestos in the *EC—Asbestos* case and the revised guidelines prohibiting the import of shrimp and shrimp products from non-certified countries in *US—Shrimp* (*Article 21.5—*

37 Anabel González, 'Bridging the Divide between Developed and Developing Countries in WTO Negotiations', PIIE, 12 March 2019, at https://www.piie.com/blogs/trade-investment-policy-watch/bridging-divide-between-developed-and-developing-countries-wto (visited on 15 July 2019).

38 'Annex I Parties include the industrialized countries that were members of the OECD (Organisation for Economic Co-operation and Development) in 1992, plus countries with economies in transition (the EIT Parties), including the Russian Federation, the Baltic States, and several Central and Eastern European States'. UNFCCC, 'Parties & Observers', at https://unfccc.int/parties-observers (visited on 15 July 2019).

39 For a comprehensive analysis of those different commitments, see Brunnée and Streck (2013), above n 3.

40 Scholars generally support that a proper interpretation of the chapeau should take into account the principle of 'common but differentiated responsibilities'. For instance, Hertel (2011); Mehling, van Asselt, Das, Droege and Verkuijl (2019), above n 4.

41 AB Report, *US—Shrimp*, para 164–65.

42 *US—Shrimp (DS58), US—Gasoline (DS2), EC—Asbestos (DS135), Argentina—Hides and Leather (DS155), Brazil—Retreaded Tyres (DS 332)*, and *EC—Seal Products (DS 400; DS401).*

Malaysia). Neither of them has a discriminatory aspect. In contrast, other such measures with a discriminatory aspect were eventually found to discriminate arbitrarily, unjustifiably, or in both respects against the products of the complaining WTO members.

A major challenge to justify differential 'export duties plus' is to articulate why the different treatment towards domestic and foreign consumers relates to the reduction of local or global pollution. In the *Brazil—Retreaded Tyres* case, although the panel acknowledged that the MERCOSUR exception and the imports of used tyres constitute discrimination, it still found that the measure as a whole met the requirements of the chapeau.[43] In particular, in its analysis of the justifiability of the MERCOSUR exception or the court injunction under the chapeau, the panel held that, as long as the achievement of the environmental purpose was not 'significantly undermined' by such discriminatory aspects, they should not constitute 'arbitrary or unjustifiable discrimination'.[44]

This quantitative approach was later rejected by the AB on the grounds that there was no support for it in the text of Article XX.[45] In the view of the AB, if the alleged rationale behind a discriminatory provision does not relate to the pursuit of, or would contravene, an objective that had been justified provisionally, the discrimination cannot be justified under the chapeau to any degree.[46] The AB accordingly found that both the MERCOSUR exception and the court injunction constituted 'arbitrary or unjustifiable discrimination' and that the injunction in addition constituted a 'disguised restriction on international trade' because the purposes for the measures bore no relationship to the claimed purpose of the import ban on retreaded tyres relating to Article XX.[47]

Following this line of reasoning, differential 'export duties plus' would constitute 'arbitrary or unjustifiable discrimination' unless China could prove that the discrimination against foreign consumers actually relates to the purpose of reducing pollution. China may not be able to succeed in most cases because, as discussed above, the reduction of pollution seems to be served irrespective of where the products are consumed. China might argue that its consumers may not be able to bear the same environmental costs as those in developed countries. This argument, however, does not seem relevant to the reduction of pollution because it is based on economic considerations. Moreover, such economic considerations could be accommodated if China chooses to impose identical 'export duties plus' in a less stringent manner. Indeed, although the Preamble to the WTO Agreement suggests that WTO members may adopt various approaches to protecting the environment 'in a manner consistent with their respective needs and concerns at different levels of economic development', it does not authorise China to discriminate consumers in developed countries. As a result, differential 'export duties plus' are prohibited in most cases.

43 Panel Report, *Brazil—Retreaded Tyres*, paras 7.356–7.357.
44 Ibid. paras 7.288–7.289; 7.348–7.349.
45 AB Report, *Brazil—Retreaded Tyres*, para 229 and para 239.
46 Ibid. para 228.
47 AB Report, *Brazil—Retreaded Tyres*, para 247 and para 251.

Again, one exception might be found in the climate change regime where, compared with Annex I parties of the UNFCCC, China together with other non-Annex I parties have only made less stringent commitments. This difference might serve as a justification for charging a lower carbon price for products consumed in China. In other words, higher carbon price might be charged for products consumed in Annex I countries because they have explicitly committed to take a greater mitigation role. To effectively tackle carbon leakage by equalising the carbon costs among China's exports and those from Annex I countries, the requirement of identical 'export duties plus', as a *de facto* economy-wide carbon tax, may in effect require China to adopt the same climate measures as those in place in Annex I countries. This result seems to be inconsistent with the principle of 'common but differentiated responsibilities'.[48] If China chooses to impose identical 'export duties plus' in a less stringent manner, the carbon cost of Chinese exports remains lower compared with those from Annex I countries. The issue of carbon leakage is thus failed to be effectively addressed.[49] Given these considerations, 'export duties plus' might be allowed to differentiate Annex I and non-Annex I parties for the purpose of fighting climate change.

It has been argued that the AB appeared to have softened its zero-tolerance stance on measures with disconnected purposes in the *EC—Seal Products* case.[50] This raises the question of whether the aforementioned economic considerations might be accommodated under the chapeau. In *EC—Seal Products*, to balance the public moral concerns on seal welfare and the protection of Inuit cultural identity, the EU had banned the sale of seal and seal-containing products while carving out exceptions, including one for such products derived from hunts conducted by Inuit or other indigenous communities (the IC exception). The AB faulted the measure based on the reason that the rationale behind the IC exception was not connected to achieving seal welfare and other 'additional factors'.[51] This finding was in contrast with the earlier decision in the *Brazil—Retreaded Tyres* case, in which the AB faulted the measure based solely on the lack of connection.[52] In this context, the additional inquiry into 'additional factors' might indicate that the AB implicitly accepted the purpose of the IC exception as legitimate. In other words,

48 For instance, it has been argued that any measure requiring non-Annex I countries to adopt mitigation policies that are 'comparable in effect to those' adopted by Annex I countries is inconsistent with the principle of 'common but differentiated responsibilities' and thus cannot be justified under Article XX.

49 For further discussion, see Chapter 6.

50 Gracia Marín Durán, 'Measures with Multiple Competing Purposes after EC–Seal Products: Avoiding a Conflict between GATT Article XX-Chapeau and Article 2.1 TBT Agreement', 19(2) *Journal of International Economic Law* (2016).

51 AB Report, *EC—Seal Products*, para 5.321.

52 Donald H. Regan, 'Measures with Multiple Purposes: Puzzles from EC—Seal Products' AJIL Unbound (25 June 2015); Julia Y. Qin, 'Accommodating Divergent Policy Objectives under WTO Law: Reflections on EC—Seal Products' AJIL Unbound (25 June 2015); Lorand Bartels, 'The Chapeau of the General Exceptions in the WTO GATT and GATS Agreements: A Reconstruction', 109(1) *American Journal of International Law* (2015), at 119.

the EU's ban might be justified under the chapeau despite the lack of a rational connection between protecting the Inuit on the one hand and protecting seals on the other.[53] This interpretation may not, however, gain support from the concluding paragraph of the AB's analysis, which seems to suggest that the rational connection requirement is decisive in determining the arbitrariness or unjustifiability of a discrimination case.[54]

Moreover, even if the AB were to allow a justification based on irrelevant purposes under the chapeau, the scope of legitimate purposes to justify discrimination under the chapeau would remain unclear. Bartels has proposed four interpretive options for justifying discrimination based on (i) one of the reasons set out in the subparagraphs of Article XX (even if the reason for such discrimination were to differ from the reason for the measure itself), (ii) reasons recognised elsewhere in the GATT 1994 or other WTO agreements, (iii) reasons recognized in international standards, and, least likely, (iv) legitimate objectives without reference to other normative considerations.[55] The economic considerations behind favourable treatment for Chinese consumers, however, do not appear to fall within any of these categories.

Although the differentiation between Annex I and non-Annex I parties might be found relevant to fighting climate change, China may need to consult with its trading partners before the adoption of such differential 'export duties plus'. In the *US—Shrimp* case, the import ban on shrimp products was found to constitute 'unjustifiable discrimination' because the US failed to engage negotiations with other WTO members 'with the objective of concluding bilateral or multilateral agreements for the protection and conservation of sea'.[56] The AB made it clear in the *US—Shrimp (Article 21.5—Malaysia)* case that WTO members need to make serious efforts, in good faith, to engage in negotiations with other members.[57] Such efforts may prevent 'export duties plus' from being 'unjustifiable discrimination'.

8.2.3. Differential 'export duties plus' might be permitted for fighting climate change

This section shows that differential 'export duties plus' for reducing local or global pollution would constitute 'arbitrary or unjustifiable discrimination' in most cases, with the exception of combating climate change. Given that Annex I parties have generally agreed to follow more stringent rules under the UNFCCC, 'export duties plus' might be permitted to differentiate Annex I and non-Annex I parties for the purpose of fighting climate change in two ways in light of the principle of 'common but differentiated responsibilities'.[58]

53 Ibid., at 117.
54 Durán (2016), above n 50, at 480.
55 Bartels (2015), above n 52, at 118.
56 AB Report, *US—Shrimp*, para 166.
57 AB Report, *US—Shrimp (Article 21.5— Malaysia)*, paras 115–134.
58 For a general view that a proper interpretation of the chapeau should take into account the principle of 'common but differentiated responsibilities', see Hertel (2011), and Mehling, van Asselt, Das, Droege and Verkuijl (2019), above n 4.

The first option for China is to argue that the same conditions do not prevail between China and Annex I parties. The UNFCCC, as a framework treaty for fighting climate change, may provide 'pertinent context' to this argument. In this way, the difference between charges on energy-intensive products destined for Chinese consumers and for consumers in Annex I countries does not even constitute 'discrimination' within the meaning of the chapeau.[59] Alternatively, if differential 'export duties plus' are found to be discriminatory, China may argue that the different commitments made by Annex I and non-Annex I parties of the UNFCCC in light of the principle of 'common but differentiated responsibilities' serves as a justification for charging a higher carbon price for products consumed in Annex I countries.

In the context of the assessment of subparagraphs (b) and (g), the differential 'export duties plus' that do not impose 'a significantly more onerous burden' on consumers in Annex I countries, for instance, a 1/4 difference between export duties (20%) and domestic charges (15%), might meet the first condition of the chapeau. Speculatively, as discussed in the previous section, the differential 'export duties plus' that impose 'a significantly more onerous burden' on foreign consumers might be justified under Article XX(b), provided that the products at issue are primarily consumed abroad. This raises the question of whether such significant level of differentiation, for instance, export duties (20%) together with domestic charges (5%), could also be justified for the purpose of fighting climate change.

Although the answer appears to be affirmative,[60] such a situation can hardly occur. In order to effectively reduce carbon emissions, China needs to impose 'export duties plus' on a range of products. Given China's huge domestic market, targeted products are very unlikely to be primarily consumed abroad. In this sense, the above speculation is actually irrelevant to the analysis of differential 'export duties plus' for fighting climate change.

After differential 'export duties plus' has met the first condition of the chapeau, they could still be found to constitute a 'disguised restriction on international trade' under the second condition. The reason is that if differential 'export duties plus' cover raw materials, the difference between charges on products destined for

59 Julia Y. Qin, 'Accommodating Divergent Policy Objectives under WTO Law: Reflections on EC—Seal Products' *AJIL Unbound* (25 June 2015), available at https://www.asil.org/blogs/accommodating-divergent-policy-objectives-under-wto-law-reflections-ec%E2%80%94seal-products (visited on 4 December 2017).

60 This result is indeed odd because it is difficult to rationalise why should a measure targeting XX(b)-related global pollution could differentiate more than the one targeting XX(g)-related global pollution under the chapeau. This odd result is, however, consistent with case law. The first condition of the chapeau is 'qualitative', whether a discriminatory aspect relates to the legitimate objective of the measure, rather than 'quantitative', how much greater a differential could be accepted (e.g. the even-handedness test). Thus, even though it is tempting to suggest that a measure targeting XX(b)-related global pollution should not be allowed to differentiate more than the one targeting XX(g)-related global pollution, this conclusion may not be supported by case law.

domestic consumption and those destined for Annex I countries could provide Chinese downstream producers with preferential access to industrial inputs. This issue is examined in the next section.

8.3. Second condition of the chapeau: 'disguised restriction on international trade'

The AB in *US—Gasoline* implies that the concepts of 'disguised restriction on international trade' and 'arbitrary or unjustifiable discrimination' may overlap because the former one 'includes disguised discrimination in international trade'.[61] The term 'disguised restriction', however, has not been clearly defined in WTO jurisprudence. If the requirement regarding 'disguised restriction on international trade' prohibits any measure that could potentially benefit domestic industry, then differential 'export duties plus' should perhaps exclude upstream products in order to eliminate any chance of favouring Chinese downstream producers. This result would, however, undermine the effectiveness of this measure because many carbon-intensive products exposed to trade are 'at or near the beginning of the value chain'.[62] The following two subsections thus argue that favouring domestic industry is not dispositive of a violation of the second condition of the chapeau. That being said, however, it is equally important to address concerns that China might circumvent WTO rules by providing Chinese producers with cheaper industrial inputs. This section therefore proposes additional limits on the use of differential 'export duties plus' for fighting climate change.

8.3.1. Distinguishing between active discrimination and passive discrimination

The AB held in *Japan—Alcoholic Beverages* that, although a protectionist aim is difficult to establish, the protective application of a measure can most often be discerned based on the 'design, architecture and revealing structure', which is in turn essential in determining whether a measure constitutes a 'disguised restriction on international trade'.[63] The term 'disguised restriction' thus appears to suggest that a challenged measure has a mixture of a claimed purpose, that is, the one to be justified under the subparagraph and a hidden purpose that is likely to be protective.[64] The question in light of these considerations is whether the requirement regarding 'disguised restrictions on international trade' prohibits only measures with an entirely or primarily hidden protective purpose or should also include, more broadly, measures with any protective purpose, even if the hidden protective

61 AB Report, *United States—Gasoline*, at 25.
62 Aaron Cosbey, Susanne Droege, Carolyn Fischer, Julia Reinaud, John Stephenson, Lutz Weischer and Peter Wooders, 'A Guide for the Concerned: Guidance on the Elaboration and Implementation of Border Carbon Adjustment', November 2012, at 13, https://www.iisd.org/pdf/2012/bca_guidance.pdf (visited on 19 August 2019).
63 AB Report, *Japan—Alcoholic Beverages II*, at 27–29.
64 Bartels (2015), above n 52, at 123.

purpose is minor compared with the legitimate purpose.[65] In the former case, China may still have policy space to impose differential 'export duties plus' on industrial inputs that are energy-intensive.

Relevant here is the panel's explicit support for the former condition in *Brazil—Retreaded Tyres*. In that case, it found that, as long as the achievement of the environmental purpose of the import ban on retreaded tyres was not 'significantly undermined' by the imports of used tyres protected by the court injunction (and that in effect favoured domestic producers of retreaded tyres), the ban did not constitute a 'disguised restriction on international trade'.[66] In other words, the panel recognised that a measure should not be considered a 'disguised restriction' under the chapeau if the hidden protective purpose—in this case that associated with the court injunction—is minor in comparison with the environmental purpose of the import ban. This quantitative approach was, however, explicitly rejected by the AB in the same case.

Nevertheless, the quantitative approach might still apply to differential 'export duties plus' because their discriminatory aspect differs from the discriminatory aspect of the measure at issue in *Brazil—Retreaded Tyres*. Unlike in the latter case, in which the Brazilian government through the court injunction rendered its import ban on used tyres discriminatory, the discriminatory aspect of export duties is inherent, requiring the adoption of a complementary measure to counter this effect. Such passively discriminatory side effects, it could be argued, deserve a more lenient approach. As the panel held in *EC—Asbestos*, favouring domestic industry is 'a natural consequence of prohibiting a given product and in itself cannot justify the conclusion that the measure has a protectionist aim, as long as it remains within certain limits'.[67] In this context, differential 'export duties plus' might be allowed to target industrial inputs if they are adopted primarily for fighting climate change.

8.3.2. The irrelevance of the hidden protectionist aim

Alternatively, as the following analysis shows, the AB does not even need to consider the hidden protective purpose of China's export duties under the chapeau. It is noteworthy that the AB has never tried to determine whether a measure at issue has a hidden protective aim under the chapeau. The AB in the *US—Gasoline* case, in finding that the discriminatory aspect of cost considerations constituted a 'disguised restriction on international trade',[68] criticised the 'omission' on the part of

65 Ibid.
66 Panel Report, *Brazil—Retreaded Tyres*, paras 217–219.
67 Panel Report, *EC—Asbestos*, para 8.239.
68 In the *US—Gasoline* case, the US, as part of an effort to prevent and control air pollution, had adopted the Clean Air Act, which required its Environmental Protection Agency to establish an individual and a statutory baseline for gasoline. Under this regime, domestic gasoline was subject to the individual baseline, while imported gasoline was automatically subject to the statutory baseline except under certain conditions. To justify the discriminatory aspect of the gasoline baselines under the

the US in failing to account for the costs to foreign refiners.[69] Similarly, in the *Brazil—Retreaded Tyres* case, when the AB found that the imports of used tyres, as raw materials in the production of retreaded tyres, constituted a 'disguised restriction on international trade' owing to the court injunction discussed earlier, it faulted the rationale for the disconnection of the injunction from the purpose of protecting public health rather than hiding a protective aim, namely to promote the domestic retreaded tyres industry.

A similar approach can also be found in other jurisdictions. In Court of Justice of the European Union (CJEU) jurisprudence, for instance, the *Ladbrokes* case concerns a measure reserved a gambling licence to a single operator for the combined aims of preventing gambling addiction and fighting fraud.[70] Although the two purposes could be justified under Article 52 TFEU, there was concern that the Member States might use these purposes of as a mask for protectionism which results in 'arbitrary state monopolisation'.[71] The court, however, did not try to examine the potential protectionist aim of the measure at issue but looked only at the most suitable purposes of the measure.[72] The ruling in the *Ladbrokes* case thus allowed a Member State to provide gambling services relating to fighting fraud as long as this function did not undermine the purpose of preventing addiction.[73] One possible reason behind the reluctance of the AB or CJEU to look into the measure's hidden protective aim could be that doing so would place an undue burden of proof on the party to demonstrate the existence or nonexistence of a protectionist aim in a measure 'which sometimes can be indiscernible'.[74]

Possibly for the same reason, the panel and the AB in the past refused to examine the 'regulatory intent' and thus rejected the 'aim-and-effect' approach. In *Japan—Alcoholic Beverages II*, the panel criticised the 'aim-and-effect' approach for its 'important repercussion on the burden of proof imposed on the complainant' because the burden was on the complainant to prove the protectionist aim of a measure. The panel found it difficult to evaluate the determinative aims of the measure owing to the common practice regarding 'a multiplicity of aims that are

chapeau, the US argued that it would have been impossible in terms of cost for domestic refiners to meet the statutory baselines. This argument was rejected by the AB, which found that the US had failed to account for the same cost considerations for foreign refiners.

69 Ibid., at 29.

70 Case C-258/08 Ladbrokes Betting & Gaming and Ladbrokes International [2010] ECR I-4757. See Stefaan Van den Bogaert and Armin Cuyvers, '"Money for Nothing": The Case Law of the EU Court of Justice on the Regulation of Gambling', 48 (4) *Common Market Law Review* (2011), at 1202.

71 Justin Franssen and Frank Tolboom, 'Practical Implications Of The Santa Casa Judgment', in Alan Littler, Nele Hoekx, Cyrille J.C.F. Fijnaut, and Alain-Laurent Verbeke (eds), *In the Shadow of Luxembourg: EU and National Developments in the Regulation of Gambling* (Brill, 2011), at 96.

72 Van den Bogaert and Cuyvers (2011), above n 70, at 1208.

73 Ibid. at 1202.

74 Panel Report, *Japan—Alcoholic Beverages II*, para. 6.16.

sought through enactment of legislation'.[75] This rejection was then implicitly affirmed by the AB in the same case.[76] Therefore, should differential 'export duties plus' on industrial inputs be justified provisionally and do not constitute 'arbitrary or unjustifiable discrimination', the AB might choose not to examine their hidden protectionist purpose under the chapeau.

8.3.3. Additional limits on the use of differential 'export duties plus'

Admittedly, the above analysis does not sufficiently address an important concern that China might circumvent WTO rules by exclusively targeting carbon-intensive industrial inputs. In this way, differential 'export duties plus' may unfairly benefit Chinese downstream producers. To prevent China from abusing such policy space, this book proposes additional limits on the use of differential 'export duties plus' for fighting climate change in two scenarios (see Figure 8.2).

First, China may adopt differential 'export duties plus' as part of its climate initiative. In this scenario, the second condition of the chapeau would prohibit an exclusive coverage of upstream products. Objective criteria should instead be used to define the coverage of goods in the 'export duties plus' regime. A good example is the recommended criteria for carbon-outsourcing countries, namely carbon intensity and trade sensitivity, to decide scope of their BTAs.[77] Differential 'export duties plus' thus should cover both upstream and downstream products from sectors with high carbon intensity and trade exposure. This additional limit would

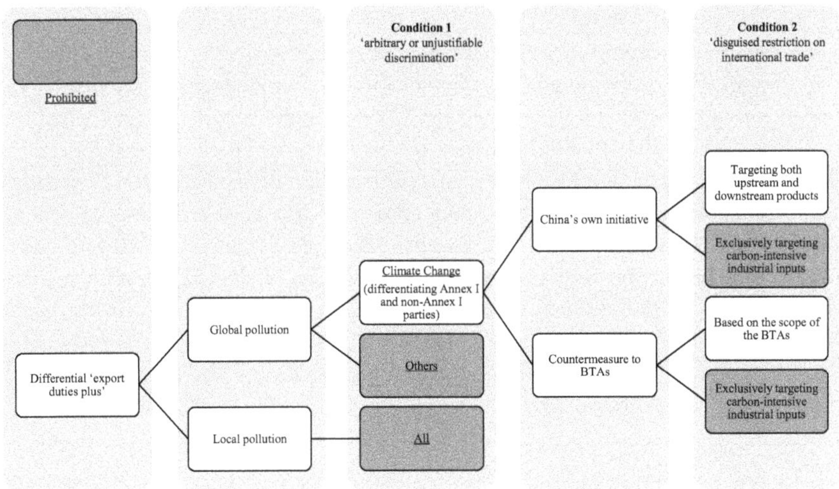

Figure 8.2 Feasibility of justifying differential 'export duties plus' under the chapeau

75 Ibid., para. 6.16.
76 AB Report, *Japan—Alcoholic Beverages II*, at 115.
77 Cosbey, Droege, Fischer, Reinaud, Stephenson, Weischer and Wooders (2012), above n 62, at 13.

prevent China from cherry-picking the carbon-intensive products that could potentially benefit Chinese downstream producers.

Second, differential 'export duties plus' may be adopted to counter a BTA. In this scenario, the second condition of the chapeau would require China to adopt its countermeasure in accordance with the scope of the BTA. The EU in 2019 issued a list of sectors that 'shall be deemed to be at risk of carbon leakage for the period 2021 to 2030'.[78] If the EU decides to impose a BTA on China's exports from the listed sectors, 'export duties plus' should at least cover those products. If the EU decides to adopt its BTA on a narrower scope of sectors,[79] to achieve a more ambitious climate target, China may also go beyond the coverage of the EU BTA, provided that the broad coverage of goods is defined in accordance with the objective criteria as discussed above.

8.4. A reality check on China's environmental policies targeting consumption

The above analysis shows that the degree of restriction on Chinese consumption is decisive to justify 'export duties plus'. On the one hand, if 'export duties plus' treat domestic and foreign consumers in an identical manner, there is a good chance of justifying them under Article XX. If, on the other hand, fewer charges are imposed on products destined for Chinese consumers, such differential 'export duties plus' might only be justified for the purpose of fighting climate change. An overview of China's environmental policies is thus offered here in order to examine the existing environmental measures that target consumption. This analysis serves in turn as a basis for policy recommendations.

To begin with, a major goal of China's environmental policies is to reach the targets set out in China's Five-Year Plan.[80] The Guidelines of the Eleventh Five-Year Plan (2006–2010) included three specific targets for pollution reduction: the air pollutant sulphur dioxide (SO_2); chemical oxygen demand (COD), which is a useful measure of water pollution; and GDP per unit of energy use, or 'energy intensity'. The Guidelines of the Twelfth Five-Year Plan (2011–2015) added another four reduction targets: ammoniacal nitrogen (N-NH3), which is a useful measure of water pollution; nitrogen oxides (NOx), a generic term for the forms of these compounds that contribute significantly to air pollution; greenhouse gases per capita and per unit of GDP, or 'carbon intensity'; and the proportion of primary energy consumption represented by non-fossil energy, or 'non-fossil energy

78 Commission Delegated Decision (EU) 2019/708 of 15 February 2019 supplementing Directive 2003/87/EC of the European Parliament and of the Council concerning the determination of sectors and subsectors deemed at risk of carbon leakage for the period 2021 to 2030 (Text with EEA relevance.), L 120/20, 8 May 2019, at https://eur-lex.europa.eu/legal-content/EN/TXT/PDF/?uri=CELEX:32019D0708&from=EN (visited on 19 August 2019).

79 It has been argued that BTAs should avoid over-broad sectoral coverage. See Cosbey, Droege, Fischer, Reinaud, Stephenson, Weischer and Wooders (2012), above n 7.

80 For further information, see Chapter 5.

consumption'.[81] These changes were followed in the Guidelines of the Thirteenth Five-Year Plan (2016–2020).

The central government distributes those pollution reduction targets to each region. Thus, for instance, in accordance with the national reduction targets established in the Guidelines of the Twelfth Five-Year Plan (2011–2015), the 2011 General Work Plan for Energy Conservation and Pollutant Discharge Reduction and the 2011 Work Plan for Greenhouse Gas Emission Control set the air and water pollution quotas, energy intensity reduction targets, and carbon intensity levels for 32 regions for the period from 2011 to 2015.[82] The 2016 General Work Plan for Energy Conservation and Pollutant Discharge Reduction in addition specifies energy consumption quotas for the 32 regions and an energy-intensity reduction target for various types of industry.

These regional targets are further distributed to each producer, with particular attention to those from the so-called 'high-polluting and high-energy consumption' industries. To increase the enforcement of these reduction targets, a new provision was added to the *Environmental Protection Law of the People's Republic of China* in 2014 that requires the establishment of a pollution permission management system under which companies can only discharge pollutants in accordance with their permissions.[83] This management system was implemented at the end of 2016 in accordance with a notice from the State Council requiring companies in the thermal power and paper industries to apply for pollution permissions.[84] In 2017, companies from major high-polluting industries began to be covered under this pollution permission management system.[85] The reduction of carbon emissions, by contrast, has been regulated under China's national emissions trading system since 2017. This system sets carbon emission quotas for companies involved in the petrochemical, chemical, building materials, steel, nonferrous metals, paper, electricity, or aviation industries that consume energy equivalent to more than 10,000 tons of standard coal.[86]

81 Guidelines of the Twelfth Five-Year Plan (2011–2015), adopted on 14 March 2011, available at http://www.gov.cn/2011lh/content_1825838_2.htm (visited on 4 December 2017).

82 Notice of the State Council on Issuing the Work Plan on Controlling Greenhouse Gas Emissions during the Period of the Twelfth Five-Year Plan (2011–2015), adopted on 1 December 2011, available at http://www.gov.cn/zwgk/2012-01/13/content_2043645.htm (visited on 4 December 2017).

83 Article 45 of the *Environmental Protection Law of the People's Republic of China.*

84 Notice of the General Office of the State Council on Printing and Distributing the Implementation Plan of the Permit for Control of Emission of Pollutants, adopted on 10 November 2016, available at http://www.gov.cn/zhengce/content/2016-11/21/content_5135510.htm (visited on 4 December 2017).

85 Ibid.

86 Notice of the General Office of the State Development and Reform Commission on Earnestly Enhancing the Key Work of Starting the Emission Trading Market in China, available at http://www.ndrc.gov.cn/zcfb/zcfbtz/201601/t20160122_772123.html (visited on 4 December 2017).

In addition to the above quantitative restrictions, China also requires companies to pay pollution fees. The recently introduced *Environmental Protection Tax Law* calls for the replacement of pollution fees by environmental protection taxes, which are easier to enforce.[87] These taxes are applied to four main categories of taxable items, including air pollutants, water pollutants, solid waste, and noise pollution.[88] The scheme of environmental protection taxes is, however, unlikely to be extended to carbon emissions as suggested by China's Minister of Finance.[89]

Although the above measures have generally increased the environmental costs in China, none of them, however, serves to specifically restrict Chinese consumption. To target consumption, one quantitative option is to restrict the access of firms in China to certain products. Thus, for instance, in late 2014, the Ministries of Commerce, Environmental Protection, and Industry and Information Technology issued Green Purchasing Guidelines to encourage the consumption of environment-friendly and energy-saving raw materials, products, and services, such as those certified by the China Environmental United Certification Center and China Energy Conservation Program.[90] Article 15 of this measure explicitly discourages companies from purchasing products on the Environmentally Unfriendly List and other high-polluting and high-energy-consumption products, though this directive is not legally binding.[91] China may consider making these requirements mandatory.

With respect to fiscal restrictions on Chinese consumption, it is noteworthy that the consumption of recycled industrial inputs is encouraged in China in the form of a VAT rebate in order to conserve natural resources and reduce pollution and carbon emissions. In 2015, the Ministry of Finance and the State Administration of Taxation provided recyclers a VAT rebate ranging from 30% to 100% relating to the use of various recycled industrial inputs, such as ferrous scrap.[92] However, although this favourable tax treatment may provide producers in China with incentives to increase resource utilisation, it may not adequately restrict Chinese consumption of high-polluting and high-energy-consumption products.

In contrast, the experience with the consumption tax in China suggests a more effective alternative for restricting domestic consumption of high-polluting and

87 The *Environmental Protection Tax Law of the People's Republic of China*, adopted on 25 December 2016, available at http://www.npc.gov.cn/npc/xinwen/2016-12/25/content_2004993.htm (visited on 4 December 2017).

88 Ibid., Article 43.

89 Xinhuanet, 'China Will Not Specifically Tax Carbon Emissions', available at http://energy.people.com.cn/n1/2016/0321/c71661-28214363.html (visited on 4 December 2017).

90 Ministry of Commerce, Ministry of Environmental Protection and Ministry of Industry and Information Technology, issuing the Green Purchasing Guideline, available at http://www.mofcom.gov.cn/article/h/redht/201412/20141200846975.shtml (visited on 4 December 2017).

91 Article 15 of the Green Purchasing Guideline.

92 Favourable Value-added tax List of Products and Services Concerning Comprehensive Utilization of Resources, available at http://www.chinatax.gov.cn/n810341/n810755/c1703758/content.html (visited on 4 December 2017).

high-energy-consumption products. The NDRC thus in 2013 called for the inclusion of those products within the scope of consumption taxes as a means to fulfil targets for reducing pollution and carbon emissions.[93] Following this suggestion, certain batteries and coatings with high levels of volatile organic compounds have since 2015 been added to products covered by China's consumption tax at a rate of 5% in order to reduce pollution and carbon emissions.[94] The Guidelines of the Thirteenth Five-Year Plan (2016–2020) call for continued improvements in China's consumption tax system,[95] and one interpretation of this commitment might be to cover more high-polluting and high-energy-consumption products.[96] Therefore, in order to increase the chance of justifying 'export duties plus', one feasible option is to broaden the existing scope of products that are subject to consumption taxes.

8.5. Conclusions

There is a good chance of justifying identical 'export duties plus' under Article XX for the purposes of reducing local pollution under subparagraph (b) or global pollution under subparagraph (g). Compared with Article XX(b), Article XX(g) provides more policy space because identical 'export duties plus' would certainly meet the 'even-handedness' requirement. Such 'export duties plus' might, however, fail the necessity test under Article XX(b) if, for instance, a less trade-restrictive alternative is available. Article XX(g) thus provides China with more policy space to adopt identical 'export duties plus' for targeting global pollution.

In contrast, differential 'export duties plus' would be generally prohibited under Article XX because they discriminate against foreign consumers. On the one hand, although Articles XX(b) and XX(g) do not necessarily require identical treatment, more charges on products for export could incentivise Chinese consumption. This result would undermine the effectiveness of 'export duties plus' to reduce pollution and thus decrease the chance of justifying them. In most cases, Article XX(g) seems to provide more policy space.[97]

93 Notice of National Development and Reform Commission on Enhancing its Work to Ensure Targets and Objectives of Energy Saving and Emission Reduction in 2013, available at http://www.ndrc.gov.cn/zcfb/zcfbtz/201308/t20130827_555124.htm l (visited on 4 December 2017).

94 Circular on Consumption Taxes on Battery Coatings, available at http://www.mof.gov.cn/zhengwuxinxi/caizhengwengao/wg2015/wg201503/201507/t20150722_1344546.html (visited on 4 December 2017).

95 Chapter 15 Section 3 of the Guidelines of the Thirteenth Five-Year Plan (2016–2020).

96 Xinhuanet, 'The Next Step of Tax Reform in China: Consumption Tax', available at http://news.xinhuanet.com/fortune/2017-08/04/c_1121428785.htm (visited on 4 December 2017).

97 In exceptional cases where the products at issue are primarily consumed abroad, the 'export duties plus' that are not even-handed under Article XX(g) might nevertheless be found necessary under Article XX(b). For further information, see Section 8.1.

If, on the other hand, differential 'export duties plus' are provisionally justified under Articles XX(b) or XX(g), they would generally fail to satisfy the first condition of the chapeau which prohibits 'arbitrary or unjustifiable discrimination between countries where the same conditions prevail'. In the case of fighting climate change, however, 'export duties plus' might be permitted to differentiate Annex I and non-Annex I parties because Annex I parties have agreed to follow more stringent rules in light of the principle of 'common but differentiated responsibilities' under the UNFCCC. China thus may argue that 'the same conditions' do not prevail between China and Annex I parties. Alternatively, the discrimination against Annex I parties might be found not 'arbitrary or unjustifiable' because the more stringent commitments made by those parties could serve as a justification for charging a higher carbon price for products consumed there.

That being said, however, it is equally important to address concerns that China might use differential 'export duties plus' to provide Chinese downstream producers with favourable access to industrial inputs and thus circumvent WTO rules. This chapter proposes additional limits on the use of differential 'export duties plus' as part of climate policy under the second condition of the chapeau prohibiting 'disguised restriction on international trade'. These limits would prevent China from cherry-picking the carbon-intensive products that could potentially benefit its downstream producers.

Finally, a reality check on China's environmental policies shows that domestic consumption has not been adequately restricted for environmental purposes. A possible reason could be that, given the WTO ban on China's export duties on high-polluting or energy-intensive products, the sole restriction on Chinese consumption would induce companies to manufacture those products for foreign consumers.[98] This is no longer a concern, however, because, as suggested in this book, 'export duties plus' could be consistent with WTO law as part of China's demand-side environmental policies. In order to increase the chance of justifying 'export duties plus', one feasible option is to broaden the existing scope of products that are subject to consumption taxes.

98 It has been argued that China may use quotas to restrict export. However, 'While it is possible to construct a policy package that uses an export quota in conjunction with consumption taxes, such a package would require continual adjustment of policies in response to changes in market conditions to avoid discriminatory outcomes'. See Bond and Trachtman (2016) above n 1, at 202. Moreover, as discussed in Chapter 4, given the three major disadvantages of quantitative restrictions compared with duties, such arguments do not seem to make economic sense as well.

9 Implications of 'Greening' the WTO ban on Chinese export duties

This final chapter begins with a review of the findings of the previous chapters in order to draw lessons regarding how best to address trade-related environmental concerns and avoid extreme judicial outcomes. Next, in Section 9.2, the interpretative techniques employed by other tribunals to temper the rigidity of *stare decisis* are identified as a moderate alternative response to an important issue behind the Appellate Body (AB) crisis. In Section 9.3, some of the findings are presented as a basis for the creation of mechanisms that would prevent China from abusing the proposed 'export duties plus'. Lastly, in Section 9.4, it is argued that the very possibility of 'greening' the World Trade Organization (WTO) ban on China's export duties does not only indicate that the WTO is not standing in the way of environmental protection but also encourage global efforts to combat climate change.

9.1. Lessons for addressing trade-related environmental concerns

This section discusses the key lessons of the conflict between China and its trading partners, in particular regarding ways to address trade-related environmental concerns that could, in turn, inform future cooperative efforts to deal with cross-border issues. The first lesson is that addressing trade-related environmental concerns often requires the balancing of environmental and economic interests—and that doing so can require some finesse. Second, environmental justification should not be used to circumvent WTO rules; this may provoke extreme responses. Third, because it could prove costly and difficult to moderate extreme outcomes, this path should probably be avoided.

9.1.1. Balancing environmental and economic interests

Environmental measures often have negative economic effects that elicit opposition, especially from developing countries. A feasible pollution control measure, therefore, must take economic considerations into account if it is to garner public support. In fact, when it comes to addressing global environmental concerns, even for countries with advanced economies such as the EU and the US, economic interests play an important role. Thus, for instance, various proposed

DOI: 10.4324/9781003162339-12

carbon border tax adjustments have included free emissions allowances or even export rebates designed to address the issues of carbon emission outsourcing and competitiveness simultaneously.[1]

While the influence of economic considerations does not necessarily delegitimise an environmental measure, policymakers need to prevent non-environmental considerations from outweighing environmental goals. A recent empirical study has shown, for instance, that China at one point reduced export VAT refund rates in earnest as a type of demand-side control measure that 'discourages exports of waste water, ammonium nitrogen, SO_2 and energy intensive products'.[2] Export duties, however, being a similar instrument, have been more often 'motivated by an attempt to protect downstream producers in China'.[3] A textual analysis of the Guidelines of China's Eleventh and Twelfth Five-Year Plans (covering the years 2006–2010 and 2011–2015) indeed suggests that, in the past, the country imposed export duties on so-called 'high-energy-intensive, high-pollution, and resources-based' products largely as a means to pursue industrial purposes.[4] A more environment-oriented policy would have also restricted the domestic consumption of those products.

Although the aforementioned duties were not primarily adopted for environmental purposes, some of them might have helped reduce pollution up to a point. Especially in the context of climate change, China's export duties on steel, aluminium, coal, chemical products, and fertilizers were applauded by some commentators, who see their potential to tackle the problem of carbon leakage in China as the largest emitter and exporter of carbon dioxide (CO_2) emissions.[5] Those positive environmental effects may have incentivised China to try its luck under Article XX. For China, while its export duties were not environment-oriented, they might have indeed reduced the pollution associated with the manufacture of targeted products.[6] Based on those good side-effects, China was trying to glamorise its duties.

9.1.2. Hard cases make bad law

China's questionable litigation tactic thus provoked the complaining governments to 'minimize China's chances of prevailing' by denying its right to impose export

1 Madison Condon and Ada Ignaciuk, 'Border Carbon Adjustment and International Trade: A Literature Review', No. 6 OECD Working Paper (2013), at 4.
2 Sabrina Eisenbarth, 'Is Chinese Trade Policy Motivated by Environmental Concerns?', 82 *Journal of Environmental Economics and Management* (2017), at 95.
3 Ibid., at 96.
4 For further information, see Chapter 5.
5 For further information, see Chapter 6.
6 For instance, China adduces two empirical studies in *China—Raw Materials* which show that 'elimination of the export duty of 20% on manganese metal would imply an increase in production by 4.28%'; 'eliminating the 40% export duty on coke would increase domestic production of coke by 2.2%'. Panel Reports, *China—Raw Materials*, paras 7.519–7.520.

duties in a manner consistent with Article XX.[7] This was an obvious tit-for-tat response, for the complainants could have based their arguments 'on the merits of China's contention that its export duties were justified for environmental reasons'.[8] Article XX provides fairly strict tests that could be used to prevent China from using the duties for protectionist purposes; thus the duties at issue in the *China—Raw Materials* and *China—Rare Earths* cases did not even pass the first-tier test under Article XX.

The extreme stance of the complaining governments also steered these cases away from a conventional issue—namely the design of an environmental measure so as to meet the requirements under Article XX—and towards a very controversial issue—the applicability of Article XX to China's WTO-plus commitments. The panel and the AB, apparently swayed by the unconvincing nature of China's arguments, ruled in favour of the complaining governments.

This outcome has incurred strong criticism over the unfairness, especially given that most WTO members remain free to impose duties on exports for any purpose.[9] More importantly, this book shows that the WTO ban on China's export duties would also have negative environmental impacts. The practice of WTO members suggests that export duties can be useful to reduce local or global pollution under certain circumstances, possibly because the theoretically first-best environmental policies are not always feasible in financial or practical terms. The environmental regulatory autonomy with respect to export duties is thus always preserved for WTO members at both the multilateral and regional levels.[10] For instance, the EU's proposal generally prohibiting the use of export duties did recognise the environmental regulatory autonomy of WTO members by incorporating Article XX.

An investigation of the policy rationales behind China's export duties shows that those duties could be part of China's climate policy to curtail carbon leakage.[11] Although this problem could also be addressed by duties on the carbon-intensive imports from China, this type of solution has never been put into practice largely owing to well-founded fear of sparking a trade war. Thus the potential role of China's export duties has been encouraged by a number of climate studies including the well-known Stern Review on the economics of climate change, its follow-up article, and a World Bank research paper.[12] In this sense, the WTO ban on China's export duties would risk undermining international cooperation on climate change and thus serves as a good example of the lawyer's adage that 'hard cases make bad law'.

7 Marco Bronckers and Keith E. Maskus, '*China–Raw Materials*: A Controversial Step Towards Evenhanded Exploitation of Natural Resources', 13(2) *World Trade Review* (2014), at 402.
8 Ibid.
9 For further information, see Chapter 3.
10 For further information, see Chapter 4.
11 For further information, see Chapter 5.
12 For further information, see Chapter 6.

9.1.3. Moderation of extreme judicial outcomes is possible, but would be difficult

With regard to expanding the desirable policy space in light of the *China—Raw Materials* and *China—Rare Earths* decisions, this book provides a comprehensive assessment of the feasibility of moderating the WTO ban on such duties through either a judicial or a political approach.[13] The conclusions reached are that the AB's decisions are not easily altered and that considerably more effort would be required to temper the negative environmental implications of the ban than would have been required to avoid producing the ban in the first place.

A judicial approach requires a new interpretation to alter the harsh ban on China's export duties. Given that the AB has never, in its more than 20 years of jurisprudence, explicitly reversed itself, a more nuanced approach has been proposed in this book that draws a line between duties that are applied exclusively to exports on the one hand and so-called 'export duties plus', which are adopted in conjunction with corresponding restrictions on domestic consumption, on the other. By permitting China to justify the use of 'export duties plus' under Article XX, this interpretation would moderate the negative environmental impact of the WTO ban.

Given the AB's membership crisis, it is probably not the best time to rely on a judicial approach. In terms of political solutions, China could follow the lead of Mongolia, which made a successful request in 2007 for a waiver of its export duty commitments on raw cashmere for the purpose of responding to 'extensive environmental damages and desertification' by limiting the growth of goat herds.[14] China's chances of obtaining such a waiver would, however, be relatively small in practice given the WTO's *de facto* consensus requirement. Thus China would also need to convince the parties that prevailed in *China—Raw Materials* and *China—Rare Earths* to view its export duties, not as a means to protect domestic industry, but in a new light, as a policy instrument designed to curb environmentally destructive practices. China's best chance for success in this effort would be to apply for a collective waiver allowing for the adoption of all climate policies that could potentially violate WTO rules. The disadvantage of such a waiver is that, as observed earlier, it could carry the unwelcome political implication that WTO law generally prevents China, and other countries, from protecting the environment in the absence of a supplementary agreement.

While waivers could be useful as a stopgap measure, China may request amendments or authoritative interpretations as a long-term solution in order to better accommodate the climate considerations.[15] The latter one is recommended because it is more flexible than amendments that generally require formal acceptance.[16] But, given the deep unpopularity of authoritative interpretations in practice, China is advised to avoid the discussion of whether authoritative

13 For further information, see Chapter 7.

14 Communication from Mongolia, 'Request for a Waiver', on 26 January 2007, G/C/W/571.

15 Susanne Dröge, 'Tackling Leakage in a World of Unequal Carbon Prices', Climate Strategies Working Paper (2009), at 68.

16 As discussed in Chapter 7, it has been argued that China's accession protocol could be seen as a bilateral treaty between China and the WTO. In this scenario, once the

interpretations are a proper instrument to correct the *China—Raw Materials* and *China—Rare Earths* decisions. Alternatively, it may request the Ministerial Conference to take a decision updating its accession protocol regarding the use of 'export duties plus' to protect the environment as a 'fudge'.[17] Moreover, in order to make such updates even more attractive to the WTO's membership at large, they could also include a redefinition of other commitments in China's accession protocol such as subsidies or technology transfer.

9.2. Loosening the grip of precedent within the WTO's legal framework

The analysis of the feasibility of various options for correcting an AB decision might serve to identify ways to resolve the persistent blocking of the appointment of AB members by the US. The latter country has justified its obstructionism in this regard with reference to 'systemic concerns' over the 'adjudicative approach and proper role' of the AB in certain cases.[18] Thus, for example, a 2016 US statement blocking the reappointment of an AB member raised concerns regarding both the *obiter dicta* in AB reports[19] and the AB's approach to reviewing WTO members' domestic laws.[20] The US, then, has generally criticised the AB for failing to perform its assigned role under WTO law, at least in certain cases. An analysis of the merit of these concerns is, however, beyond the scope of this book.

The discussion here takes up a more general issue, namely the WTO's precedent system, which the US raised at the beginning of 2018. This issue plays an important role in the current AB crisis in relation to fears on the part of the US that the AB's allegedly incorrect interpretations would be further exacerbated by the *de facto stare decisis* regime underlying the WTO's dispute resolution mechanisms.[21] In other words, owing to the rule of precedent in the WTO, what the US views as a problematic approach would impact future cases. So it was that, late in 2018, the US even began to challenge the precedential value of the AB's decisions at the DSB meeting.[22] From the perspective of the US, the AB's decisions cannot be treated as precedent under WTO law.

17 For general discussion of the decision-making in the WTO, see Pieter Jan Kuijper, 'WTO Institutional Aspects', in Daniel Bethlehem, Isabelle Van Damme, Donald McRae, and Rodney Neufeld (eds.), *The Oxford Handbook of International Trade Law* (Oxford, 2009). Mary Footer, 'Principal rule-making', in *An Institutional and Normative Analysis of the World Trade Organization* (Martinus Nijhoff, 2006).

18 Statement by the United States at the Meeting of the WTO Dispute Settlement Body Geneva, 23 May 2016, https://www.wto.org/english/news_e/news16_e/us_statment_dsbmay16_e.pdf (visited on 1 January 2019).

19 Ibid., at 3.

20 Ibid.

21 Tetyana Payosova, Gary Clyde Hufbauer, and Jeffrey J. Schott, 'The Dispute Settlement Crisis in the World Trade Organization: Causes and Cures', March 2018, https://piie.com/system/files/documents/pb18-5.pdf (visited on 1 January 2019).

22 Statements by the United States at the Meeting of the WTO Dispute Settlement Body Geneva, 18 December 2018, https://geneva.usmission.gov/wp-content/uploads/sites/290/Dec18.DSB_.Stmt_.as-deliv.fin_.public.pdf (visited on 1 January 2019).

However, even the US has recognised that the AB's decisions 'can provide valuable clarification of the covered agreements'.[23] In this sense, complete dismissal of the precedential value of the AB's decisions would inevitably undermine their capacity to clarify WTO law, thereby further rendering interpretation inconsistent.[24] Put another way, legal clarification would obviously be of no benefit in future cases if it were limited to the case at hand. This result seems to be contrary to the mandate of the WTO's dispute settlement system, which calls for 'providing security and predictability to the multilateral trading system'.[25]

Indeed, one of the problems of the old GATT dispute settlement system, which did not include the AB, was inconsistency among the clarifications provided in panel reports.[26] To avoid this outcome, WTO members, including the US, have frequently cited AB reports in their submissions in what amounts to a clear recognition of their precedential value in ensuring that clarifications remain consistent.

This perception echoed during the reform negotiations of the investor-state dispute settlement (ISDS) system, which in its current form has been criticised for 'inconsistency and lack of coherence' in regard to its arbitral awards to an extent that could further undermine 'the reliability, effectiveness and predictability of the ISDS regime and its credibility'.[27] The consensus decision from the US and other United Nations Commission on International Trade Law (UNCITRAL) members last year to move forward in considering possible ISDS reforms shows that the US seeks a precedent system that, on the one hand, avoids 'unjustified inconsistency' and, on the other, accommodates 'divergent decisions' justified by 'for example, rules of treaty interpretation or different facts and evidence before the tribunal'.[28] The reasoning is that 'in certain cases you may have the same treaty, same provision, and you may have different treatment of it'.[29] However, given that the AB has both upheld all of its prior decisions, at least explicitly, and also repeatedly reversed decisions by the panel that have departed from the AB's reports, the US

23 Office of the United States Trade Representative, '2018 Trade Policy Agenda and 2017 Annual Report', March 2018, https://ustr.gov/sites/default/files/files/Press/Reports/2018/AR/2018%20Annual%20Report%20FINAL.PDF (visited on 1 January 2019), at 28.

24 Simon Lester, 'What Is the Precedential Value of Appellate Body Reports?', 1 March 2018, https://worldtradelaw.typepad.com/ielpblog/2018/03/what-is-the-precedential-value-of-appellate-body-reports.html (visited on 1 January 2019).

25 'The dispute settlement system of the WTO is a central element in providing security and predictability to the multilateral trading system'. Article 3.2 of the DSU.

26 Lester (2018), above n 24.

27 UNCITRAL, 'Possible reform of investor-State dispute settlement (ISDS): Consistency and related matters', 28 August 2018, http://www.uncitral.org/uncitral/en/commission/working_groups/3Investor_State.html (visited on 1 January 2019), at 3.

28 Ibid., at 2.

29 Anthea Roberts, 'UNCITRAL and ISDS Reforms: Concerns about Consistency, Predictability and Correctness', 5 June 2018, https://www.ejiltalk.org/uncitral-and-isds-reforms-concerns-about-consistency-predictability-and-correctness/ (visited on 1 January 2019).

has reason to suspect that the AB would not support a more nuanced precedent system. Therefore, in order to create a situation in which 'divergent decisions' are available, the US has sought to deny the precedent system in the WTO as a whole, even at the cost of interpretative consistency, though it could have made good use of authoritative interpretations as a means to correct judicial interpretation.[30]

It has been demonstrated in this book that the US could achieve its objective (perhaps ironically) by supporting the judicial or political corrections of the *China—Raw Materials* and *China—Rare Earths* decisions.[31] With regard to the proposed judicial correction, for instance, the technique of distinguishing, which has been commonly used by tribunals at the international, regional, and national levels, would inject valuable flexibility into the WTO's precedent system. Together with the proposed political options, they could help alter other questionable precedents that are more troubling for the US without undermining the predictability of the WTO system.

Although the AB is currently not able to review any new appeals,[32] the proposed judicial correction remains relevant for the 'multi-party interim appeal arbitration arrangement' (MPIA) or for panel decisions.[33] If the AB is revived in the future, it may consider the use of distinguishing in order to temper the rigidity of its precedent system.[34]

9.3. Preventing circumvention of WTO rules: aluminium sector as an example

While this book challenges the WTO ban on China's export duties for the sake of the environment, it is equally important to acknowledge concerns that China might use export duties to unfairly favour its downstream producers and thus circumvent WTO rules. A more sophisticated approach is thus offered to balance environmental and economic interests. It begins with a distinction between export duties and the 'export duties plus' that are imposed in combination with restrictions on Chinese consumption. The environmental exceptions under GATT

30 Only one request has yet been made for an authoritative interpretation which was rejected by the US itself.

31 For further information, see Chapter 7.

32 The AB no longer had a quorum to hear new appeals because the mandates of two of the three remaining members was expired on 10 December 2019.

33 The participants of MPIA include, currently, Australia; Brazil; Canada; China; Chile; Colombia; Costa Rica; the European Union; Guatemala; Hong Kong, China; Iceland; Mexico; New Zealand; Norway; Pakistan; Singapore; Switzerland; Ukraine and Uruguay. Other WTO members may join the MPIA at any time. European Commission, 'Interim Appeal Arrangement for WTO Disputes Becomes Effective', 30 April 2020, https://trade.ec.europa.eu/doclib/press/index.cfm?id=2143 (visited on 1 November 2020).

34 Compared with a clear change in jurisprudence, a change made in disguise, which seems to be preferred by the AB, is more likely to reduce predictability. See Frieder Roessler, 'Change in the Jurisprudence of the WTO Appellate Body During the Past Twenty Years', No. 72 EUI Working Papers (2015), at 14.

Article XX would only apply to the latter one, which are by nature much less protectionist than those imposed exclusively on exports. Furthermore, Chapter 8 suggests that 'export duties plus' should generally treat domestic and foreign consumers in an identical manner in order to stand the best chance of satisfying the requirements of Article XX. For the purpose of fighting climate change, however, given the different commitments that are made by Annex I and non-Annex I parties under the UNFCCC, the treatment between the two categories might thus differ under Article XX (Figure 9.1). This proposed solution is very unlikely to be abused in practice as shown in the below example of 'export duties plus' covering aluminium sector.

The production of primary aluminium metal consists of bauxite mining, refining bauxite into alumina, and smelting alumina into aluminium.[35] Various environmental issues are associated with these operations. In the first stage of bauxite mining, for instance, the activities of clearing and removal of land may cause air pollution.[36] Moreover, bauxite washing may also cause serious water quality problems.[37] In contrast, the energy demand associated with the extraction of bauxite is much lower compared with the other two stages.[38] To refine bauxite, for instance, could be energy-intensive.[39] The red mud disposal and storage involved in the refining process may also cause the pollution of soil and water.[40] The third stage of smelting is the most energy-intensive one largely owing to the electrolysis process involved.[41] This process may also cause air pollution.[42] Given the strong

35 Aluminium metal is further processed into thousands of final products.

36 Noor Hisham Abdullah, Norlen Mohamed, Lokman Hakim Sulaiman, Thahirahtul Asma Zakaria, and Daud Abdul Rahim, 'Potential Health Impacts of Bauxite Mining in Kuantan', 23(3) *Malaysian Journal of Medical Sciences* (2016), at 2.

37 Ibid. Also see BBC, 'Bauxite in Malaysia: The Environmental Cost of Mining', 19 January 2016, available at https://www.bbc.com/news/world-asia-35340528 (visited on 20 July 2019).

38 Possibly because drilling or blasting operations are generally not required owing to the soft earthy nature of many bauxite deposits. See U.S. Department of Energy, 'U.S. Energy Requirements for Aluminum Production: Historical Perspective, Theoretical Limits and Current Practices', February 2007, available at https://www.energy.gov/sites/prod/files/2013/11/f4/al_theoretical.pdf (visited on 20 July 2019), at 16.

39 'This broad range of energy intensity reflects both bauxite quality (alumina content) and refinery design'. Ibid.

40 Valentina Dentoni, Battista Grosso and Giorgio Massacci, 'Environmental Sustainability of the Alumina Industry in Western Europe', 6 *Sustainability* (2014), at 9478.

41 The production of one tonne of sawn primary aluminium ingot requires 37 GJ of thermal energy and 58 GJ of electricity, whereas the processes of bauxite and alumina only requires (i) 0.02 GJ and 10 GJ of thermal energy, and (ii) 0.003 GJ and 0.65 GJ of electricity. J.A. Moya, A. Boulamati, S. Slingerland, R. van der Veen, M. Gancheva, K.M. Rademaekers, J.J.P. Kuenen andA.J.H. Visschedijk, 'Energy Efficiency and GHG Emissions: Prospective Scenarios for the Aluminium Industry', Publications Office of the European Union, 2015, available at http://publications.jrc.ec.europa.eu/repository/bitstream/JRC96680/ldna27335enn.pdf (visited on 20 July 2019), at 7–8.

42 Stephen Claude Martin and Claude Lariviere, 'Community Health Risk Assessment of Primary Aluminum Smelter Emissions', 56(5) *Journal of Occupational and Environmental Medicine* (2014).

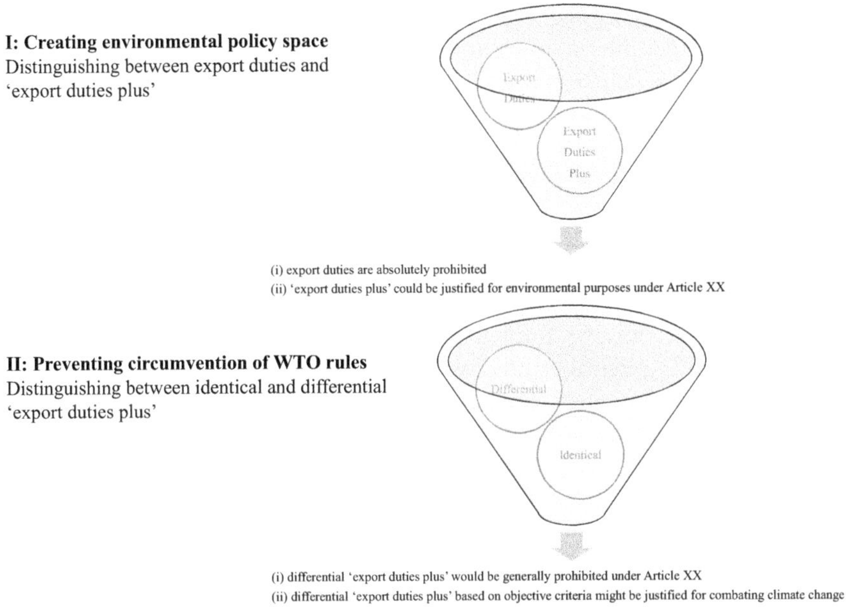

Figure 9.1 A more sophisticated approach to balance environmental and economic interests

growth in China's aluminium sector, 'export duties plus' could be imposed on (i) bauxite, alumina, or aluminium to reduce local or global pollution, and (ii) alumina and aluminium to fight climate change.

Such 'export duties plus' may be designed to treat domestic and foreign consumers in an identical manner. As a result, Chinese downstream producers would not gain favourable access to bauxite, alumina, or aluminium. A Swedish tax on natural gravel provides a similar example. This tax has been introduced by Sweden since 1996 in order to conserve natural gravel which is crucial for providing clean drinking water.[43] Unlike those taxes adopted in Denmark and the UK where exports are relieved from the taxes,[44] both the extraction consumed in Sweden and extraction for export are covered by the same natural gravel charges.[45] Identical 'export duties plus' thus would not raise concerns over circumvention.

If China decides to impose differential 'export duties plus', the analysis provided in Chapter 8 suggests that they might only be allowed for the purpose of fighting climate change. Bauxite thus should be excluded even though the production of it may cause air pollution.[46] With respect to the differential 'export duties plus' on

43 Patrik Söderholm, 'Taxing Virgin Natural Resources: Lessons from Aggregates Taxation in Europe', 55(11) *Resources, Conservation and Recycling* (2011).
44 ECOTEC Research & Consulting, 'Study on Environmental Taxes and Charges in the EU', April 2001, http://ec.europa.eu/environment/enveco/taxation/pdf/ch11_aggregated_taxes.pdf (visited on 1 April 2019), at 213.
45 Ibid., at 205. Exporters are not allowed to reclaim the natural gravel tax.

alumina and aluminium, the 'even-handedness' requirement under Article XX(g) prohibits 'a significantly more onerous burden on foreign consumers or producers'.[47] Hypothetically, one may argue that a 1/4 difference between export duties (20%) and domestic charges (15%) might be permitted, whereas a 1/2 difference (20% export duties plus 10% domestic charges) might be prohibited. Chinese downstream producers thus are unlikely to have considerable advantages of acquiring alumina and aluminium. In addition, the second condition of the chapeau regarding 'disguised restriction on international trade' would prohibit China from exclusively targeting alumina according to the objective criteria of carbon-intensity and trade sensitivity.[48] The advantages of Chinese aluminium producers would thus be further weakened by charges on their aluminium exports, though, admittedly, the additional benefit may not be completely eliminated. This result, however, as the panel held in *EC—Asbestos*, 'in itself cannot justify the conclusion that the measure has a protectionist aim, as long as it remains within certain limits'.[49]

Another scenario is that differential 'export duties plus' are used to counter a carbon border adjustment. For instance, the EU's carbon border measure may cover the listed sectors that could be 'at risk of carbon leakage for the period 2021 to 2030'.[50] Comparable 'export duties plus' should then be imposed to cover those products. If the EU's measure focuses on a narrower scope of sectors by, for instance, only targeting cement, steel, and primary aluminium,[51] to achieve a more ambitious climate target, China may go beyond this coverage by including alumina and other products based on the objective criteria of carbon intensity and trade sensitivity.

47 AB Report, *China—Rare Earths*, para 5.134.

48 In 2018, 2% alumina and 16% aluminium were exported from China. Reuters, 'China Dec Alumina Exports at 177,430 Tonnes – Customs', 23 January 2019, https://www.reuters.com/article/china-economy-trade-alumina/china-dec-alumina-exports-at-177430-tonnes-customs-idUSB9N1ZB001(visited on 1 April 2019). Reuters, 'China December Aluminum Production Surges to Record Monthly High', 21 January 2019, https://www.reuters.com/article/us-china-economy-output-aluminium/china-december-aluminum-production-surges-to-record-monthly-high-idUSKCN1PF0C2 (visited on 1 April 2019).

49 Panel Report, *EC—Asbestos*, para 8.239.

50 Commission Delegated Decision (EU) 2019/708 of 15 February 2019 supplementing Directive 2003/87/EC of the European Parliament and of the Council concerning the determination of sectors and subsectors deemed at risk of carbon leakage for the period 2021 to 2030 (Text with EEA relevance.), L 120/20, 8 May 2019, at https://eur-lex.europa.eu/legal-content/EN/TXT/PDF/?uri=CELEX:32019D0708&from=EN (visited on 19 August 2019).

51 It has been argued that carbon border measures should avoid over-broad sectoral coverage. See Aaron Cosbey, Susanne Droege, Carolyn Fischer, Julia Reinaud, John Stephenson, Lutz Weischer and Peter Wooders, 'A Guide for the Concerned: Guidance on the Elaboration and Implementation of Border Carbon Adjustment', November 2012, at 13, https://www.iisd.org/pdf/2012/bca_guidance.pdf (visited on 19 August 2019).

9.4. Final remarks

The proper balance between trade liberalisation and environmental protection has long been a matter of debate.[52] A key issue in this discussion concerns the policy space of WTO members to adopt trade-related measures designed to address environmental concerns, especially those with an extraterritorial reach. It has been argued that WTO law would not prevent countries from taking such unilateral actions as carbon border adjustments, and therefore the WTO is no excuse for countries with powerful markets to forego incentivising their less environmentally advanced counterparts to join in international cooperative efforts.[53] So it is also argued here that the WTO's legal regime is likewise no excuse to prevent the latter ones such as China from actively taking steps to protect the environment.

The findings in this book particularly stand to benefit global efforts to combat climate change in three respects. First, given that a large portion of China's carbon emissions results from the manufacture of products for export, 'export duties plus' that reduce this source of emissions would contribute to the achievement of global carbon reduction targets. Second, the proper use of export duties as a climate measure by China would set a good example for other pollution-outsourced countries, such as India, where 20% of the emissions are related to exports.[54] As it is, while China has been working to reduce its emissions, it has done so in part by pushing some of its more carbon-intensive activities onto such neighbouring countries as Cambodia, Vietnam, and India.[55] In this game of 'whack-a-mole', export duties could represent an appealing option for carbon-outsourced countries seeking to join in the global effort to combat climate change. Third, 'export duties plus' would also address the competitive concerns of Western nations so that they would be better able to win public support for more ambitious climate actions.[56] For instance, while the 'Carbon Border Tax' involved in the European Green Deal has been proposed to ensure a level playing field for EU companies, an important goal of this measure is to strengthen the current

52 The link between trade and environmental protection was recognized as early as 1970. See WTO, 'Early Years: Emerging Environment Debate in GATT/WTO', https://www.wto.org/english/tratop_e/envir_e/hist1_e.htm (visited on 1 January 2019).

53 For instance, Barbara Cooreman, *Global Environmental Protection through Trade: A Systematic Approach to Extraterritoriality* (Edward Elgar, 2016), at 281.

54 Brad Plumer, 'You've Heard of Outsourced Jobs, but Outsourced Pollution? It's Real, and Tough to Tally Up', 4 September 2018, https://www.nytimes.com/2018/09/04/climate/outsourcing-carbon-emissions.html (visited on 1 January 2019).

55 Ibid.

56 Aaditya Mattoo and Arvind Subramanian, 'Four Changes to Trade Rules to Facilitate Climate Change Action', No.10 PIIE Policy Brief (2013), https://www.piie.com/publications/policy-briefs/four-changes-trade-rules-facilitate-climate-change-action (visited on 4 September 2019). The more recent development shows that the EU might indeed have prepared to impose a carbon border tax. See Alan Beattie, 'Carbon Border Tax Sends Signals for Trade Deals', FT, 29 May 2019, https://www.ft.com/content/016adba8-82ed-11e9-b592-5fe435b57a3b (visited on 15 June 2019).

Emissions Trading System.[57] Moreover, the option of export duties as a countermeasure could also be extended to other countries that are covered by carbon border adjustments. This offer representing good faith from the West, then, would both temper political opposition from other countries and increase the chances that their extraterritorial actions would be justified under Article XX.[58]

We should never let the perfect become the enemy of the good. The world's slow progress in fighting climate change is in part attributable to countries' obsession with the first-best climate policies, such as an effective carbon tax.[59] While the debate over the enormous difficulties involved with adopting the ideal environmental tools shows no sign of abating, the problems associated with climate change are worsening more rapidly than experts had expected just a few years ago. A recent IPCC report thus has called for 'rapid, far-reaching and unprecedented' actions on the part of all nations.[60] China's 'export duties plus' targeting carbon consumption could be among these actions.[61]

57 Ursula von der Leyen, 'A Union that Strives for More: My Agenda for Europe', 16 July 2019, at 5, https://ec.europa.eu/commission/sites/beta-political/files/political-guidelines-next-commission_en.pdf (visited on 1 August 2019).

58 For instance, the US Rep. Bill Pascrell has proposed to draw the link between climate change and national security. 'Pascrell Calls for National Security Investigation of Carbon Pollution', 12 March 2019, https://pascrell.house.gov/news/documentsingle.aspx?DocumentID=3855 (visited on 1 April 2019).

59 Justin Gillis, 'Forget the Carbon Tax for Now', 27 December 2018, https://www.nytimes.com/2018/12/27/opinion/carbon-tax-climate-change.html (visited on 1 January 2019).

60 'Limiting global warming to 1.5°C would require rapid, far-reaching and unprecedented changes in all aspects of society'. See IPCC, 'Summary for Policymakers of IPCC Special Report on Global Warming of 1.5°C Approved by Governments', 8 October 2018, https://www.ipcc.ch/2018/10/08/summary-for-policymakers-of-ipcc-special-report-on-global-warming-of-1-5c-approved-by-governments/ (visited on 14 November 2018).

61 As suggested by the same report, demand-side solutions would play a key role in mitigating climate change through enabling lifestyle and behavioural change. IPCC, 'Chapter 4: Strengthening and Implementing the Global Response', at 8, https://www.ipcc.ch/site/assets/uploads/sites/2/2019/05/SR15_Approval_Chapter_4.pdf (visited on 23 August 2019).

Moreover, according to an EU research project, given that 'upward drivers of GHG emissions come from consumption', demand-side measures can complement current climate actions focusing on production. European Commission, 'Carbon Emission Mitigation by Consumption-based Accounting and Policy', 2013, https://cordis.europa.eu/project/rcn/110539/factsheet/en (visited on 23 August 2019).

Index

For Product Safety Concerns and Information please contact our EU representative GPSR@taylorandfrancis.com
Taylor & Francis Verlag GmbH, Kaufingerstraße 24, 80331 München, Germany

www.ingramcontent.com/pod-product-compliance
Ingram Content Group UK Ltd.
Pitfield, Milton Keynes, MK11 3LW, UK
UKHW021722240926
475702UK00029BA/1764
9780367753955